An Introduction to Natural Language Processing Through Prolog

Learning About Language
General Editors
Geoffrey Leech & Mick Short, Lancaster University

Already published:

Analysing Sentences 2nd edition
Noel Burton-Roberts

Patterns of Spoken English
Gerald Knowles

Words and Their Meaning
Howard Jackson

An Introduction to Phonology
Francis Katamba

Grammar and Meaning
Howard Jackson

An Introduction to Sociolinguistics
Janet Holmes

Realms of Meaning: An Introduction to Semantics
Th. R. Hofmann

An Introduction to Psycholinguistics
Danny D. Steinberg

An Introduction to Spoken Interaction
Anna-Brita Stenström

Watching English Change
Laurie Bauer

Meaning in Interaction: An Introduction to Pragmatics
Jenny Thomas

An Introduction to Cognitive Linguistics
Friedrich Ungerer and Hans-Jörg Schmid

Exploring the Language of Poems, Plays and Prose
Mick Short

Contemporary Linguistics: An Introduction
William O'Grady, Michael Dobrovolsky and Francis Katamba

An Introduction to Natural Language Processing Through Prolog

Clive Matthews

LONGMAN

London and New York

Contents

Preface

Research into Natural Language Processing (NLP) – the use of computers to process natural language – has exploded in the last couple of decades into one of the most vigorous areas of current work on language and communication. However, even in these days of ever growing computer literacy, NLP is often seen as an off-putting subject for many students. This is a pity since not only is the work stimulating, but also many of the fundamental ideas and techniques involved in NLP are not difficult to understand. The present book is an attempt to present some of these basic concepts in a relatively simple way so as to allow those with only a minimal computational background entry into this exciting field.

There are two broad types of introductory textbook that one might write on NLP. The first would provide a broad survey of the field outlining, say, its history, various practices and more important research projects. It would be little concerned with technical detail. The second sort of text, however, would approach the subject more with an eye to this technical side, concerned, in particular, with showing how computer programs can be written to perform various language processing tasks. This book is of the latter type.

There are various reasons why I have chosen to go with this second approach. For example, although programming can be frustrating at times, when everything comes together, it can also be hugely exhilarating. In my experience, students tend to respond very positively – and, so, become motivated by – the dynamic aspect of writing and running successful programs. But this aside, a programming approach is invaluable in the way it meshes with other aspects of linguistic study. For instance, the difficulties involved in carrying out even seemingly trivial tasks is a valuable lesson in coming to understand something of the complexity of language processing (both in humans and with computers). This is something which is often talked about but rarely experienced. Further, being forced to produce precise (and relatively complete) statements regarding the language understanding process is a useful corrective to much of the hand waving which happens in other areas of modern linguistics. With NLP, it is not possible to say 'assuming a suitable account of X'. Not only are we forced into producing a suitable account but also into stating it in the explicit form that a literal minded computer can work with. Further, the emphasis in NLP on linguistic behaviour as a *process* is a useful adjunct to other areas of linguistic thinking where the emphasis tends to be more on the static forms of knowledge underlying this behaviour rather than the operations manipulating this information. A final benefit of introducing NLP through programming is the understanding it brings to a broad range of issues to do with the general nature of cognitive processes and the computational theory of the mind.

Once the decision has been made to introduce NLP through a programming approach, the next decision is which programming language to use. There are a number of possibilities but the one chosen has been Prolog. One reason for this choice is that it is one of the major programming languages used by NLP researchers. Consequently, implementation details in the literature are frequently stated in Prolog so that it is useful to have some knowledge of the language in order to be able to follow the discussion. However, perhaps more importantly for our current purposes is the oft expressed view that Prolog is one of the more 'user friendly' programming languages to learn. Although this claim is, perhaps, exaggerated – learning to program in any language is never easy – it is true that beginners can learn to write fairly interesting programs in a relatively short time using Prolog. This, again, makes the learning process that much more enjoyable.

Although it is probably possible to pick up some feel for the subject without experimenting with a computer, the assumption is that most readers will be following the text with access to a computer running Prolog. As such, the relatively easy availability of Prolog is a further advantage to using the language. There are many different implementations of the language for all types of machine currently available from main frame to personal computer. If you do not already have access to Prolog, advice is probably best sought from specialist software suppliers who will be able to help with details of which versions are currently available and prices. It is worth bearing in mind that, apart from commercial packages, it is possible to obtain quite serviceable public domain implementations at very little cost. Some quite sophisticated versions are also available over the World Wide Web.

At present, Prolog does not have an official standard. Consequently, different implementations can vary quite widely in what features they make available. However, most versions do consist of a common core of features, sometimes referred to as 'standard' or 'Edinburgh' Prolog. It is in terms of this core that most Prolog textbooks introduce the language and this text is no different.

Consequently, the programs in this book should run with little, if any, modification on most commercially available packages. One of the most popular exceptions to these remarks is Turbo Prolog, although it is often quite easy to modify some of the simpler programs to work within the Turbo environment. A number of excellent textbooks have appeared in much the same area as the current work in the last few years. However, these texts tend to assume a more computer literate audience than the one that is assumed here. For example, both Gazdar and Mellish's *Natural Language Processing in Prolog* and Covington's *Natural Language Processing for Prolog Programmers* assume that the reader already has taken a basic course in Prolog programming. Pereira and Shieber's *Prolog and Natural-Language Analysis* gives an excellent detailed introduction to Prolog but it is highly compact and probably too sophisticated for those with no previous experience of programming. Gal *et al.*'s *Prolog for Natural Language Processing* also includes a short introduction to Prolog programming but this usually proves insufficient for complete novices. What I have tried to do here is produce, in one volume, a comprehensive introduction to Prolog at an elementary level to enable the reader with no previous computing experience to understand and write various NLP programs which go beyond the merely trivial. Since the reason for using Prolog is mainly for the purpose of illustration, I have not always been concerned with questions relating to elegance or efficiency of implementation *qua* Prolog programming. Such considerations are left for more sophisticated texts.

Because a sizeable proportion of the text is taken up with an introduction to Prolog, this has meant that it has been impossible to provide anything like a complete coverage of work in all the various areas of NLP. For example, there is no coverage of either semantics or pragmatics. Rather, the emphasis is on syntactic processing. Even within this restricted domain there is much that has been left out. This said, my experience is that there is more than enough material to keep students occupied through a (12 week) semester. Once this material has been covered, the student will be in a good position to move on to some of the more advanced texts mentioned above and, eventually, to the research literature itself.

The text is structured into three sections. The first, consisting of the first two chapters, offers a brief overview of potential NLP applications and some discussion as to why producing NLP systems is such a complex task. The second section, from chapters 3 to 7, is the introduction to Prolog programming. The core chapters to this section are 3, 4 and 5. Indeed, once the material in chapter 5 has been mastered, the third section which describes various NLP techniques will become accessible. This third section runs from chapters 8 to 12. Chapter 11 is, perhaps, the core of this section providing, as it does, an exploration of a fairly wide range of syntactic constructions using Definite Clause Grammars. The linguistic coverage in this section is somewhat more complex than in previous chapters. The final chapter is also quite difficult but this is more the result of compression than of actual content. As with all books of this type, the exercises form an integral part of the learning process and should not be skipped. Answers to many of the questions are included in an appendix. Complete program listings are given at the end of each chapter since the program code is often spread across a number of pages during the discussion in the chapter.

A number of friends and colleagues have helped me greatly over the preparation of the book and it is with pleasure that I would like to thank them here. In particular, thanks go to Jeremy Fox who provide considerable support and helpful comment, especially through the slow times. Laurie Buxton went through much of the text and (as he would probably want to point out) virtually all the best-written bits are the direct result of his interventions. Gerald Gazdar kindly looked at a very early draft. His comments made me rethink and rework to such an extent that what is here bears very little relation to this earlier attempt; for that we must all be grateful. Vic Rayward-Smith also kindly looked at some of the earlier drafts and provided a number of insightful comments. My editors, Mick Short and (especially) Geoff Leech, tidied up matters considerably and helped make the whole more coherent than it might have been. Finally, thanks to Longman for their patience as deadline followed deadline. As always, the blame for any shortcomings to be found in the text rest with the author. All I can say is that I did my best.

The University of East Anglia has provided a pleasant environment in which to teach and write. Thanks to the Computing Centre for help in ways too numerous (and, in some cases, embarrassing) to mention. Thanks also to John Hutchins, our inestimable linguistics librarian – and machine translation expert – for managing to provide such a fine collection despite ever tighter budgets. The Inter-Library Loan Office managed to provide any missing materials with good humour and grace. Thanks also to all those students who, over the years, have had to struggle through various versions of the text providing invaluable feedback and who, through their enthusiasm, made the task ultimately so fulfilling. Finally, I would like to thank the University for providing me with the study leave which allowed for the completion of the writing.

The last thank you must also be the largest since it goes to my family; my wife Anne and children Felicity, Joshua and Mathilde. They have had to put up with too much for too long. Perhaps, we can go and fly the kites now as I promised. My only worry is that I no longer have an excuse for not mending that stool. Finally, I should like to dedicate this book to my parents, Audrey and Ralph Matthews.

PART I

Introduction

CHAPTER 1

Natural Language Processing

In almost every aspect of our daily experience, we are touched by the computer revolution. Computers control our cars, heating systems and washing machines; they are crucially involved in the production of our newspapers and weather forecasts, our bank statements and supermarket bills, the special effects on our television screens and the music from our sound systems; and concepts derived from computing subtly shape and organise our perceptions of the world. However, pervasive as computers already are, their potential is so great that they are destined to play an ever more integral role in our lives.

If society is to enjoy the full benefits of these advances, all of its members will need equal access to the technology. This is not always the case at present. Today's computer user has to be an expert of sorts, becoming 'computer literate', in order fully to exploit current applications. The problem is that many potential users have neither the time, inclination nor aptitude necessary to acquire this knowledge. For them, the computer is a forbidding object, best left in the hands of specialists, and only to be experienced indirectly. A large part of the next stage of the computer revolution will be involved in overcoming this literacy barrier.

It is most unlikely that the solution to this problem will be a simple increase in educational resources since the results will be highly variable; if computer literacy is partially a matter of aptitude, there will always be some who will remain challenged by the technology. A far more radical alternative is to turn the problem on its head and design computers that are 'human literate'. In this way, we will be able to interact with them on *our* terms rather than theirs so that users will require no special training to operate them. Since a large part of human communication is conducted effortlessly through **natural languages** such as English, Japanese or Swahili, the ability of computers also to be able to converse in such languages will be one of the crucial components in making them 'human literate'. The capacity of a computer to 'understand' a natural language is referred to as **Natural Language Processing** (NLP). This book is an introduction to some of the elementary programming techniques involved in designing and building a computer with an NLP capability. The rest of this chapter explores some of the potential applications of NLP technology. As a broad division, it is useful to think of two types of application; those that will facilitate the flow of information between man and machine (section 1.1) and those where the aim is to improve communication between man and man (section 1.2). As section 1.3 outlines, NLP can also benefit the study of linguistics irrespective of its practical applications.

1.1 Natural Language Interfaces

Most computer applications are intended as aids to human activities rather than as free-standing agents. For this reason it is important that the **interface** between human and computer be **user-friendly**, in the sense of being easy to learn, use and understand. The history of computing is, in part, a story of increasingly friendly interfaces. For some applications, the logical extension of this process is the provision of natural language interfaces.

Natural language interfaces are not necessarily the best solution for all applications. For example, graphical interfaces linked to a pointing device such as a mouse are an efficient and user-friendly method in many cases. However, where the input to the system is textual, a natural language interface has various advantages as some of the examples in this section show.

A **database management system** enables the information in a database to be altered, sorted, and retrieved at the command of the user. There are innumerable questions and requests that a user might want to issue to such a system. Here is a sample.

Which cities' sales were greater than we targeted for?
Produce a graph of last year's sales for Cambridge by week.
Change this year's target for Norwich from £12,250 to £13,000.
When do our earliest records for Seiler PLC date from?
Display all those under target for the last two years in bold print throughout.

In the early days of computing, commands such as these could only be expressed through a **machine language**, the 'native' language of the computer. The following gives an idea of what such instructions look like.

```
0100101100000100
1010000111010100
0000000110010011
0011110011111001
```

Each line is a direction to perform one of the machine's basic operations – compare, copy, add, multiply and so on. They are expressed in **binary code** – combinations of 0s and 1s. These basic operations are so primitive that even to get the machine to perform a simple task, such as adding two numbers together, requires several lines of code. Since every detail of how to carry out more intricate commands must be fully specified, machine language is far too cumbersome a language in which to express the types of instruction required of a database management system.

Matters are not much improved with **assembler languages**. These use mnemonic expressions for the instructions. For instance, the previous lines of machine code written in assembler might look as follows.

```
LOAD 3, A
LOAD 4, B
ADD 3, 4
LOAD 3, C
```

Assembler statements must be translated into machine language before they can be executed by the computer. This is performed automatically by a program called a **compiler**.

Assembler languages are closely allied to machine code and are only marginally more friendly. **High-level programming languages** such as FORTRAN, COBOL or BASIC are an improvement. They allow the replacement of chunks of assembler/machine code with single expressions. For instance, the previous example might now be reduced to:

```
ADD A, B GIVING C
```

Again, this instruction has to be compiled into machine code before it can be executed by the machine although this is hidden from the user.

Programming languages allow maximal control over the computer. The price paid is the high degree of expertise required to exploit them. User-friendliness, on the other hand, tends to be achieved at the expense of control and flexibility. Consider the use of **pull-down menus**. These allow the user to choose from a finite number of pre-selected commands using some kind of pointing device. The technique can even be adapted to produce natural language input, built up from words and phrases selected from a series of menus. The following illustrates such an interface where the user has constructed the sentence *What were the stock prices for the Channel Tunnel for each quarter in 1995?* from the various options available.

WHAT		
is the current quote for is the option price for *WERE THE STOCK PRICES FOR* are the estimated earnings for are the headings for	IBM *CHANNEL TUNNEL* Coca-Cola Co. Euro-Disney	

on the London exchange on the American exchange on the New York exchange on the Tokyo exchange	for each month in *FOR EACH QUARTER IN* for the last 12 days for the last month	1993 1994 *1995* 1996

Menu-based interfaces are easy to learn and use, efficient and robust. However, a menu-based format only works well if there are a fairly limited number of choices. They also restrict the range of expression; for example, the question *What were the stock prices for Channel Tunnel for each quarter in 1991?* can only be phrased this way in the illustrated menu system. For many applications, such restrictions are unproblematic and a menu-based interface is an effective choice. With large databases, however, the constraints are probably too limiting; for example, imagine a database containing financial information on five hundred companies and how many screens this would take to display.

The only alternative to these problems is to try and make the interface language easier to use. **Database query languages** are the result. The following shows the equivalent of 'Which cities' sales were greater than we targeted for?' in such a language.

```
SELECT city, sales, target FROM gb WHERE sales >
target
```

gb is the name of the file containing the relevant data and city, sales and target the names of the fields of information in each record. Assuming that the user knows how the database is structured, it is relatively easy to ask simple questions with a query language. However, such languages are unforgiving of mistakes; using town instead of city, for instance, would fail to produce the required information. Further, more complex questions soon start to become quite opaque; the following is equivalent to 'Which customers have greater than average balances?'

```
SELECT name, balance FROM customers
     WHERE balance >
          (SELECT avg(balance) FROM customers)
```

The progression from machine to database query languages is one of ever greater approximation to English. It would seem that the natural conclusion to this process is the use of English itself as the interface language. This way flexibility would be married to user-friendliness and efficiency. Flexibility because there is no constraint on what can be expressed in English; user-friendliness because English is our natural means of communication in most situations; and efficiency because it is always possible to express any instruction more concisely in English compared with any programming language. This is an impressive list of advantages which makes a natural language interface an attractive proposition.

This, however, is not the end of the story. A natural language front-end, by itself, is unlikely to make a database management system any more accessible to the non-specialist user. The problem is that information retrieval requires a certain degree of expertise in order to be effective. One needs to know, for instance, the most relevant data for a particular purpose, whether any other data should be taken into account, how it might be best presented and so on. In other words, it is not much use being able to ask a question in English if you do not know *which* question you should be asking in the first place. A solution to this is for the natural language front-end to interface with an **expert system**, a program able to provide the necessary guidance and through which the database will be indirectly accessed.

Expert systems need not be confined to advice on information retrieval. Examples have been built in various fields including, medical diagnosis, the interpretation of military intelligence reports and the design of experiments in molecular genetics. They are attractive for a number of reasons; allowing access to expertise at times and in places where a human expert would be unavailable or too expensive; freeing-up the human expert for more taxing problems; improving the consistency of decision making and so on.

The ideal form of any interface depends not only on the nature of the application but also on how often the system is accessed by its typical user. The same applies to expert systems; interfaces engaged by experts on a regular basis do not need to be as user-friendly as those used on a more casual basis by a broader-based clientele. There are numerous potential extensions to the technology of this latter type; from systems selling insurance and providing financial advice to computerised travel agents. It is in these cases that a natural language interface will be the optimal solution for reasons already mentioned.

The development of expert systems has led to an interesting extension which will also benefit from a natural language front-end. Many expert systems allow the user to ask for an explanation as to how a particular conclusion was reached. This allows the user to examine, and so gain confidence in, the system's conclusions. It also provides an interesting educational tool since a non-expert user can also use this facility to follow how an expert goes about solving such problems. **Computer-aided instruction** extends this pedagogic potential by taking an active role in the learning process. Some tutor the knowledge contained in current expert systems, others in completely different domains. A tutoring system needs a formidable array of knowledge; not only knowledge about the subject matter being tutored but also how to tutor it. This in turn requires some knowledge of the learner's current level of understanding since this will partially determine the pedagogic strategy. All of this makes designing a tutoring system a complex task but one which is rich in potential.

The tutor-learner interface plays an important role in the overall success of computer-aided instruction since it is the means by which various explanations, tasks, and feedback are communicated to the learner. An ill-designed interface will distract the student from the central task of learning as well as leading to potential confusion and misunderstanding. As in the previous examples, a graphical interface is often the most suitable means of communication for some topics. However, if the subject matter is best presented textually, then a natural language interface is, once more, probably the best choice.

This section has indicated a number of ways in which NLP may help to improve communication between computers and their users through the provision of user-friendly interfaces. In each case the interface was to programs involved in non-linguistic tasks. The use of NLP for specifically linguistic applications is the topic of the next section.

1.2 The Linguistic Application of NLP

Typically, computer-aided instruction has involved tutoring formal topics such as mathematics, physics and electronics. However, some systems have taken foreign languages as their subject matter. In these cases, NLP is not only involved in the interface design but represents the core of the application itself; the linguistic knowledge on which NLP relies provides the basis for instruction, whilst NLP is involved in assessing the student's responses in order both to determine the student's level of attainment as well as providing appropriate feedback.

Aside from the standard problems involved in any NLP application, language tutoring has to resolve a number of specific issues. For example, the grammatical knowledge encoded in an NLP program is unlikely to be in a suitable form for instruction; the ideal form of pedagogic grammar and how this is to be related to the computational grammar are interesting questions. Also of some interest is how to handle ill-formed input. Any NLP system will have to cope with mistakes. However, because of the nature of the users, a foreign language tutoring system will tend to encounter far more and of greater severity. Processing these errors is also an important pointer to the student's current state of knowledge. However, it often proves extremely difficult to interpret ill-formed input, sometimes because it is unclear what the intended form was, sometimes because the error could have been due to a number of causes.

Most current foreign language tutors are rather primitive in design and only in a prototype stage of development. However, a number of other natural language applications have reached a level of development where they are now commercially available. Their attraction lies in the possibility of the computer taking over various mundane linguistic tasks so freeing up time to allow the user to concentrate on more complex and interesting problems.

Machine translation, the use of computers to translate from one language into another, has been a long term goal of NLP. It has, however, had a somewhat chequered history. After considerable funding from the early 1950s, research almost ceased in the mid-1960s following adverse assessments of its potential. Advances in the late 1970s saw a resurgence of interest and the appearance of the first commercial systems so that machine translation is once more a vibrant area of research.

The output from a machine translation system can often appear disappointing. The following passage was translated from Russian.

> A contemporary airport is the involved complex of engineer constructions and techniques, for arrangement of which the territory, measured sometimes is required by thousands of hectares (for example the Moscow Airport Domodedovo, Kennedy's New York Airport).

Clearly, this is not a very stylish rendering into English. However, its meaning is reasonably clear and for many purposes such a rough and ready translation may be quite satisfactory. In any case, post-editing by a human translator can fairly quickly produce a more elegant translation.

As the previous example shows, machine translation does not eliminate the need for a human translator. The benefit lies in the increase in productivity that machine aided translation can generate. In this sense, machine translation is best thought of as a means of improving communication between humans rather than improving any man-machine interactions. Exactly how great those gains in productivity will be largely turns upon how much post-editing is required and this will vary depending upon both the type of text and the required quality of the final output. Although it is unlikely that there will be any great advantages in the use of machine translation for literary texts, there are enough 'mundane' documents – scientific and technical articles, commercial transactions, weather reports, patents and so on – where the production of adequate translations at much faster rates than is possible 'by hand' will be of great benefit.

The shortage of human translators in relation to the huge amount of written material which modern technology now allows us to produce means that machine translation is destined to become ever more important. But machine translation by itself can only overcome part of the informational bottleneck. Texts still need to be processed for their content and keeping abreast of incoming information, translated or not, is now a major problem.

The computer, which has partly been responsible for this deluge of information, also offers a means of controlling it through automatic text analysis or **content scanning**. One area where this has been developed involves the processing of shipping messages in order to update a database which keeps a plot of the position of merchant ships throughout the world. In the event of an emergency, those ships nearest to the event can be quickly located and dispatched to help. The output of current content scanning systems still requires human checking for errors but, as with machine translation, this process still achieves greater speed and accuracy than purely manual methods.

A considerable amount of textual material is now produced through word processing or desk-top publishing packages. NLP can also be used to provide various kinds of support for the writing process within these packages. Writing aids can be divided into two main types, those providing **text critiquing** facilities of previously written material and those, sometimes called **writer's assistants**, which provide support in the compositional process.

Text critiquing provides information on lexical, grammatical and stylistic features of the text. Lexical feedback usually means spell checking. However, it could be extended, say, to pick up on clichés and sexist language. Stylistic feedback, on the other hand, is normally of a statistical nature, listing analyses of word and sentence lengths, sentence types, parts of speech and so on.

Most currently available critiquing packages involve very little NLP. Many spell checkers, for example, utilise a simple string matching procedure. Such programs are invaluable but the results can still be frustrating. For example, a proposed list of replacement words usually includes a number that could not possibly be candidates either because the proposed word is of the wrong syntactic category or is incorrectly inflected for the particular context. Further, spell checkers will not reject a word if it is correctly spelt but of the wrong syntactic category as in *I bought this four Mary*; similarly for semantically deviant text: *John cooked the seat*. Ideally, a spell checker would also recognise the difference between those words that have been misspelt by accident – perhaps, by hitting the wrong key or transposing two letters – and those misspelt through ignorance. Perhaps, the former might be automatically corrected whilst the latter could be brought to the user's attention. A solution to each of these shortcomings depends upon access to NLP capabilities.

A writer's assistant provides a support system for textual composition via such functions as showing the structure of a text and its relation to its underlying ideas, allowing the exploration and manipulation of ideas and texts, as well as the specification of various stylistic constraints. They may be especially important in those situations where a text has to be written in a hurry or based only on a rough outline of ideas. For large organisations, their use will make it easier to achieve conformity to a company style, consistency in terminology and so on.

1.3 NLP as a Tool for Linguistic Research

The previous two sections have emphasised some of the commercial applications of NLP. However, NLP can also provide a valuable tool for linguistic research. One obvious area is in grammar development. Writing a grammar with broad coverage for a particular language is a complex task. In many frameworks, this complexity is the result of analysing constructions in terms of the interaction of a number of separate structural components. The problem is that the interactions between these various modules are often so complex and subtle that it is difficult for the grammar writer to be sure that the proposed grammar describes the language in the intended way. Manually checking the consequences of the grammatical description on paper is usually too time consuming and prone to error.

An invaluable tool in this situation is a **grammar development system**, a computer environment which allows for the creation of a grammar for a language. In addition, such systems also provide various testing facilities and the ability to be able to correct any faults. One core element of such systems is a parser, a program which provides structural analyses of sentences which can then be checked for accuracy and consistency. Also important is a language generator which can be used to produce a representative sample of sentences defined by the grammar in order to check that no ungrammatical examples are included. Both parsing and language generation are central concerns of NLP.

NLP also provides a useful alternative perspective on much linguistic theorising. Partly as a consequence of its historical development, a great deal of recent linguistics has concentrated on providing a characterisation of the linguistic knowledge of a speaker – sometimes referred to as *competence* – without saying much about how this knowledge is put to use as linguistic behaviour – sometimes referred to as *performance*. This is not to say that performance has been dismissed as being irrelevant to the concerns of linguists, but that since performance is (partly) determined by competence, the study of competence has been argued to take logical priority over the study of performance. NLP, with its concern with the *processes* by which linguistic structures are constructed, has helped focus interest on questions of how competence grammars could form the basis of linguistic behaviour, a not unreasonable concern. However, although some have argued for the adoption of one type of competence grammar over another because of its processing advantages, conclusions in this area are fraught with uncertainty as new techniques are discovered which provide solutions to what previously seemed insoluble problems.

What is not in question is the salutary effect research on NLP has had on our overall appreciation of the complexity of the various tasks involved in the production and comprehension of even the simplest of linguistic utterances. Although it had been apparent for a number of years that the processing of language must involve access to, and manipulation of, considerable amounts of complex information, it was only by trying to build functional NLP systems that the daunting complexity of this process became apparent. This is the subject matter of the next chapter.

1.4 Further Reading

Many introductory texts on NLP devote surprisingly little discussion to the potential applications of NLP technology. An exception is Shwartz (1987; see also Shwartz 1984). Bennet *et al.* (1986) also contains a useful survey as do a number of articles in Reitman (1984). The best source of information, however, is to be found in two reviews of the commercial potential of NLP; Johnson (1985) – now somewhat dated – and Obermeier (1989). See also Johnson and Guilfoyle (1989). Further details of individual projects and some of the technical issues involved can be found in the various conference proceedings of the Association of Computational Linguistics (ACL) especially those on Applied Natural Language Processing. For details of the ACL and its publications write to the ACL, PO Box 6090, Somerset NJ, 08875, USA. An entertaining account of 'human literate' computing can be found in Schank (1984).

The account of natural language interfaces in the chapter mainly follows Shwartz (1987). More information can be found in Perrault and Grosz (1986), Bates (1987) and Copestake and Sparck Jones (1990). Apart from Shwartz (1987), Tennant (1987) discusses menu-based NLP interfaces. There is a large general literature on human-computer interface design; Baecker and Buxton (1987) is a useful source of readings.

Introductions to expert systems can be found in Jackson (1986), Hayes-Roth *et al.* (1983) and Alty and Coombs (1984). Various articles in Shapiro (1987) are also useful, including Hayes-Roth (1987) for a general survey, Rennels and Shortcliffe (1987) on medical advice systems and Franklin *et al.* (1987) on military applications. Wenger (1987) and Polson and Richardson (1988) provide booklength descriptions of computer-aided instruction. Briefer accounts can be found in Woolf (1988), Kearsley (1987) and Lesgold (1987). Swartz and Yazdani (1992) is a collection of papers on the computer-aided instruction of foreign languages; see also the special issue of the *Journal of Artificial Intelligence in Education* (1994; volume 5.4) on language learning.

Amongst a wide range of sources, machine translation is discussed in Hutchins (1986), Hutchins and Somers (1992), King (1987), Nirenberg (1987), Wilks (1987) and Slocum (1988). Text critiquing is discussed in Dale (1989) whilst Heidorn *et al.* (1982) describes the EPISTLE system. Sharples and O'Malley (1988) address some of the issues involved in designing a writer's assistant.

For examples of a grammar development tool see Evans (1985) and Erbach (1992). See also discussion in Shieber (1984 and 1988). Dalrymple *et al.* (1987) and Antworth (1990) both present examples of tools for morphological analysis based on two-level morphology (Koskenniemi, 1983). Chapter 1 of Winograd (1983) is a good introduction to the notion of language as a process.

The best introduction to NLP, especially in the context of this book, is Allen (1995). Smith (1991) is also valuable as is Winograd (1983) for information on syntactic processing. Other general texts are McTear (1987) and Beardon *et al.* (1991). Useful survey articles on NLP are Ritchie and Thompson (1984), Winograd (1984), Ramsay (1986), Gazdar and Mellish (1987), Ballard and Jones (1987), Carbonell and Hayes (1987), Joshi (1991) and Gazdar (1993). Grosz *et al.* (1986) is a wide ranging collection of core readings in NLP.

CHAPTER 2

The Challenge of Natural Language Processing

To behave intelligently requires knowledge. This is as true of playing chess as it is of processing language. The difficulty in creating intelligent machines lies in discovering and then expressing the relevant knowledge in a machine-usable form. Perhaps surprisingly, it has proved far easier to design programs which perform intellectual tasks that humans typically find hard rather than those that we all carry off effortlessly. Accordingly, the world chess champion has now been beaten by a computer but cannot *discuss*, even at the most childish level, the course of the game with his conqueror.

Beyond the fact that they are extraordinarily complex, the exact form and content of the various knowledge structures that underlie our linguistic abilities are still unclear. What is apparent is that language understanding requires mastery of both linguistic and non-linguistic knowledge. This chapter illustrates something of the difficulty of the NLP task by examining the range of different knowledge structures that are necessary for processing even the simplest of texts.

2.1 Knowledge of Linguistic Structure

Understanding a language means being able to match linguistic sounds to meanings. If English only consisted of a small number of sentences, say fifty, this would be easy. Each sentence could be stored in a list and paired with its meaning. Comprehension would simply involve locating the relevant sentence in the list and retrieving its associated meaning. However, the sheer number of sentences that each of us is potentially able to understand means that learning a language cannot consist solely of the rote memorisation of these sentences. What is acquired is the language's **grammar**, the structural system which underlies each sentence. Grammatical knowledge is central to language processing.

It is usual to identify five levels of grammatical structure. The **lexicon** contains information about the language's vocabulary; for instance, that *dictionary* is a noun and refers to a certain kind of book. **Morphology** deals with the internal structure of words; for example, that *unbelievable* is made up of three elements *un + believe + able*. **Phonology** concerns the sound system of the language; for example, that words in English may begin with the sounds 'str-' but not 'ktr-'. **Syntax** relates to the combination of words within a sentence; for instance, that *The village team lost in extra-time* is a possible sentence of English but not *Team in lost extra-time village the*. Finally, **semantics** deals with the linguistic meaning of sentences; for instance, that if *Few men like reading fiction* is true, then so is *Few men like reading romantic novels*.

These brief characterisations give no hint of the intricate and abstract nature of the structural principles underlying each component. A flavour of this may be gained by briefly considering two aspects of syntactic structure.

Sentences consist of words, strung together, one after another. This can be perceived whenever we hear an utterance. What cannot be observed is the **phrasal structure** of a sentence. For instance, in the sentence:

The knight challenged the king

the article *the* and the noun *knight* form a unit, *the knight*, referred to as a **noun phrase** or **NP**. Similarly for *the* and *king*. In addition, the verb *challenged* and the NP *the king* combine to form a **verb phrase** (**VP**), *challenged the king*. Finally, the VP and the NP *the knight* combine to make the sentence (**S**).

Phrasal structure can be represented using a labelled **tree diagram**.

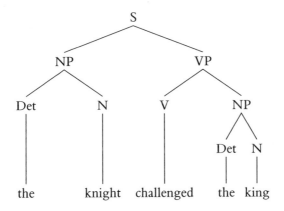

where Det = determiner, N = noun and V = verb

The tree consists of a number of **nodes**, each labelled with the name of a lexical or phrasal category or with a lexical item. The nodes are connected by **branches**, represented by the straight lines. Those branches which link categorial nodes should be read as 'consists of'. For example, the top-most part of the tree:

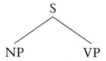

is interpreted as saying that 'the sentence consists of a noun phrase followed by a verb phrase'. A branch between a lexical category and a word:

should be read as 'is a'; in this case, '*knight* is a noun'.

An alternative representation to a tree diagram is a **labelled bracketing**.

[$_S$ [$_{NP}$ [$_{Det}$ the] [$_N$ knight]] [$_{VP}$ [$_V$ challenged] [$_{NP}$ [$_{Det}$ the] [$_N$ king]]]]

Although tree diagrams are easier to read, the programs in later chapters will use a labelled bracketing format to represent phrasal structure.

The phrasal structure of a language is described by **phrase structure rules**. Each rule states what a particular category may consist of. For example, the rule:

NP → Det N

is read as saying 'a noun phrase can consist of a determiner immediately followed by a noun'. The categorial information that *the* is an article, *knight* a noun and so on is expressed in the lexicon.

Numerous questions arise regarding the nature of phrase structure; what is the structure of more complex phrases such as *the large knight with the red favour*, do all phrases (category names aside) have the same structure? Are there elements in a phrase which are obligatory, and so on? Answers to these questions will either be implicitly or explicitly represented in the set of phrase structure rules for the language.

Syntactic structure is not exhausted by the linear order and phrase structure of lexical items. Consider the following sentence.

Strawberries, I like

The NP *strawberries* is functioning semantically as the object of the verb – it names the things that are liked. Usually, objects follow, rather than precede, their verb as in:

I like strawberries

The problem here is to account for how an NP can function as an object without appearing in the usual object position. One way of doing this is to assume that the sentence's structure includes a canonical object position following the verb, albeit one with no lexical content, and that the NP *strawberries* is linked to this position by means of co-indexing both NPs as is shown in the following tree.

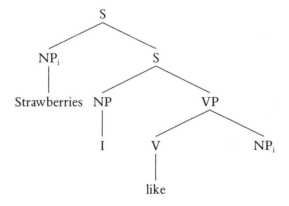

The NP with no lexical content is referred to as an **empty category**. As with phrase structure, various questions arise regarding the nature of empty categories; Where can they appear? Can other categories apart from NPs be empty? Are empty categories always linked to a non-empty phrase? Are there any constraints on which phrases they can be linked to, and so on?

This discussion has only indicated a small part of the complex and abstract nature of syntactic structure. Similar points could have been made with any of the other levels of linguistic structure. Indeed, the complexity is such that a full grammatical description of even a well studied language such as English is still some way off. Since, for reasons previously noted, language processing involves the construction of linguistic structures based upon grammatical knowledge, this lack of understanding partially explains the slow progress of NLP technology. This said, considerable advances have been made in the last few decades. The most notable successes have been in the area of syntax and this is where current NLP programs are strongest.

However, syntactic analysis is only one stepping stone towards the overall goal of being able to *interpret* linguistic input. In fact, assigning a meaning to a text has proved a far harder task than was initially expected. In part, this has been due to difficulties in representing semantic structure. More problematic, though, has been the realisation that the meaning of a statement depends to a large degree upon its context of utterance so that language understanding becomes the result of combining both linguistic and non-linguistic knowledge. The inclusion of more broad-based knowledge into the process widens the scope of NLP beyond the merely linguistic into areas of general cognitive processing, areas which are even less well understood than those involving specifically linguistic structures. This is the topic of the next section.

2.2 Ambiguity and Contextual Knowledge

The meaning of a sentence is a function not only of its constituent words but also of the way in which they are syntactically combined. This is known as **compositionality**. One implication of compositionality is that if a sentence can be syntactically analysed in more than one way, it will be ambiguous. Take the sentence:

Joshua hit the boy with the sword

This can be variously analysed depending upon whether the prepositional phrase (PP), *with the sword*, is an immediate constituent of the NP:

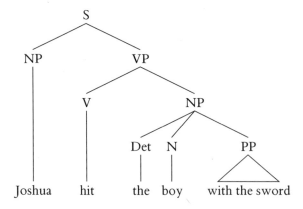

or the VP:

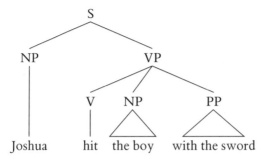

The sentence is also ambiguous; it can either mean that Joshua hit a boy who possessed a sword or that Joshua hit the boy with the aid of a sword. These two readings can be seen as consequences of the different syntactic structures just outlined; the first meaning corresponding to the first tree, the second meaning to the second tree. Ambiguity of this kind is called **structural ambiguity**. There are various other sources of ambiguity. **Lexical ambiguity** occurs when words can be interpreted in more than one way. For example, *tree* may refer to a certain type of plant, a diagram of a branching nature as in a phrase structure tree, or a wooden structure used for special purposes as in a shoe tree. **Scope ambiguities** arise when a sentence contains multiple quantifier expressions – *every*, *most*, *a*, *nine* and so on. For instance, the sentence:

Many children have read a book by Enid Blyton

has two possible interpretations; one where many children have read some book or other by Enid Blyton (although not necessarily the same one in each case) and another where there is some one book by Enid Blyton, say *Puzzle for the Secret Seven*, which many children have read.

Although ambiguous sentences have more than one meaning, in typical conversation a speaker will usually intend to convey only one of them. The problem for the listener is in deciding on which one. Clearly, linguistic knowledge is of no help here since it is the linguistics which gives rise to the ambiguity in the first place. Rather, disambiguation depends upon knowledge of the **context** of utterance. Contextual knowledge is a broad notion covering not only knowledge of the previous utterances in the conversation but also the utterance's location in time and space, the beliefs, desires and intentions of the participants, as well as the utterance's place within a general set of assumptions about the nature of the world, sometimes referred to as **encyclopaedic knowledge**. Encyclopaedic knowledge is a rich combination of information ranging from knowledge particular to the individual to knowledge common to a whole culture or society. To see how context is relevant to disambiguation, consider the following example.

Olivier presented the gift in blue wrapping paper

This has the same structural ambiguity as the earlier example *Joshua hit the boy with the sword*. It can mean, therefore, either that Olivier presented a gift that was wrapped up in blue paper or that Olivier made the presentation whilst he (Olivier) was wrapped up in blue paper. Of these two interpretations, the first more closely fits our general expectations about the world; on the one hand, gifts are often presented in special paper, whilst, on the other, such paper is rarely used as a form of apparel. Accordingly, unless a hearer had additional contextual information – perhaps, that Olivier likes to dress audaciously – it would be reasonable to assume the first meaning if this sentence was uttered in a conversation.

Encyclopaedic knowledge can also be used to resolve lexical ambiguity. For example, with:

The blossom on the tree is beautiful this year

the arboreal meaning of *tree* is likely to be preferred over the phrase structure or shoe tree interpretations since the latter are unlikely to be covered in blossom. Similarly with scope ambiguities. If part of your encyclopaedic knowledge is that Margaret Mitchell only wrote one book, *Gone with the Wind*, then the potentially ambiguous:

Many people have read a book by Margaret Mitchell

will be interpreted as meaning that many people have read *Gone with the Wind* rather than that many people have read some book or other from Margaret Mitchell's oeuvre.

In the last example, contextual knowledge was used not only to disambiguate between competing interpretations but also to fix the specific reference – i.e. *Gone with the Wind* – of the indefinite NP *a book by Margaret Mitchell*. Contextual knowledge is similarly required in fixing the reference of **indexical** expressions such as *here, there, now* and *tomorrow*. Out of context, the sentence:

Anne is coming here tomorrow

has only an *indeterminate* meaning along the lines that somebody called 'Anne' is going to be in some location the day after the utterance of this sentence. Embedded within a context of use, however, it will have a very particular meaning; for instance, that Anne Giggleswick is coming to 8 Kentwell Road, Glemsford, Suffolk on 16th November 1984.

With indexicals, context is used to construct a meaning which is *under-determined* by the linguistics of the expression. Similarly, discourse context is crucial in interpreting elliptical utterances. **Ellipsis** refers to the omission of words or phrases from a sentence which have already been previously referred to or mentioned. So, in the following exchange:

Claude: When will the book be completed?
Isabelle: Soon

Isabelle's elliptical response may be understood as expressing 'the book will be completed soon' as recoverable from Claude's previous utterance. Without the context of Claude's utterance, Isabelle's response is so vague as to be practically meaningless.

Different types of contextual information may combine to determine the specific meaning of an utterance. For example, the context of discourse in the following means that Audrey's elided utterance *Mary, then?* may be interpreted either as asking whether Mary ate the trifle or whether David ate Mary.

Audrey: Did David eat the trifle?
Bruce: No
Audrey: Mary, then?

Encyclopaedic knowledge will determine that, since David is unlikely to be a cannibal, the first interpretation is the more likely.

In each of the previous cases, contextual information was used to disambiguate or fully specify the literal meaning of a sentence. However, sentences can also be used to convey thoughts other than their explicit meaning. For example,

It's overly warm in here

is literally an *assertion* that the temperature in a particular location – to be determined by the context – is too high with respect to some level – again to be determined by the context. However, in some situations an utterance of this sentence could be understood as a *request*, say, to open a window. In other circumstances, the same sentence could be used as an *explanation* – for example, as to why the speaker has just taken off his jacket – or as a *warning* – for instance, that there are likely to be bacteria flourishing in the fridge – and so on. In these cases, which particular meaning the utterance has must be inferred on the basis of what is believed to be the speaker's emotions, desires, goals and intentions.

Encyclopaedic knowledge also plays a central role in establishing the links between utterances which give a discourse its coherence. For example, in:

> David has bought a new squash racquet. Unfortunately, the strings broke in the very first game.

general knowledge about squash racquets means that a hearer will feel justified in assuming that *the strings* of the second sentence refers to part of *the squash racquet* mentioned in the first sentence. The use of such 'bridging' assumptions to fix the interpretation of an expression means that discourse can be more compressed than would be the case if its cohesive links had to be expressed explicitly.

Without contextual information, then, an utterance conveys only an indeterminate meaning. Providing an NLP program with access to the relevant knowledge in order to construct the precise meaning intended is, however, a major undertaking. For instance, characterising a representative sample of encyclopaedic knowledge is a huge task. Imagine, say, coding up everything that you know about books – the title is printed down the spine, they come in hard and soft covers, they often have a dedication, and so on – and then multiply this for all the myriad objects and situations of our experience. The point is that any one of these assumptions may eventually play a role in the interpretation of some utterance or other. Problems of volume aside, there are other fundamental issues relating to the organisation of such large bodies of information and how best to represent them within a computer.

If successful language understanding depends upon access to such broad classes of non-linguistic knowledge, developing an NLP system with a human-like capacity for conversation would appear to be an almost impossible undertaking. However, some of the problems can be reduced by restricting the domain of discourse. For example, a program designed to act as a front-end to an expert system on plant diseases will only need to know the arboreal interpretation of *tree*. Further, although this move will not remove all vague or ambiguous input, a fairly constrained subset of background knowledge will usually be sufficient to determine the intended interpretation.

The knowledge structures discussed in the last two sections have mainly been examples of **declarative knowledge**. Declarative knowledge refers to factual knowledge and is often described using the locution 'know that . . .'. For example, speakers of English *know that* a noun phrase may consist of a determiner followed by a noun or that squash racquets have strings. Declarative knowledge is of little use, however, unless it is also known how to use it. This is the topic of the next section.

2.3 The Process of Language Understanding

Section 2.1 introduced a piece of syntactic information expressed by the phrase structure rule *NP → Det N*. This states that a noun phrase can consist of a determiner followed by a noun. However, such knowledge is of little use to an NLP program unless it can *use* this information to work out that, say, *the king* is an example of such a phrase. The process by which the syntactic structure of an expression is determined is known as **parsing**. Parsing is an example of **procedural knowledge**, knowledge about *how* to do something.

Typically, parsers work by manipulating the declarative knowledge of the grammar in various ways. Here is one way that a parser might work. Suppose the parser has access to the grammatical information expressed by the following phrase structure rules:

S → NP VP
NP → Det N
VP → V NP

and a lexicon with the relevant categorial information for each word of the input sentence *The knight challenged the king*. Further, imagine that the processor proceeds by inspecting the sentence, one word at a time, from left to right. The first word examined will be *the*. Looking this up in the lexicon, the parser will find that it is classified as a determiner. With this information, the parser is able to construct the following branch of a tree.

The next word is the noun *knight*. Proceeding as before, the parser will end up with two branches.

On the basis of the phrase structure rule *NP → Det N*, these two branches may now be combined into a single NP-tree.

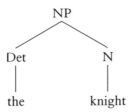

Continuing the process, the next word in is the verb *challenged*, followed by the determiner *the* and finally the noun *king*. The result will be as follows.

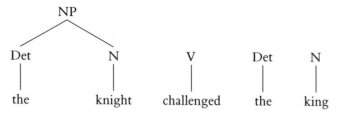

As before, the Det and N branches may be combined into an NP-tree, which, in turn, may be combined with the V branch to form a VP-tree as licensed by the rule *VP → V NP*. The result is now a two tree 'forest'.

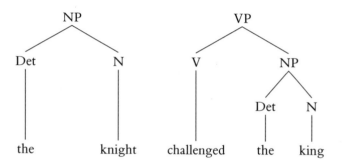

Finally, these two trees may be combined into an S-tree given the rule *S → NP VP*, so completing the parse.

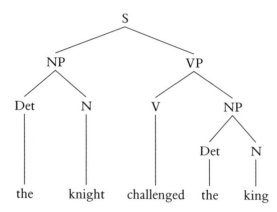

Because of the direction that the phrase structure tree is 'grown' during the process, the parsing strategy just outlined is referred to as a **bottom-up** approach. Other strategies, including **top-down**, are equally possible as later chapters will show.

Parsing is not always the simple process that this example may have suggested. One problem involves ambiguity again, although of a somewhat different nature to that discussed earlier. Each of the sentences in the previous section were **globally** ambiguous in that the sentence as a whole was ambiguous. Ambiguity may also arise *temporarily* as part of the parsing process. Consider the sentence:

Have the children cleared up the toys?

When the parser initially processes the first word, *have*, it has no way of knowing whether it is to be interpreted as an auxiliary verb (as in this case) or as a main verb as in the following imperative:

Have the children clear up the toys

Indeed, it is only upon encountering *cleared* that the parser will know that *have* should be analysed as an auxiliary in the first sentence. Ambiguities that are resolved by later material in the sentence in this way are referred to as **local** ambiguities. Local ambiguity pervades natural language as much as global ambiguity.

There are various ways to handle local ambiguity. One possibility is for the parser simply to choose one of the options when the ambiguity arises and see how things work out. If subsequent material shows the decision to have been wrong, then the parser goes back and tries one of the alternatives. The main problem with this approach lies in the computational cost that it incurs. For example, the parser must keep a record of the places where alternatives have still to be tried and what those alternatives are. Further, exploring these alternatives often involves the parser in reduplicating previous effort as it rediscovers structures that had been successfully identified during the original selection. For sentences containing a number of local ambiguities this computational burden may become quite considerable. This is not to say that these problems cannot be overcome or, at least, reduced with more sophisticated parsing techniques. The point is simply to indicate something of the potential complexity of parsing.

Just like syntactic analysis, utterance interpretation is a process. The previous section showed that understanding the meaning of an utterance involves being able to draw **inferences** based upon the context of utterance as in the following interchange.

Adrian: Would you like a cup of coffee?
Bruce: Coffee would keep me awake

Adrian has to decide whether Bruce's reply to his question is intended as a yes or no. The literal meaning of the reply, however, expresses neither. Rather, Adrian must use the utterance in conjunction with the context to infer the answer. If part of the context includes the assumption that Bruce would like to stay awake, then Adrian may conclude that Bruce is accepting the offer of coffee. On the other hand, if Adrian knows that Bruce wants to go to sleep soon, then the utterance will be taken as a refusal.

Before this inferential process may begin, however, the context itself needs constructing. This is a complex and little understood process. There are various sources from which a particular set of contextual assumptions may be chosen. For example, apart from those derived from the current utterance, they may come from previous stages of the conversation; through monitoring the physical environment; or as part of the speaker's current set of preoccupations. In some cases encyclopaedic knowledge may be tapped via the lexical items of the utterance. For instance, the use of *coffee* will provide access to a large body of general knowledge about coffee. Some of this information will be common to most members of the community – 'coffee is (usually) drunk hot' – but some will be idiosyncratic to the hearer – 'Anne Giggleswick only drinks decaffeinated coffee'. It has been suggested that encyclopaedic knowledge is partly organised into chunks of stereotypical assumptions, sometimes called **frames** or **schemes**, about common objects or situations. So, the word *concert* will not only introduce the concept of a musical performance into the context but also information about typical places where they are held, the time of day they tend to occur, what happens in the interval and so on.

A context may be built up from any of these sources. The problem is deciding upon which of these possible assumptions are to form the actual context. For example, not everything that the hearer knows about coffee will be relevant for the interpretation of Bruce's utterance. There are further complications since some assumptions may not be derivable from memory at all but have to be inferred by the hearer. For example, whether or not Bruce wants to stay awake might not be part of Adrian's background knowledge. However, if he knows that Bruce has to finish some work before going on holiday in the morning, then it would be reasonable to assume that he wants to remain awake in order to complete it and so adds this to the context.

The two processes briefly examined in this section, parsing and context construction, are psychological processes which an NLP program must attempt to replicate in some way. The next section considers some reasons as to why research in NLP should pay close attention to how the human language processor achieves its goal of understanding language.

2.4 Psycholinguistics and NLP

NLP can be treated as a branch of computational psychology. From this perspective, only those techniques consistent with what is known about how humans process language are permissible. Alternatively, NLP could be pursued more as a branch of engineering, so that *any* means of accomplishing the goal of language understanding would be acceptable, as long as it worked. However, even from this latter standpoint, NLP research cannot be completely divorced from psycholinguistic concerns.

On the one hand, the human processor provides a valuable case study in understanding how language comprehension might be achieved, not only because it is the *only* example of a language processing system that we have, but also because it is so spectacularly successful. On the other hand, NLP systems are designed to interact with the human system. If the former are not sensitive to the processing quirks of the latter, then problems of misunderstanding may arise. It is this latter point which is pursued here.

In section 2.2 it was shown how context may be used to determine a single interpretation for structurally ambiguous utterances. However, even in situations where the context does not favour one reading over the other, potential ambiguity often goes unrecognised by hearers. Consider the following example:

Nicole said Claude left yesterday

Most people will interpret this as meaning that the leaving was done yesterday. However, there is an alternative reading, that where the saying happened yesterday. The ambiguity arises because the adverb *yesterday* may attach to either the upper or lower VP.

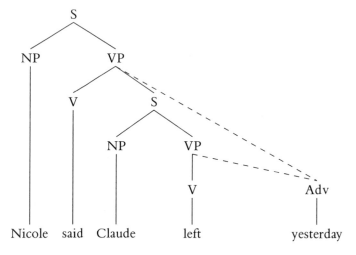

Why is it that even in a neutral context most people fail to notice this ambiguity? The assumption is that the answer lies with the structure of the parser. In other words, ignoring contextual effects, the design of the parser favours certain types of analysis over others. In this case, the **parsing preference** seems to be for attaching a word or phrase to the lowest possible node to the right. Other examples show that this is a systematic preference. So, with:

> Louise figured that Richard wanted to take the dog out

take out is preferred over the equally possible *figure out* and with:

> Caroline said that Shula had just given birth in her car

give birth in her car is preferred to *said in her car*. Of course, semantic and contextual information may override this preference as in the following example:

> Rebecca drove through the village in her car

Here the reading *drove in her car* will be favoured given the encyclo-paedic link between driving and cars and the incongruence of the alternative parse, *the village in her car*.

It is not always the case that phrases are preferentially attached to the lowest node. For instance, in the following:

> Richard wanted the necklace for Ruth

the natural interpretation is *wanted for Ruth* rather than the reading *the necklace for Ruth*. Note, however, that a change of verb may switch this preference:

> Richard included the necklace for Ruth

Parsing preferences have been used to explain the phenomena of **garden path** sentences. These are sentences where the parser's preferences result in the wrong analysis, so, leading it 'up the garden path'. In some cases, this may only cause the parser to stumble temporarily as in:

> The granite rocks during an earthquake

In other cases, the parser seems to come to a complete halt as in the (grammatical) example:

> The horse raced past the barn fell

[This sentence has the same structure as the non-garden path example *The horse ridden past the barn fell.*]

At a practical level, NLP systems must be sensitive to these parsing preferences. For example, if the parser fails to emulate the attachment preferences itself, then it may fail to recover the intended message. Or, consider garden path sentences. For humans these cause comprehension problems. However, for computer systems they are more likely to be problematic for the generation of sentences. **Language generation** involves choosing the right words, phrases and syntactic structures by which to express an intended meaning. However, even though *The horse raced past the barn fell* is grammatical, a program must be sensible to the fact that expressing this meaning this way will cause comprehension problems for the human user.

As a final example of the psycholinguistic constraints on an NLP system, consider ill-formed input. A surprising amount – some estimates say around 25 per cent – of input to such systems is deviant for various reasons; errors in typing, spelling, punctuation, word order, agreement, as well as sentences which are anomalous, contradictory, incomplete and so on. Humans are almost as equally adept at understanding such examples as their well-formed counterparts. Indeed, in many cases, processing is so effective that we are unaware that an utterance contained any mistakes. It is even possible to make sense out of the most garbled of texts as anybody who has read a poor translation into English knows.

> Nowadays, in our country Sweden, there is so well of all sort of eating that man light come to big overweight.

NLP programs are often designed only to handle well-formed input. However, ideally the techniques developed for this task should also be capable of extension towards handling ill-formed input. In many cases, contextual information and the ability to be able to infer what was likely to have been said provides the key to such understanding. Nevertheless, it is also likely that the structure of the grammar and its associated parser plays a considerable role in this process.

The argument of this section has been that NLP must take into account psycholinguistic research for practical reasons. There is perhaps a more general reason as well. Since the aspects of processing examined here are assumed to be consequences of the structure of the human processor, it may be that techniques developed purely on engineering grounds are unable to exactly mimic the relevant behaviour without a great deal of *ad hoc* machinery. Indeed, it might be that the only system which could completely replicate human linguistic abilities would be one that copies the human design almost exactly. If this were so, NLP and psycholinguistics might be best thought of as different sides of the same coin.

It is not possible in a single chapter to convey anything but the most cursory of impressions of the complexity of the language processing task. Clearly, if NLP research could not proceed until a firm understanding of each of the various components involved had been acquired, it would be some years before the programme could even start. Fortunately, progress can be made in a more piecemeal fashion. In part, this is due to the modular nature of the process. For example, understanding the nature of syntactic structure and processing can proceed to some considerable extent without a complete understanding of the nature of semantic structures and processing. Also it is possible to consider the application of NLP techniques within fairly restricted domains of discourse so as to greatly reduce the problems of access to non-linguistic knowledge.

The rest of this book is an elementary introduction to just one area of NLP: syntactic processing. Before this can be started, the programming language Prolog needs to be introduced. This is the topic of the next five chapters.

2.5 Further Reading

There are many overviews of the topics covered in this chapter. Crystal (1997) provides a wide range of material on a vast array of topics although often in fairly limited detail. More comprehensive introductions to linguistics can be found in Fromkin and Rodman (1988), Akmajian *et al.* (1990) and O'Grady *et al.* (1992, 1997). Collections of survey articles on various aspects of linguistics can be found in Lyons *et al.* (1987), Oshern *et al.* (1990) and Newmeyer (1988). Pinker (1994) is a most entertaining and wide ranging account of the nature of language from a biological perspective. Valuable discussion of the nature of interpreting language in a context can be found in Brown and Yule (1983) and Blakemore (1992). Introductions to psycholinguistics are presented by Matthei and Roeper (1983), Garnham (1985) and Garman (1990). Dowty *et al.* (1985) is an interesting interdisciplinary collection of articles on natural language parsing from various perspectives including the computational.

The relationship between linguistic theory and NLP is not quite as clear cut as might be expected. For some discussion on this point see especially Shieber (1988). See also Sag (1991) and Halvorsen (1988).

PART II

The Fundamentals of Prolog Programming

CHAPTER 3

Facts

Prolog is the first practical example of a **logic programming** language; indeed, its name is short for '**pro**gramming in **log**ic'. The idea behind logic programming is that symbolic logic can be used to express knowledge and that logical inference can then be employed to manipulate it. An **inference** is a conclusion drawn on the basis of certain facts or assumptions. From this perspective, solving a problem is thought of as trying to infer a desired conclusion from a particular set of assumptions.

This brief characterisation might make Prolog sound more forbidding than it is in reality. First, it is relatively easy to express the various statements required to form a knowledge base and, secondly, the inferencing mechanism is provided 'for free' as part of the system. This chapter provides clarification of these points by introducing some simple examples of Prolog programming.

A number of different versions of Prolog are now available to suit a variety of needs. Although they vary in terms of the special features offered, nearly all have a common core which is sometimes referred to as 'Edinburgh Prolog'. It is this 'standard' Prolog which forms the basis of the following presentation.

3.1 Facts

A Prolog program consists of a number of statements defining various relationships which hold between the objects in the area of interest. These are the assumptions from which the inferences will be drawn. Defining relationships in this way is sometimes referred to as 'programming by declaration'.

By way of illustration, we will express some trivial information about certain world languages and their speakers. For example, we might want to say that Boris speaks Russian. One way of representing this in Prolog is with the following expression.

```
speaks(boris, russian).*
```

---

* Prolog text is printed throughout in Courier font.

We might also want to state the information that English is spoken in the United Kingdom. This could be represented in Prolog as:

```
spoken_in(english, uk).
```

These are both examples of a Prolog **fact**. A fact asserts or declares that certain objects are related to one another in a particular way.

A fact consists of two parts. First comes the name of the relation. This is called the **predicate**. Then, inside round brackets, come the names of the objects involved in the relationship, each separated by a comma. These names are called **arguments**. In the examples above, speaks and spoken_in are predicates and boris, russian, english and uk arguments. A predicate and its arguments is sometimes called a **literal**. Here are some other examples of Prolog facts with a gloss of their intended meaning.

```
noun(computer).        i.e. 'Computer' is a noun

means(fils,son).       i.e. The meaning of 'fils' is 'son'

word(fils,noun,masculine).
                       i.e. 'fils' is a masculine noun.
```

A predicate may take any number of arguments (including none at all). This number is referred to by talking of the **arity** of the predicate. For example, spoken_in has an arity of 2, noun an arity of 1 and word an arity of 3. For stylistic variety, predicates will occasionally be referred to as being binary (arity of 2) or ternary (arity of 3). A unary predicate (arity of 1) is often called a **property**.

There are a number of syntactic conventions that need to be followed when writing Prolog facts. For example, the predicate name must start with a lower case letter. Accordingly, the following is not well-formed:

```
Speaks(boris, russian).
```

Predicates may not contain any spaces; it is for this reason that the underscore, _, has been used for the predicate spoken_in since spoken in is ill-formed. Expressions with these properties are called **atoms**. Atoms may take other forms which will be introduced as necessary.

Arguments are more varied in their appearance. For the present, only atoms as described above and integers – that is, positive or negative whole numbers – will be considered as possible argument names. Atoms and integers are sometimes referred to as **constants**.

Note that each fact must finish with a full stop. This is so that the Prolog interpreter knows where the fact ends. It is easy to forget the full stop in the initial stages of programming. Many versions of Prolog have a syntax checker which will signal such an error on loading the program. [However, see section 6.7.] The meaning of a fact is left entirely at the programmer's discretion and plays no role in the functioning of the program. Consequently, it does not matter what names are used for either predicates or arguments. For example, it is possible to express the earlier statement about Boris with the fact:

```
climbed(tenzing, everest).
```

Here the *speaks*-relation is named by the predicate climbed and Boris and Russian with the atoms tenzing and everest, respectively. Although representing the information this way will not affect the running of the program, it does not aid the programmer's understanding of what the fact is supposed to represent. For this reason, names should be chosen whose interpretation is intended to approximate to the equivalent English words.

It is important to note that with respect to Prolog 'fact' simply refers to a particular type of syntactic expression. There is no requirement that facts should actually be *true*. As long as the syntax of the expression is correct, any statement may be made in Prolog, even those that are false such as:

```
speaks(boris, piro).
```

Whenever a constant is used as an argument within a program it is, as its name suggests, taken to represent the same object. Therefore, each distinct object must have a distinct name. For example, the two facts:

```
speaks(john, swahili).
speaks(john, warlpiri).
```

must be understood as jointly stating that one and the same person, who is being called john, speaks these two languages. This representation cannot be used for the case where two different people who both happen to be called 'John' are involved. In such a situation different names must be used. One possibility would be to add an integer at the end of the name.

```
speaks(john1, swahili).
speaks(john2, warlpiri).
```

Another possibility would be to add surnames and link them with an underscore.

```
speaks(john_hart, swahili).
speaks(john_spink, warlpiri).
```

Predicate symbols also receive a constant interpretation in a program. Their identification, however, not only depends upon their spelling but also upon their arity. For example, the following two facts involve different predicates because of the different number of arguments taken.

```
language(english).
language(english, indo_european).
```
i.e. English is an Indo-European language

It is important that a fact's arguments appear as an ordered sequence since relations are often ordered. For instance, English is spoken in the United Kingdom but the United Kingdom is not spoken in English. It is arbitrary which ordering of arguments is chosen. All that matters is that, once a choice has been made, it is adhered to throughout the program. Often the ordering chosen is that which most closely approximates to the ordering in the equivalent (active) English sentence.

Because the order of arguments is fixed, names of the same type of object will appear in the same position for each instance of a fact with a particular predicate. It is possible to use this to refer to a particular argument position. For example, rather than saying 'the first argument position' for the predicate spoken_in it might be referred to as the 'language position'.

A set of facts with the same predicate symbol and same number of arguments defines the relation for which the predicate stands. Such a collection of facts is called a **procedure**. Below is a procedure for the predicate spoken_in.

```
spoken_in(english, uk).
spoken_in(english, usa).
spoken_in(english, australia).
spoken_in(spanish, peru).
spoken_in(quechua, peru).
spoken_in(piro, peru).
```

A set of procedures makes up a **program**. The program below consists of two procedures, one defining the predicate spoken_in as above and the other the predicate speaks.

```
spoken_in(english, uk).
spoken_in(english, usa).
spoken_in(english, australia).
spoken_in(spanish, peru).
spoken_in(quechua, peru).
spoken_in(piro, peru).
```

```
speaks(boris, russian).
speaks(hank, english).
speaks(john, english).
speaks(jacques, french).
speaks(helmut, german).
```

A program can be thought of as a description of a particular world of objects. How complete that description is depends upon the requirements of the program.

Question 3.1

Expand the previous program by adding the data that German is spoken in Austria and Switzerland, French in Canada, Belgium and Switzerland and Spanish in Spain and the Canary Islands.

Question 3.2

How might the information that Bess Spooner and Ben Spooner speak English be represented in Prolog?

Question 3.3

Using the Prolog fact:

```
word(dog, noun).
```

as a basis, express the lexical categories of the following words. Note that in some cases a word may be associated with more than one category.

every, gave, under, the, she, tree, small, can, old, very, quickly, Bloomfield, time

Question 3.4

Express the following English sentences as Prolog facts:

(1)   Dravidian is (the name of) a language family.
(2)   Tamil is a Dravidian language.
(3)   Latin is an extinct language.
(4)   Tok Pisin is a pidgin language of Papua New Guinea.
(5)   'pordo' is the Esperanto for 'door'.
(6)   'tante' is a singular, feminine noun.
(7)   Kanji is a writing system for Japanese.
(8)   Chamorro is spoken in Guam by 51,000 people.
(9)   Mary speaks Warlpiri and Samoan.
(10)   The plural of 'ox' is 'oxen'.

Question 3.5

Given the description in this section, which of the following are well-formed Prolog facts?

```
(1)  language(icelandic, indo european).
(2)  Language(icelandic, indo_european).
(3)  language(dinka)
(4)  related(bulgarian, warlpiri).
(5)  2_languages(john).
(6)  languages_2(john).
```

Question 3.6

The following is a part of the family tree for the Germanic branch of the Indo-European languages. It shows the 'genetic' relationships between various modern languages and their ancestral forebears. Each language is a descendent of those languages higher up in the tree to which it is linked by ascending branches. For example, Old English is a descendent of both Anglo-Frisian and West Germanic but not High German. Using the predicate daughter_of – for example daughter_of(anglo_frisian, west_germanic) – represent this tree as a set of Prolog facts.

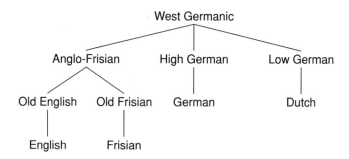

3.2 Asking Simple Questions in Prolog

The discussion in the following sections will be with respect to the following simple program which consists only of a single procedure, spoken_in.

```
spoken_in(english, uk).
spoken_in(english, usa).
spoken_in(english, australia).
spoken_in(spanish, peru).
spoken_in(quechua, peru).
spoken_in(piro, peru).
```

If you are following this book with a computer, you will need to create a file containing these facts. Exactly how to create and edit a file varies from system to system and you will have to consult your reference manual for particular information.

The file will need a name. Let it be example. The file will also need a **file type** which will identify the file as a Prolog file. Here pl will be used as the file type so that the full name of the file is example.pl. Notice the full stop separating the file name from the file type. Your own version of Prolog may use a different file type name such as pro; your reference manual should provide details.

Assuming that the reader is able to create the program file example.pl, the next step is to load Prolog from the operating system. Again, how this is achieved will vary with the implementation. When Prolog has been successfully loaded the Prolog prompt will appear on the screen; this is a question mark followed by a hyphen:

```
?-
```

The form of the prompt indicates that the system is in query mode, ready to accept questions from the user.

First, however, the file example.pl needs loading. This can be achieved by typing the following:

```
?- consult('example.pl').
```

Note that the name of the file has to be in single quotes so that the dot between the file name and file type is not misparsed as a terminating full stop. Note also that the whole expression must finish with a full stop. Pressing the RETURN key will result in Prolog replying yes. This indicates that the file has been successfully located and loaded.

```
?- consult('example.pl').
   yes
```

An alternative way of loading the file is by typing:

```
?- ['example.pl'].
```

This notation is especially useful if more than one file needs loading since the relevant files can simply be listed between the square brackets, each separated by a comma:

```
?- ['file1.pl', 'file2.pl', 'file3.pl'].
```

With example.pl successfully loaded, questions can now be asked of the program.

The simplest queries in Prolog correspond to *yes-no* questions in English. In other words, they ask for confirmation of some statement. Accordingly, Prolog replies with a yes or no depending on whether Prolog can confirm the statement or not. For example, the Prolog equivalent of the English question 'Is English spoken in the United Kingdom?' is:

```
?- spoken_in(english, uk).
```

After having pressed the RETURN key, Prolog will reply with a yes since it is able to confirm that, according to its program, English is spoken in the United Kingdom. On the other hand, the question:

```
?- spoken_in(piro, uk).
```

will result in a no response since the system is unable to verify that Piro is spoken in the United Kingdom.

A yes-no question in Prolog looks just like a fact except that it is preceded by the system prompt. Indeed, both facts and questions have the same syntax. In order to distinguish between the two, a question will be called a **goal**. The difference between a fact and a goal is that the former asserts that a certain relationship holds whilst the latter questions whether it holds or not.

Recall that the idea behind logic programming is that solving a problem involves trying to infer a desired conclusion from a set of assumptions. The set of assumptions is the program and the desired conclusion the goal. That part of Prolog which attempts to infer the goal from the program will be referred to as the **interpreter**, **inference engine** or more generally just 'Prolog'. As already noted, the programmer does not need to specify an inference engine since one is already built into Prolog. It is this that provides the answer yes or no.

The interpreter works by attempting to **satisfy** the goal that constitutes the question. Sometimes this will be referred to as **calling** or **invoking** the procedure. A goal is satisfied if it can be shown (by the interpreter) to follow from the program. The simplest example of a goal following from a program is if it **matches** with a fact. In other words, the reason why the *goal* spoken_in (english, uk) is satisfiable is because it matches with the *fact* spoken_in(english, uk). In this case, the goal and fact match because they are identical; both predicates are spelt the same and have the same arity and each corresponding argument is identical. Note how the matching is syntactic in nature; it is determined purely by identity of syntactic form and not meaning.

The interpreter searches for a match by checking each fact in turn. The facts are examined in the same top-down order as they appear in the file. If a match is found, the system reports the satisfaction of the goal by printing yes on the screen. A goal that is not satisfiable is said to **fail**. In such cases no is returned to the screen.

This description explains Prolog's responses to the earlier questions. Given the goal spoken_in(english, uk), a match is possible with the very first fact in the program; hence, Prolog's yes. With the second goal, spoken_in(piro, uk), there is no possible match and so Prolog replies with a no.

```
?- spoken_in(piro, uk).
            ?- spoken_in(english, uk).

                    spoken_in(english, uk).
                    spoken_in(english, usa).
                    spoken_in(english, australia).
                    spoken_in(spanish, peru).
                    spoken_in(quechua, peru).
                    spoken_in(piro, peru).
```

No match

The satisfaction of a goal is determined solely by which facts are in the database. If there is no match with a fact in the program, the goal fails. This explains Prolog's response to the question:

```
?- spoken_in(spanish, spain).
   no
```

The no refers to this goal not being a consequence of the program. In other words, Prolog assumes that anything it has not been told about does not hold. This is sometimes referred to as the **closed world assumption**.

Question 3.7

Assuming the program example.pl, why do each of the following goals fail?

(1) ?- spokenin(english, uk).
(2) ?- spoken_in(peru, spanish).
(3) ?- speaks(boris, russian).

3.3 Compound Questions

It is possible to ask questions containing multiple goals. These are
called **compound questions**. This is achieved by separating each of
the goals by a comma – read as 'and' in this context. For example:

```
?- spoken_in(english,uk), spoken_in(english,
australia).
```

is the equivalent of the English question 'Is English spoken in the
United Kingdom and is English spoken in Australia' or, more
idiomatically, 'Is English spoken in both the United Kingdom and
Australia?' There can be any number of goals in a compound question.

For Prolog to reply yes to a compound question, each of the
goals must be satisfied. The satisfaction of each individual goal is
determined just as described in the last section for a single goal.
Theoretically, it does not matter in which order the goals are evaluated, indeed, they could proceed in parallel. The actual procedure
that the Prolog interpreter adopts is to attempt to solve the goals
from left to right as written. By now the reader should be able to
see that Prolog will respond yes to the above question since both
goals are satisfiable.

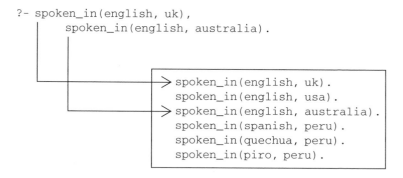

It is also possible to pose **disjunctive** queries using a semi-colon
– pronounced 'or' – in place of a comma. For instance, the query:

```
?- spoken_in(english, peru); spoken_in(spanish,
peru).
```

is the Prolog version of the English 'Is English spoken in Peru or is
Spanish spoken in Peru' or, slightly more idiomatically, 'Is English
or Spanish spoken in Peru?' A disjunction of goals is satisfied if
either one of the goals is satisfied. In the above, Prolog will reply
with a yes since, although the first goal fails, the second is satisfied.

```
?- spoken_in(english, peru);
        spoken_in(spanish, peru).
```

```
                    spoken_in(english, uk).
                    spoken_in (english, usa).
                    spoken_in (english, australia).
                  → spoken_in (spanish, peru).
                    spoken_in (quechua, peru).
                    spoken_in (piro, peru).
```

No match

Question 3.8

What will Prolog reply to the following questions and why?

(1)   ?- spoken_in(english, usa).
(2)   ?- spoken_in(biro, peru).
(3)   ?- spoken_in(german, germany).
(4)   ?- spoken_in(german, germany); spoken_in(piro, peru).
(5)   ?- spoken_in(english, uk), spoken_in(english, usa),
       spoken_in(piro, peru).

3.4 Questions with Variables

The questions so far have simply asked for confirmation of some
number of goals. This can be fairly limiting. Imagine, for instance,
trying to find out which languages are spoken in Peru if you did
not already suspect which they might be. In such a situation, you
would have to ask various yes-no questions, changing the name of
the language argument each time.

```
?- spoken_in(english, peru).
   no

?- spoken_in(german, peru).
   no

?- spoken_in(spanish, peru).
   yes
```

This is a clumsy method. Further, if we are unaware that, say, Piro
is a language, we will never be able to formulate the question
which will confirm that this is one of Peru's languages.

The kind of question that needs asking in this case is the Prolog equivalent of the English question 'Which languages are spoken in Peru?' One way of expressing the meaning of such a question is with the formula:

(which X: X a language) is such that X is spoken in Peru

The X here is called a **variable** and stands for the object which we cannot name. In this case, the X is restricted to the names of languages by the bracketted clause. To answer this question, a value needs to be found for X which makes 'X is spoken in Peru' true. In this case 'Spanish' is a possible answer since 'Spanish is spoken in Peru' is true.

Variables of this kind are similar to those found in algebraic equations such as:

$$x + 3 = 5$$

To solve an equation like this means finding a particular value for the variable such that substituting the one for the other results in a true formula. In this case, x stands for 2 since '2 + 3 = 5' is true.

The use of variables in Prolog is analogous to these two cases. The corresponding version of the earlier question is:

```
?- spoken_in(X, peru).
```

Here X is a Prolog variable. Since the variable appears in the first argument position of the predicate spoken_in, it is a variable over languages. Posed this question, Prolog will reply:

```
X = spanish
```

Pressing the RETURN key again results in Prolog answering yes. In other words, the interpreter has found a value for the variable which makes the question true.

Prolog distinguishes between constants and variables by the case of the initial letter of the name; constants start with a lower case letter and variables with an upper case letter (or the underscore). Constants and variables together are called **simple objects**.

As with constants, the choice of variable names is at the discretion of the programmer. The above shows that a single algebraic-type letter will suffice. However, it is usually better to choose a more meaningful name. For example, the previous question could equally have been expressed as:

```
?- spoken_in(Language, peru).
   Language = spanish
   yes
```

A question containing a variable is a goal which, just as in the previous examples, Prolog attempts to evaluate by matching with a fact in the program. However, matching through identity which was the cause of satisfaction with the previous goals is no longer possible; none of the facts in the program contain a variable. But recall that variables are surrogate names, only there because the object of interest cannot be named. If the variable were replaced with an actual name – a constant – a match with a fact would be possible. So, the goal spoken_in(Language, peru) would match with the fact spoken_in(spanish, peru) if the variable Language were to be replaced with the constant spanish. But, this is just what is required since it produces a value for the variable which makes the original question satisfiable. In such a case, the variable is said to be either **instantiated** or **bound** to the value spanish. A variable is **uninstantiated** if it is not currently associated with a value. If instantiating a variable to a constant results in a match, then Prolog outputs the instantiation on the screen just as we might write '2' as the answer to the algebraic problem $x + 3 = 5$.

The attempt to satisfy a goal with variables proceeds in the same top-down way through the program as described previously. Accordingly, in the current example, the first match is with the fact spoken_in(spanish, peru).

```
?- spoken_in (Language, peru).
```

```
                    spoken_in(english, uk).
                    spoken_in(english, usa).
                    spoken_in(english, australia).
               ───> spoken_in(spanish, peru).
Language = spanish  spoken_in(quechua, peru).
                    spoken_in(piro, peru).
```

Variables can be placed in any argument position.

```
?- spoken_in(spanish, Country).
   Country = peru
   yes
```

Also, more than one variable may appear in the same goal:

```
?- spoken_in(Language, Country).
   Language = english
   Country = uk
   yes
```

The value of a variable only applies to those instances of the variable *in the same goal*. This is the same as in algebraic equations. For example, although the variable x appears in both the following equations, there is no requirement that the same value be associated with both occurrences.

$$x + 3 = 5$$
$$4 - x = 1$$

However, within the same equation, as in:

$$x + 3 + x = 7$$

the variable must take the same value in both instances. The same applies with Prolog. For example, the variable `Language` in the compound question:

```
?- spoken_in(Language,uk), spoken_in(Language,
australia).
```

must take the same value. But the same variable in two separate questions need not as Prolog's replies show.

```
?- spoken_in(Language, uk).
   Language = english
   yes

?- spoken_in(Language, peru).
   Language = spanish
   yes
```

As with constants, distinct variable names stand for distinct objects. Instantiating the variable to a value results in all other instances of the variable within the same goal being similarly instantiated. Accordingly, there is no possible match for the query:

```
?- spoken_in(X, X).
```

because there are no `spoken_in` facts where the first and second arguments are identical.

There is a special variable in Prolog called the **anonymous variable**. This is represented by the underscore, `_`. It is used on those occasions when we do not care what value is assigned to a variable, only that an assignment exists. Accordingly, Prolog will not print out the value. For example, we might want to ask the question 'Is

Piro spoken somewhere?' without wanting to know exactly where. In this case the anonymous variable can be used:

```
?- spoken_in(piro, _).
   yes
```

One distinguishing feature of the anonymous variable is that it need not be instantiated to the same value if it appears more than once in a goal; each occurrence of the variable is unique. Note the difference between Prolog's responses to the following questions:

```
?- spoken_in(X, X).
   no
?- spoken_in(_, _).
   yes
```

The second question is satisfiable through different instantiations from the two occurrences of the anonymous variable.

Finally, note that variables can only be used in argument positions. It is not possible, for example, to use variables in place of predicate names. Accordingly, expressing the question 'What relationship do Spanish and Peru stand in?' as in the following query is ill-formed.

```
?- Relationship(spanish, peru).
```

Question 3.9

What does Prolog reply to the following questions and why?

(1) ?- spoken_in(Swahili, uk).
(2) ?- spoken_in(spanish, Country).
(3) ?- spoken_in(English, UK).
(4) ?- spoken_in(_123, uk).
(5) ?- spoken_in(_, australia), spoken_in(_, peru).

Question 3.10

Suppose the order of the database were changed to:

```
spoken_in(english, australia).
spoken_in(piro, peru).
spoken_in(quechua, peru).
spoken_in(english, uk).
spoken_in(spanish, peru).
spoken_in(english, usa).
```

What differences would there be compared with the answers to the previous question?

Question 3.11

How might the problem of not being able to use variables for predicate names be overcome?

3.5 Finding Alternative Answers: Backtracking

Given the information in the program example.pl, there is more than one answer to the question:

```
?- spoken_in(Language, peru).
```

However, so far Prolog has only provided a single answer. This section shows how Prolog finds the others.

The reader who has been following the text with a computer will have noticed that when Prolog displays a value for a variable the cursor remains in position immediately following the answer. This indicates that the system recognises that there might be alternative answers and is waiting for further instructions. If the user is satisfied with the given answer, then pressing the RETURN key abandons the search for more solutions. However, typing a semicolon – recall that this means 'or' – tells the interpreter to search for an alternative answer. If one can be found, the new value for the variable will be displayed on the screen, if not the system replies with a no – here meaning 'no more answers can be found'. The following shows a possible interaction with the program.

```
?- spoken_in(Language, peru).
   Language = spanish;
   Language = quechua;
   Language = piro;
   no
```

Repeated use of the semi-colon has resulted in Prolog finding all the possible values that could satisfy the goal.

It is of some importance to understand how Prolog finds alternative solutions. Basically, the interpreter tries to resatisfy the original goal. In effect, this means reverting back to the state of the original goal. To achieve this, any variables that became instantiated during the original satisfaction of that goal will revert to their uninstantiated state. Once the original goal has been recovered in this way, the program can be searched for another solution. The search proceeds as before except for one difference, the place where the search starts from. If it were to start from the top of the program, then the same values would be found each time. What needs to happen is that values already found should be ignored. This is achieved by the search restarting from the point in the program of the last match.

With this in mind, Prolog's responses to the previous question can now be traced. As was seen in section 3.4, Prolog's initial answer is with Language bound to spanish.

```
?- spoken_in (Language, peru).
```

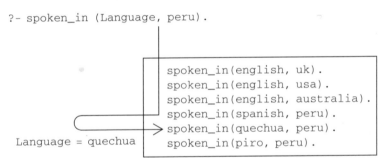

```
                          spoken_in(english, uk).
                          spoken_in(english, usa).
                          spoken_in(english, australia).
                        > spoken_in(spanish, peru).
Language = spanish        spoken_in(quechua, peru).
                          spoken_in(piro, peru).
```

Asking for an alternative solution by typing in a semi-colon forces Prolog to backtrack. Reverting to the original goal, Prolog attempts to resatisfy it but starting the search after the point in the procedure where the previous solution was found. In this case the next match is as indicated.

```
?- spoken_in (Language, peru).
```

```
                          spoken_in(english, uk).
                          spoken_in(english, usa).
                          spoken_in(english, australia).
                          spoken_in(spanish, peru).
                        > spoken_in(quechua, peru).
Language = quechua        spoken_in(piro, peru).
```

Seeking an alternative solution involves undoing the new binding of Language to quechua to revert (once more) to the original goal and continuing the search from the last point of satisfaction. This time the match is as follows.

```
?- spoken_in (Language, peru).
```

```
                          spoken_in(english, uk).
                          spoken_in(english, usa).
                          spoken_in(english, australia).
                          spoken_in(spanish, peru).
                          spoken_in(quechua, peru).
                        > spoken_in(piro, peru).
Language = piro
```

A further search is unsuccessful since there are no more facts left to check and Prolog relays this information by reporting no.

The process of reverting back to a previous goal in an attempt to resatisfy it is called **backtracking**. If more than one goal has already been satisfied, Prolog backtracks to the most recently satisfied goal. If this cannot be resatisfied, then Prolog backtracks to the next most recent and so on until no more possibilities are left. Of course, backtracking of itself does not guarantee that there are any further solutions.

The use of the semi-colon allows the user to force backtracking. However, backtracking may happen automatically, instigated by the system itself if, during the satisfaction process, some possible instantiation leads to a dead end. To see an example, consider how the following, somewhat vacuous, question would be answered:

```
?- spoken_in(Language,Country), spoken_in
(Language,peru).
```

Note that the variable Language appears in both goals so that whatever instantiation of Language satisfies the first goal must also satisfy the second. Prolog begins by attempting to satisfy the first goal. It can do this by matching with the first fact of the program with the instantiations:

```
Language = english
Country = uk
```

These instantiations mean that the second goal now becomes spoken_in(english, peru). Of course, this goal will fail. The system now automatically backtracks to the first goal to see if there is an alternative answer. Resatisfaction is possible with the instantiations:

```
Language = english
Country = usa
```

However, this results in the second goal becoming spoken_in (english,peru) once again. It is only after backtracking twice more that the instantiation:

```
Language = spanish
Country = peru
```

results in the second goal becoming spoken_in(spanish, peru) which is satisfiable. Since both goals have now been satisfied, so has the compound question.

In attempting to search for an answer to a question, Prolog proceeds systematically, satisfying the goals from left to right and looking through the program for matches from the top to the bottom. This methodical approach means that, on occasion, various wrong decisions will be made and blind alleys entered. Backtracking allows the system to rescue itself from such situations. The overall effect is that if a solution exists to the question given a particular program, Prolog will, certain cases aside, eventually find it.

Question 3.12

Trace Prolog's behaviour in the following interaction:

```
?- spoken_in(english,Country).
   Country = uk;
   Country = usa;
   Country = australia;
   no
```

3.6 Using Variables in Facts

Variables can also be used in facts, although then their interpretation changes. A variable used in a question is understood as being *existentially* quantified. In other words, the question will be true if there exists *at least one* instantiation of the variable which satisfies the goal. The variable, in effect, is standing for at least one constant. A variable in a fact, on the other hand, is taken as standing for all constants; it is *universally* quantified. So, for example, the fact:

```
spoken_in(Language, un).
```

is interpreted as meaning that all languages are spoken at the United Nations. Seeing how Prolog matches goals with such a fact shows why this is the case.

Suppose Prolog is asked the following question:

```
?- spoken_in(english, un).
```

This will match the fact above just as spoken_in(Language, un) would match with spoken_in(english, un) if the former were a goal and the latter a fact. Hence, Prolog will reply with a yes. Note that since the variable was not in the goal, no value is printed on the screen; after all, the query is a yes-no question. The point here is that it does not matter what constant name is put in the first argument position in the question since it will always match the variable in the fact. This is why the variable in the fact stands for all languages.

Question 3.13

Write a program which gives the translation of an English word in various other languages. You should be able to ask questions equivalent to 'What is the Spanish for "mountain"?', 'Which language has "montagne" as the translation for "mountain"?' or 'What is the English for the German word "Berg"?'.

3.7 Further Reading

Limitations of space preclude a full description of Prolog and the reader is referred to one of the many textbooks for more complete coverage. Two outstanding texts are Bratko (1990) and Sterling and Shapiro (1986). Also useful are Clocksin and Mellish (1987) and Covington, Nute and Vellino (1988). Coelho and Cotta (1988) provide an interesting collection of programs. Ross (1989) introduces more advanced techniques. These references also cover the next four chapters.

CHAPTER 4

Rules and Complex Names

This chapter introduces two extensions to Prolog which greatly increase its expressive power.

4.1 Rules

Imagine a program consisting of the following set of facts.

```
spoken_in(english, uk).
spoken_in(english, usa).
spoken_in(english, australia).
spoken_in(french, france).
spoken_in(french, canada).
spoken_in(french, belgium).
spoken_in(german, germany).
spoken_in(german, austria).

speaks(john, english).
speaks(jacques, french).
speaks(helmut, german).
```

Suppose, further, that information about which speakers can be understood in which countries needs to be added. The only way this can be achieved at present is by adding a series of new facts to the program.

```
understood_in(john, uk).
understood_in(john, usa).
understood_in(john, australia).
understood_in(jacques, france).
understood_in(jacques, canada).
understood_in(jacques, belgium).
understood_in(helmut, germany).
understood_in(helmut, austria).
```

However, these facts only restate information which is already implicit in the original program. Take the first of the new facts. The reason why we want to say that John is understood in the United Kingdom is because he speaks English and English is spoken in the United Kingdom. But this information is already recorded as part of the definitions of the speaks and spoken_in predicates. In other words, it is possible to work out understood_in(john, uk) on the basis of previously stated facts. Prolog can also do this through the use of a **rule**.

Rules are a way of defining new relations in terms of others that have been previously defined. The rule for understood_in can be defined as follows.

```
understood_in(Person, Country) :-
        speaks(Person, Language),
        spoken_in(Language, Country).
```

Here : - is pronounced 'if' and the comma as 'and'. In other words, the definition says that a person is understood in a country if they speak a language which is spoken in that country. The definition works because both the predicates speaks and spoken_in have already been defined as a series of facts.

A rule consists of two parts; a **conclusion** which appears to the left of : - and a number of **conditions** which appear to the right. The conclusion is referred to as the **head** of the rule and the conditions as the **body**. The head consists of a single literal whilst the body may consist of any number of literals, as long as each is separated from the others by a comma. The rule terminates with a full stop in the same way as a fact. Facts and rules will be referred to as **clauses**. It is possible to think of facts as a special case of a rule, one where the conclusion is not conditional upon anything else.

If the head of a rule uses the same predicate as a set of facts, then they (partially) define the same relation. Accordingly, a procedure can be redefined as a set of clauses defining a predicate.

Adding the understood_in-rule to the program example.pl enables such questions as the following to be asked.

```
?- understood_in(john, australia).
   yes

?- understood_in(jacques, australia).
   no

?- understood_in(helmut, Country).
   Country = germany;
   Country = austria;
   no
```

```
?- understood_in(Person, Country).
   Person = john
   Country = uk;
   Person = john
   Country = usa;
   Person = john
   Country = australia;
   Person = jacques
   Country = france;
   Person = jacques
   Country = canada;
   Person = jacques
   Country = belgium;
   Person = helmut
   Country = germany;
   Person = helmut
   Country = austria;
   no
```

The last example shows that with the rule, Prolog is able to extract the same information as was originally expressed as a series of individual facts.

Consider another predicate which can be defined on the basis of the present set of predicates. Assume that world_language(Lang) holds of any language, Lang, just in case it is spoken in more than one country. The obvious way to define this might seem to be with the following rule.

```
world_language(Lang) :-
            spoken_in(Lang, Country1),
            spoken_in(Lang, Country2).
```

The idea here would be that using two different variable names for the country arguments ensures that two different countries are being referred to. However, this involves a misunderstanding. Although it is the case that, within the same rule, the same variable must be assigned the same value. The reverse is not the case; two different variables need not be assigned different values, there is nothing inconsistent with them both taking the *same* value. Accordingly, Piro will turn out to be a world language on this definition where Country1 and Country2 both happen to be assigned the value peru. For the definition to work as desired, an extra condition needs adding, namely that Country1 and Country2 have different values. This can be achieved through the use of two special predicates not(Goal) and =. not(Goal) holds just in case Goal does not hold. =(pronounced 'equals') holds between two expressions X and Y just in case they both match. Accordingly, the expression:

```
not(X = Y)
```

is satisfiable only if X and Y are not the same. not and = are examples of **built-in predicates** since they are *pre-defined* by the system. Chapter 7 has much more on built-in predicates. The amended definition for world_language now becomes:

```
world_language(Lang) :-
            spoken_in(Lang, Country1),
            spoken_in(Lang, Country2),
            not(Country1 = Country2).
```

The third clause of the body of the rule ensures that, whatever the values are for Country1 and Country2, they must not be the same. As a result, Piro is no longer defined as a world language but English is.

Question 4.1

Define the predicate language(Language) in terms of the predicate spoken_in.

Question 4.2

On the basis of a set of speaks facts, define someone as bilingual if they speak more than one language.

Question 4.3

Assume a predicate language defined as follows (where the third argument represents the number of speakers in thousands).

```
language(english, uk, 51000).
language(piro, peru, 10).
language(manx, isle_of_man, 0).
```

Define the predicate extinct(Language). Define living(Language) in terms of extinct(Language).

Question 4.4

A phrase structure tree such as:

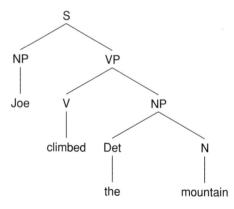

can be partially represented in terms of the predicate `immediately_dominates`.

```
immediately_dominates(s, np1).
immediately_dominates(np1, joe).
immediately_dominates(s, vp).
immediately_dominates(vp, v).
immediately_dominates(v, climbed).
immediately_dominates(vp, np2).
immediately_dominates(np2, det).
immediately_dominates(det, the).
immediately_dominates(np2, n).
immediately_dominates(n, mountain).
```

[Note how the two NP nodes have had to be distinguished.]

A node X **dominates** another node Y if X is higher up the tree than Y. X **immediately_dominates** Y if X is the next highest node dominating Y. Assuming that `immediately_dominates` has been defined, express the following tree-theoretic notions as Prolog rules:

(i)   Node X is the **mother of** node Y if X immediately dominates Y.
(ii) Node X is the **daughter of** node Y if Y immediately dominates X.
(iii) Node X is the **sister of** node Y if they have the same mother.
(iv) X is the **root** node of a tree if it is not immediately dominated by any other node.
(v)   X is a **leaf** or **terminal** node if it does not immediately dominate any other node.

(iv) and (v) will require the use of the built-in predicate `not` used in the previous question.

[Domination represents the 'up-down' dimension of a tree. A complete representation of a tree would also need to record the left-to-right or **precedence** relations between the nodes. A node X **precedes** Y if it appears to the left of Y and **immediately precedes** it if it occurs immediately to the left of Y. It is left as a further exercise for the reader to finish the coding of the tree by adding a set of `immediately_precedes` facts.]

Question 4.5

Using the definition of `immediately_dominates` as in the previous question, define a subject as an NP immediately dominated by S and an object as an NP immediately dominated by VP.

Question 4.6

Assuming a definition of `immediately_dominates` as in question 4.5, define the notion of dominates so that Prolog will respond `yes` to the following questions:

```
?- dominates(vp, np2).
?- dominates(s, n).
```

Does your solution extend to arbitrarily large trees? If not, why not?

4.2 How Prolog Answers Questions Using Rules

Only a small change to the account in section 3.2 is necessary to explain how Prolog evaluates goals against programs containing rules. Consider the question:

```
?- understood_in(john, australia).
```

Prolog attempts to satisfy this goal by finding a match with a clause in the program. The only possible match is with the head of the rule:

```
understood_in(Person, Country) :-
            speaks(Person, Language),
            spoken_in(Language, Country).
```

with `Person` instantiated to the value `john` and `Country` to `australia`. This results in the following **instance** of the rule:

```
understood_in(john, australia) :-
            speaks(john, Language),
            spoken_in(Language, australia).
```

Since a rule is a conditional statement, the truth of the head is dependent upon the truth of its conditions. This means that satisfying the head of a rule is dependent upon the satisfaction of its body. In other words, the literals of the body become **subgoals** to satisfying the original goal. In the current case this means that the goal understood_in(john, australia) will be satisfied just in case the subgoals speaks(john, Language) and spoken_in (Language, australia) can be satisfied. Prolog attempts to solve these subgoals in the same left-to-right order as with conjunctive queries. With the variable Language instantiated to the value english, the first subgoal matches with the fact speaks(john, english). Given the binding of Language to english, the second subgoal becomes spoken_in(english, australia) which directly matches a fact. Since both subgoals have been satisfied, so has the dependent goal, namely the original question. Accordingly, Prolog replies with a yes.

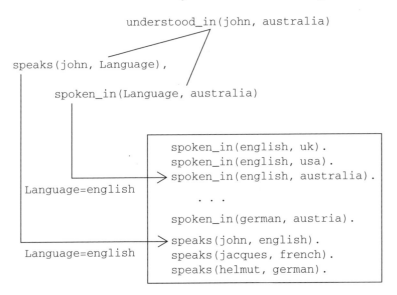

The previous description needs amending slightly to take into account the local scope of variables. As discussed in the last chapter, variables with the same name are only treated as instances of one another if they occur within the same clause. With this in mind, consider what happens when Prolog is presented with the following question.

```
?- understood_in(Person, Country).
```

It so happens that the relevant rule also uses the same variable names and so a match is clearly possible. However, this is fortuitous; the variable names could just as easily have been different in either rule or question. Further, the local nature of variables means that they should not be thought of as instances of the same variables since one pair occurs in a goal and the other in a rule. Accordingly, Prolog chooses an instantiation of the rule where the variable names are different from any already under consideration. In this case, since Person and Country are the variables 'in play', these are the ones that need renaming in the rule. Let us use Person1 and Country1 for the new names (although internally Prolog will use variables such as _235). This results in the following instance of the rule

```
understood_in(Person1, Country1) :-
            speaks(Person1, Language),
            spoken_in(Language, Country1).
```

But does the goal still match with the head of the renamed rule? Yes; a variable can match with anything, including another variable.

In effect, `Person` becomes linked to `Person1` and `Country` to `Country1`. As a consequence, if `Person1` becomes bound to a value, `Person` automatically becomes instantiated to the same value. Similarly for `Country` and `Country1`. In this case, the two sub-goals `speaks(Person1, Language)` and `spoken_in(Language, Country1)` will be satisfied with the instantiations:

```
Person1 = john
Language = english
Country1 = uk
```

Accordingly, the head of the rule is also satisfied. Since this was originally matched with the initial goal `understood_in(Person, Country)`, this latter is also satisfied. The value output for the variables is `Person = john` since `Person = Person1` and `Country = uk` since `Country = Country1`. The renaming of variables will be returned to in section 5.2.

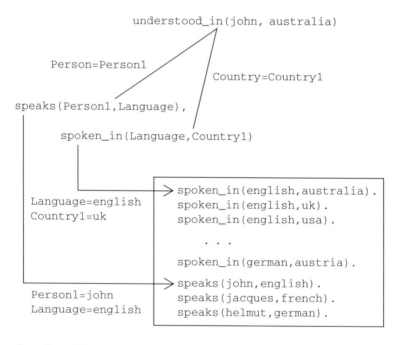

Question 4.7

Do a pen and paper trace of Prolog's response to the question:

```
?- understood_in(helmut, Country).
   Country=germany
   yes
```

How, if at all, would the satisfaction process differ if the order of the rule's body was reversed?

```
understood_in(Person, Country) :-
        spoken_in(Language, Country),
        speaks(Person, Language).
```

4.3 Structured Objects

The names used so far in argument positions have been unstructured objects consisting either of a constant or a variable. Prolog also allows structured names called **compound names**. This is like English. For example, we can refer to the language English either with the unstructured name 'English' or with a more complex expression such as 'the language of the United Kingdom'. This latter expression could be expressed in Prolog as:

```
language(uk)
```

This complex expression can then act as an argument to a predicate.

```
speaks(john, language(uk)).
```

With compound names, the item before the brackets is called the **function** (symbol) and the items inside the brackets the function's **arguments**. The syntactic conventions are similar to those already given for Prolog facts; the function symbol must be an atom, the arguments must appear inside round brackets, separated by commas. The arguments themselves are names – either constants, variables or other complex names. As with facts, a function is identified in terms of its name and arity. The arguments of functions may also be other compound expressions. For example:

```
language(queen(england))
```

is a compound expression which might be translated as 'the Queen of England's language' which is another, albeit complex, name for English. Both predicate and function names can be referred to by the general term **functor**.

Notice how similar the syntax of a clause and a compound name are. Both consist of a name with some number of arguments inside round brackets. This, in fact, means that the syntax of Prolog can be given a remarkably simple description.

All data objects in Prolog are **terms**. A term is any one of the following:

(a) an atom
(b) an integer
(c) a variable
(d) a structure

Constants – i.e. atoms and integers – and variables are simple objects. A **structure** consists of a functor – which must be an atom – followed by a number of terms inside round brackets and separated by commas.

Whether a structure is interpreted as a predicate plus arguments or a function plus arguments depends upon the context – if it is in an argument position then it is a function. For example in:

```
language(language(england)).
```

The first instance of language is a predicate whilst the second is a function.

The matching of function-argument structures is just like that for predicate-argument structures; in both cases the functors must match, as well as each of the arguments. The matching can get quite complicated if variables are involved. Prolog provides a special predicate = – pronounced 'equals' – which checks whether two terms match:

```
?- language(X) = language(language(queen(eng-
land))).
X = language(queen(england))
yes
```

Question 4.8

Using a function-argument structure for the first argument, redefine the speaks predicate so as to be able to capture the fact that both Bess Spooner and Ben Spooner speak English.

Question 4.9

Define a 2-place predicate word which captures the categorial information associated with the following French nouns.

chat – masculine, singular	'cat'	
trompettes – feminine, plural	'trumpets'	
lune – feminine, singular	'moon'	
journaux – masculine, plural	'newspapers'	

Question 4.10

Define a 2-place predicate word for the following noun paradigm from Old English ('cyning' = 'king'). Use compound names to express the gender, number and case information.

cyning – masculine, singular, nominative
cyning – masculine, singular, accusative
cyninges – masculine, singular, genitive
cyninge – masculine, singular, dative
cyningas – masculine, plural, nominative
cyningas – masculine, plural, accusative
cyninga – masculine, plural, genitive
cyningum – masculine, plural, dative

Question 4.11

Using a compound name, amend the description of the phrase structure tree of question 4.5 in order to overcome the problem noted in defining the predicates `subject` and `object` in question 4.6. These predicates will need redefining in order to accommodate the changes in representation.

Question 4.12

What will Prolog's responses be to the following questions?

(i)   `?- spoken_in(english,uk) = spoken_in(english,uk).`

(ii) `?- spoken_in(english, Country) =`
                           `spoken_in(Language, uk).`

(iii) `?- spoken_in(Language,Country) =`
                    `spoken_in(language(queen),usa).`

(iv) `?- spoken_in(language(Person), uk) =`
                    `spoken_in(Language, Country).`

(v)   `?- spoken_in(language(queen(uk)), Country) =`
                `spoken_in(language(queen),australia).`

Question 4.13

Phrase structure can be represented in terms of function-argument structures. For example,

    `np(det(the), n(violin))`

represents the following tree structure:

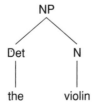

With this as a guide, express the phrase structure tree in question 4.4 as a compound name applied to a (1-place) predicate `tree`.

CHAPTER 5

Lists and Recursive Rules

The previous two chapters have presented the basics of Prolog. In this chapter two powerful extensions are introduced. One is a special kind of data-structure, a list, the other a type of rule that is essential for defining relations involving lists. Lists will form the basic data-structure for later NLP programs where they will be used to represent sentences.

5.1 Lists

There is more than one language spoken in Peru. This state of affairs has previously been represented with a set of facts.

```
spoken_in(spanish, peru).
spoken_in(quechua, peru).
spoken_in(piro, peru).
```

This is a rather repetitive form of representation. Further, it might be useful, on occasion, to be able to refer to the whole group of Peruvian languages. This is not possible with the data as represented above. One solution would be to gather the languages together under a function name, say, group.

```
spoken_in(group(spanish,quechua,piro), peru).
```

Three facts are now reduced to one and in a form that makes it possible to refer to the whole group of Peruvian languages.

```
?- spoken_in(Languages, peru).
   Languages = group(spanish,quechua,piro)
   yes
```

One problem with this solution is that it does not extend to other cases. For example, the instance of group found in:

```
spoken_in(group(english, welsh), uk).
```

although intended to represent the same notion is not the same function as that used in the previous fact, since it does not take the same
number of arguments. What is required is a more open-ended form
of expression which can be used to represent any number of items.
The data-structure that achieves this is a **list**. Lists are sequences of
items which usually – although not necessarily – bear some relation to one another. For example, a list may consist of the letters in
a word, or of the words in a sentence, or of the languages of Peru.

There are two sorts of list; the **empty list** which has no elements and **non-empty lists** which contain one or more items. The
empty list is represented in Prolog by the atom []. Non-empty lists
are represented as a sequence of terms, separated by commas, and
enclosed by square brackets:

```
[spanish, quechua, piro]
[c,h,r,i,s,t,m,a,s]
[every, copy, was, sold]
```

All non-empty lists are divided into two parts; the **head** which
is the first element of the list and the **tail** which is the remainder of
the list. The empty list is unique in having neither a head nor a tail.
It is important to remember that the tail of a list is also a list.

By way of analogy, imagine a list as a stack of plates. The top
plate is the head of the stack. If this top plate were removed, the
remainder – the tail – would still be a stack of plates (assuming
that there are any left). Note that the only plate which is directly
accessible is the top plate – the head – and this is equally true of a
list. To get at plates lower down in the stack, the top plates must
be removed first; we shall see later that the same applies to lists.
Finally, the only place that a new plate can be added to the stack is
on top as a new head; this is also true of a list.

In order to be able to refer to the head and tail of a list a special
separator symbol, |, is used. The head appears to the left of the
vertical bar and the tail to the right. For instance:

```
[spanish | [quechua,piro]]
```

Note how the tail is a list as shown by the square brackets. Using
the equality predicate introduced in the last chapter is a useful way
of gaining familiarity with the bar notation:

```
?- [Head|Tail] = [spanish,quechua,piro].
   Head = spanish
   Tail = [quechua,piro]
   yes
```

Note that single term lists also match:

```
?- [Head|Tail] = [english].
   Head = english
   Tail = []
   yes
```

but not the empty list:

```
?- [Head|Tail] = [].
   no
```

The bar notation permits any number of items before the bar as long as each is separated by a comma.

```
?- [Head1, Head2|Tail] = [spanish,quechua,piro].
   Head1 = spanish
   Head2 = quechua
   Tail = [piro]
   yes
```

This flexibility allows various different, although equivalent, representations of a list; for instance:

```
[spanish, quechua, piro]
[spanish, quechua, piro|[]]
[spanish, quechua|[piro]]
[spanish|[quechua,piro]]
[spanish|[quechua|[piro|[]]]]
```

The last of these examples is especially important since it shows that every element of a list is the head either of the list itself or of one of its sublists. This fact will be crucial in the definition of list predicates to be introduced in the next section.

Variables can also be used in lists. Using a variable for a tail represents a list of arbitrary length. For example, the list:

```
[a, b|Tail]
```

represents all those lists with a and b as the first two elements.

Finally, note that a list is an *ordered* sequence of items. In other words, two lists are the same only when they contain the same elements *in the same sequence*. This explains Prolog's response to the question:

```
?- [spanish,quechua,piro] = [piro,spanish, quechua].
   no
```

In terms of Prolog's syntax, lists are technically function-argument structures. Accordingly, they may appear as arguments to other functors. For instance, the languages of Peru can now be wrapped up into a list and used as an argument of the spoken_in predicate.

```
spoken_in([spanish,quechua,piro], peru).
```

Further, because of this function-argument structure, lists may also have other lists as arguments. For example, the following list groups some of the languages of Europe into their family classifications:

```
[ [english,german,dutch],
    [french,spanish,italian],
      [irish,breton]]
```

The representation is indented in order to make the structure a little clearer; the list consists of three members each of which is a list. A more meaningful form of representation might make each of the sublists an argument to a function naming the particular language family:

```
[germanic([english,german,dutch]),
     italic([french,spanish,italian]),
         celtic([irish,breton])]
```

This whole structure could then appear as an argument to a predicate such as euro_languages.

```
euro_languages([germanic([english,german,dutch]),
               italic([french,spanish,italian]),
               celtic([irish,breton])]).
```

Question 5.1

English is spoken in more than one country. Using the list notation change the spoken_in facts that were used at the beginning of section 4.1 to take this into account.

Question 5.2

Using a list to represent the countries where a language is spoken, what would the fact for Latin look like? Can you write a rule which would use such a fact to define an extinct language?

Question 5.3

Represent the sentence *The climber cut the rope* as a list of words where each word is represented as a list of letters.

Question 5.4

Represent the following phrase structure rules using a binary predicate `rule` whose first argument is the left-hand category with the second argument the list of right-hand categories.

    S → NP VP
    NP → Det N
    NP → Det N PP
    VP → V NP
    PP → P NP

Question 5.5

Which of the following matchings hold? For those that do, give the instantiation of variables.

(a) `[Head|Tail] = [english,spanish,french]`
(b) `[piro,quechua,german] = [piro, quechua,german|[]]`
(c) `[piro,quechua,german,[]] = [piro, quechua,german|[]]`
(d) `[Head, Head1, Head2] = [french,german, english]`
(e) `[Head, Head1] = [french,german,english]`
(f) `[Head,Head1|Tail] = [Head|Tail1]`
(g) `[] = [Head|Tail]`
(h) `[english] = [english|[]]`
(i) `[[english]] = [english|[]]`
(j) `[[english,french],spanish] = [Head|Tail]`
(k) `[[english,Item],piro] = [[Item1,quechua]|Tail]`
(l) `[french,[quechua,german]] = [Head|Tail]`

Question 5.6

The following predicate – partially indented to show its structure – represents a small part of the Uto-Aztecan branch of the language tree for the Mesoamerican Indian languages of Central America. The function names refer to language groups. Reconstitute the family tree from this representation.

```
uto_aztecan([
        corachol([cora,huichol]),
        aztecan([
                nahuatl([nahuatl,pipil]),
                pochutec([pochutec])
                                ])]).
```

5.2 Recursive Rules

A data structure is **recursive** if it contains other structures like itself. Lists, therefore, are recursive structures since, the empty list aside, the tail of a list is also a list. Because of this structure, rules defining relations which relate to lists also need to be recursive. A number of examples are introduced in this section.

5.2.1 member

One of the simplest relations relating to lists is member(Element, List) which holds just in case Element is one of the items of the list List.

```
?- member(quechua, [spanish,quechua,piro]).
   yes
?- member(english, [spanish,quechua,piro]).
   no
```

How might member be defined? For a list with three elements as above, the following three facts would suffice.

```
member(Element, [Element| _]).
member(Element, [_, Element|_]).
member(Element, [_, _, Element|_]).
```

Recall, however, that the original motivation for using a list structure is its ability to combine *any* number of items together. The above procedure, then, will not handle all possible cases of membership. Indeed, clearly, this approach, in principle, cannot be generalised to cover all cases. Fortunately, a more compact definition is possible based upon the following observation. If an item is a member of a list, then either it is the head of the list or a member of its tail. Translating this statement into Prolog gives the following two clauses:

```
member(Element, [Element| _]).

member(Element, [_ |Tail]) :-
           member(Element, Tail).
```

The fact covers the case where the item is the head of the list and the rule where the item is a member of the tail. The anonymous variable is used in those positions where the actual value is of no concern. This compact definition will suffice for any list.

Rules where the predicate being defined by the head also appears in the body of the rule are called **recursive** rules. At first glance, recursive definitions appear circular. A definition is **circular** if it assumes that which is being defined as in the following:

'Human' means being born of human parents

Here, the meaning of 'human' is (partially) defined in terms of itself and so can only be understood if one already knows the meaning of 'human'. Clearly, circular definitions are to be avoided.

The definition of member is saved from circularity by two details. First, the fact member(Element, [Element | _]) is non-recursive. This represents the **base** or **terminating condition**. It is this clause that allows the potential spiral of definitions to be broken. Secondly, although the predicate member appears in both the head and tail of the rule, note that the second argument differs between the two occurrences. Accordingly, the head is not defined exactly in terms of itself. In fact, because the list in the tail occurance of member is shorter than that in the head, the predicate is defined in terms of a simpler version of itself. The relevance of these remarks will be best appreciated by considering how the definition of member works in practice.

Imagine Prolog is posed the following question:

```
?- member(piro, [spanish,quechua,piro]).
```

Given this goal, the interpreter attempts to find a match with a clause in the program. The first potential match is with the base clause. This clause, however, requires that the head of the list be the same as the first argument. Since this is not so, no match is possible. A match can be achieved, however, with the head of the rule assuming the instantiation of variables:

```
Element = piro
_ = spanish
Tail = [quechua,piro]
```

to give the following instance of the rule:

```
member(piro, [spanish|[quechua,piro]]) :-
            member(piro, [quechua,piro]).
```

Note how the subgoal that forms the tail of the rule is just like the original goal except that the list is one item shorter.

The only potential match for the new subgoal is with the head of the rule once again, although with a subtle difference compared with the previous occasion. The goal member(piro, [quechua, piro]) is to be assessed *independently* of the goal member(piro, [spanish,quechua,piro]) since it is a different goal. To achieve this, the various variables involved need to be kept distinct through renaming. Using the convention introduced in section 4.2, renaming of those variables which are already being used will lead to the following copy of the rule.

```
member(Element1, [_|Tail1]) :-
          member(Element1, Tail1).
```

Matching of the goal member(piro, [quechua,piro]) with the head of this version of the rule is possible given the binding of variables:

```
Element1 = piro
_ = quechua
Tail1 = [piro]
```

resulting in the new instance of the rule:

```
member(piro, [spanish|piro]) :-
          member(piro, [piro]).
```

and the new sub(sub)goal:

```
member(piro, [piro])
```

This goal now matches directly with the fact – since piro is the head of the list [piro] – and so is satisfied. Since member(piro, [piro]) has been satisfied, so is the dependent member(piro, [quechua, piro]) which, in turn satisfies the original goal member(piro, [spanish, quechua,piro]). Accordingly, Prolog will respond with a yes.

Prolog's proof of a query can be represented by a **proof tree**. A proof tree shows the satisfaction dependencies between the various goals. Each goal is linked via branches to its immediate subgoals upon whose satisfaction it depends. Any goal matching with a fact is indicated with a tick. The proof tree for the current example is:

```
member(piro, [spanish, quechua,piro])
                  |
     member(piro, [quechua,piro])
                  |
        member(piro, [piro])
                  |
                  √
```

The tree clearly shows how the satisfaction of the bottom goal determines the satisfaction of the top – i.e. initial – goal. It also shows how the definition of member works. Each time the rule is applied, the head of the list is stripped off. This continues until the relevant item eventually appears as the head of the list when the terminating clause can apply.

Satisfaction, then, is ultimately determined by matching with the non-recursive terminating clause. Notice also how each recursive call to the predicate results in a simpler subgoal, the list being searched being one element shorter. The upshot of this is that if the element in question is a member of the list, it will eventually appear as the head of a list. On the other hand, if it is not a member, then all the elements will be removed one by one until the empty list is reached. In this case the process comes to a halt since no further match is possible; both clauses of the definition of member require that the list have a head and tail and the empty list has neither. The result is that the sequence of subgoals bottoms out in failure, failure which percolates back up to all the dependent goals. The following proof tree shows such a case for the question:

```
?- member(english, [spanish,quechua,piro]).
```

Failure to match with a clause is represented with a cross:

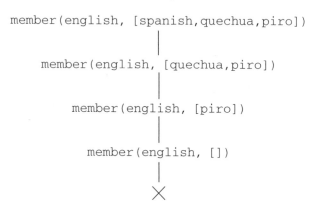

Question 5.7

The predicate language(Language) defined in question 4.1 will no longer work if the first argument of the spoken_in facts is changed to a list. Using member, redefine language to take this into account.

Question 5.8

The members of a list may also be lists. Define a predicate belongs (Element, List) which is satisfied as long as Element appears somewhere in the list List.

```
?- belongs(piro, [[english, german], french, [spanish,
piro]]).
   yes
```

Question 5.9

Explain Prolog's response to the following question:

```
?- member(spanish, List).
   List = [spanish|_23];
   List = [_22, spanish|_27]
   yes
```

Question 5.10

Using `member`, define the predicate `subset(List, List1)` which holds if all the members of `List` are also members of `List1`.

Question 5.11

One of the most famous Artificial Intelligence (AI) programs is called ELIZA. Dating from 1966, it is able to carry out a limited conversation based upon a highly unsophisticated technique. ELIZA simply scans the input sentence for certain keywords. If it finds one, it responds with a pre-stored reply. For example, on spotting *not* in a sentence such as *I am not going to lose*, ELIZA might reply with *Are you sure about that?* Devise a simple program which uses this technique. Suggestion; define a predicate `reply(Input, Output)` where `Output` is the associated response to some keyword, `Word`, which is a member of `Input`. Some suggested keyword-response pairs are:

Keyword	Response
I	Is it important to you?
you	Why am I important?
feel	Do you often feel that way?
father	Tell me more about your family

It is also useful to have a neutral response if the input does not contain one of the keywords such as *Can you expand on that?* or *Go on.* [ELIZA was originally conceived by Joseph Weizenbaum and an entertaining account of the program and the effects it had on Weizenbaum's thinking on the potential use of computers can be found in Weizenbaum (1976).]

Question 5.12

Lists are only one form of recursive data structure. As another consider the 3-place functor `tree(Node, Left, Right)` which can be used to represent a binary branching tree; where `Left` and `Right` are the left and right subtrees of the node `Node`. For example, the simple tree:

would be represented as:

```
tree(np, tree(det,[],[]), tree(n,[],[]))
```

The empty tree is represented with the empty list. The structure is recursive since it contains other tree structures inside itself. Using this notation represent the following tree:

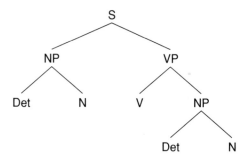

Question 5.13

Assuming the following circular definition of bird:

```
bird(X) :-
      flies(X).
flies(X) :-
      bird(X)
```

what will the proof tree for the following question look like?

```
?- bird(tweety).
```

5.2.2 concat

Another useful relationship involving lists is concat. concat is short for 'concatenate' and names the relationship which holds between three lists where the third list is the result of adding the first two lists together.

```
?- concat([english,german],[spanish,quechua],
Result).
   Result = [english,german,spanish,quechua]
   yes
```

In some texts the predicate name append is used rather than concat.

As with member, the definition of concat is recursive. It is based upon the following observations. When the empty list is added to another list, the result is that list. This is the terminating condition of the definition and can be expressed by the fact:

```
concat([], List, List).
```

As far as concatenating a non-empty list is concerned, the head of the first list will be the head of the concatenated list, where the tail of this latter list is the result of concatenating the tail of the first list to the second. This is the recursive element of the definition. A diagram may help to clarify this verbal characterisation.

[HEAD|LIST1]　　　　LIST2　　⇒　　[HEAD|LIST3]

LIST3

This can be expressed by the recursive rule:

```
concat([Head|List1], List2, [Head|List3]) :-
        concat(List1, List2, List3).
```

These two clauses suffice to define the relation.
　The following tree shows the proof for the question:

```
?- concat([english,german],[spanish,quechua],
Result).
      Result = [english,german,spanish,quechua]
      yes
```

The bindings of the various variables are indicated to the right.

```
concat([english,german],[spanish,quechua],Result)
    |
    |            Result = [english|List3] =
    |                [english,german,spanish,quechua]
    |
concat([german],[spanish,quechua],List3)
    |
    |            List3 = [german|List6] =
    |                [german,spanish,quechua]
    |
concat([],[spanish,quechua],List6)
    |
    |            List6 = [spanish,quechua]
    |
    |
    √
```

Notice how the first argument list progressively becomes smaller until it shrinks to the empty list. At this point, the base clause applies. The instantiations for each of the variables during the computation allows a value for the original variable to be computed by simply substituting in the other results. The effect is as though each item is stripped from the first list and then added, in reverse order, to the other list.

concat is an example of a **reversible predicate**. A reversible predicate is one where any argument may be computed from the others. This makes the definition extremely flexible. For example, with judicious use of variables, concat may be used to isolate a prefix list:

```
?- concat(Prefix, [d,e,f], [a,b,c,d,e,f]).
   Prefix = [a,b,c]
   yes
```

or a suffix list:

```
?- concat([a,b,c], List, [a,b,c,d,e,f]).
   List = [d,e,f]
   yes
```

or, with induced backtracking, the list may be decomposed into all its possible sublists:

```
?- concat(List1, List2, [a,b,c,d]).
   List1 = []
   List2 = [a,b,c,d];

   List1 = [a]
   List2 = [b,c,d];

   List1 = [a,b]
   List2 = [c,d];

   List1 = [a,b,c]
   List2 = [d];

   List1 = [a,b,c,d]
   List2 = [];
   no
```

The reader is urged to trace through the computations of these last three questions as an aid to familiarisation of the definition of concat.

Question 5.14

Assuming the definition of `concat`, define two predicates `prefix(Prefix, List)` and `suffix(Suffix, List)` where `Prefix` is a prefix and `Suffix` a suffix of `List`. Then try and define an alternative, recursive definition of these two predicates.

Question 5.15

Define the membership relation using `concat`. To distinguish it from the previous definition, call the predicate `member1`. Compare the proof trees for the two questions:

```
?- member(piro, [spanish,quechua,piro]).
?- member1(piro, [spanish,quechua,piro]).
```

Question 5.16

Using `concat`, define the relationship `concat3(L1, L2, L3, L4)` where `L4` is the result of concatenating the three lists `L1`, `L2` and `L3`.

Question 5.17

The plural form of most English nouns are produced by either adding *s* or, if the noun ends in a sibilant, *es*. There are a few exceptions to this; for example, nouns ending *Consonant* + *y* change the *y* to *i* and add *es* (*cry-cries*); some nouns ending *f(e)* change the *f* to a *v* and add *es* (*loaf-loaves*); and some plurals are simply irregular (*sheep-sheep*, *ox-oxen*, *foot-feet*).

Define the predicate `plural(Singular, Plural)` such that `Plural` is the plural form of the noun `Singular`. Suggestion: classify each noun into one of the plural classes and then use `concat` to suffix the relevant ending onto the singular form. Note that because `concat` is used the words will need to be represented as lists. For cases like *loaf-loaves*, define the predicate `delete_last` so as to delete the *f* from the singular form before adding *ves*.

The program should handle the following nouns:

> *sheep, ox, child, foot, mouse, woman, thief, wolf, cliff, roof, box, gas, porch, cry, spy, radio, echo, potato, computer, book, tree, shirt*

5.2.3 `dominates`

The success of the recursive definitions of `member` and `concat` depends upon the recursive call resulting in a simpler subgoal in each case as the list argument becomes smaller. There is another class of recursive definitions, not involving lists, where the recursive call does not result in a simpler subgoal but, rather, one with the same degree of complexity. As with the other recursive definitions, the chain of subgoals is continued until the boundary condition is reached.

As an example of such a procedure consider the definition of the predicate `dominates` which was set as an exercise in question 4.6. Recall that the problem was to define the predicate so as to apply to a phrase structure tree such as:

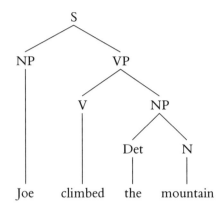

represented in terms of the predicate `immediately_dominates`.

```
immediately_dominates(s, np1).
immediately_dominates(np1, joe).
immediately_dominates(s, vp).
immediately_dominates(vp, v).
immediately_dominates(v, climbed).
immediately_dominates(vp, np2).
immediately_dominates(np2, det)
immediately_dominates(det, the).
immediately_dominates(np2, n).
immediately_dominates(n, mountain).
```

A node N1 will dominate another node N2 if, either N1 immediately dominates N2 or if it is linked to N2 through a chain of intermediate nodes, each immediately dominating the other. The first case is easily represented with the rule:

```
dominates(Node, Node1) :-
      immediately_dominates(Node, Node1).
```

For the example in question, the second case could be handled as a series of three rules where the body consists of a chain of `immediately_dominates` predicates as follows.

```
dominates(Node, Node2) :-
      immediately_dominates(Node, Node1),
      immediately_dominates(Node1, Node2).
```

```
dominates(Node, Node3) :-
        immediately_dominates(Node, Node1),
        immediately_dominates(Node1, Node2),
        immediately_dominates(Node2, Node3).

dominates(Node, Node4) :-
        immediately_dominates(Node, Node1),
        immediately_dominates(Node1, Node2),
        immediately_dominates(Node2, Node3),
        immediately_dominates(Node3, Node4).
```

This solution suffers from the same drawbacks as the piecemeal definition of member presented in section 5.2.1; it is unwieldy and, more importantly, does not extend to the general case. As with member, the solution is to use a recursive rule based on the observation that node N1 will dominate N3 if there is some intermediate node N2 such that N1 immediately dominates N2 and N2 dominates N3.

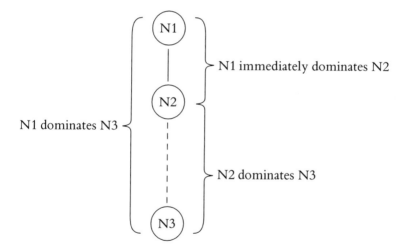

This is easily expressed by the rule:

```
dominates(Node1, Node3) :-
        immediately_dominates(Node1, Node2),
        dominates(Node2, Node3).
```

Note that the terminating condition for this recursive procedure is a rule rather than a fact as in previous examples.

A proof tree of Prolog's solution to the question:

```
?- dominates(s, mountain).
```

looks as follows.

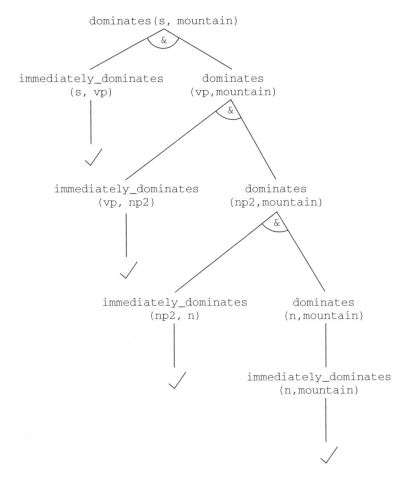

The main difference between this tree and previous examples is that the call to the recursive definition of dominates spawns two subgoals. These are indicated by **&-nodes** which are represented by a curved arc spanning the branches joining the subgoals labelled with &. The immediate daughters of each &-node must be satisfied for it to be satisfied.

As the tree shows, the repeated calls to dominates are in no sense simpler than previous calls to the predicate. The tree also shows how the definition maintains the original insight that domination can be seen as a series of chained immediate dominance relations.

Question 5.18

Define the following list relations. Some of the later definitions may require the use of some of the earlier predicates.

(a) `Element` is the last member of `List`:

> `last(Element, List)`

(b) `List1` is the same as `List` but with the first instance (if any) of `Element` in `List` deleted:

> `delete(Element, List, List1)`

(c) `List1` is the same as `List` but with all instances (if any) of `Element` in `List` deleted:

> `delete_all(Element, List, List1)`

(d) `List1` is the same as `List` but with all instances (if any) of `Element` in `List` replaced by `Element1`:

> `replace_all(Element, Element1, List, List1)`

(e) `Element` and `Element1` are consecutive members of `List`:

> `consec(Element, Element1, List)`

(f) `List1` is the reverse of `List`:

> `reverse(List, List1)`

(g) `List` is a palindrome:

> `palindrome(List)`

(h) `List1` consists of the same members as `List` but not necessarily in the same order:

> `same(List, List1)`

Question 5.19

Write a program which translates lists of numerals – from 0–9 – into their corresponding words:

```
translate([2,6,7,1], [two,six,seven,one])
```

With a suitably extended lexicon the same program should also be able to produce word-for-word translations of natural languages, e.g. substituting French words for English:

```
translate([john,likes,mary], [jean,aime,marie])
```

Question 5.20

Define the relation `member_tree(Node, Tree)` for the recursive binary tree representation used in question 5.12.

CHAPTER 6

Developing Prolog Programs

The previous three chapters have introduced the basics of Prolog from a fairly theoretical point of view. This chapter is somewhat more practical in its concerns, introducing, as it does, a number of issues relating to program development.

6.1 The Meaning of Prolog Programs

To write a computer program requires understanding the meaning of the statements of the programming language being used. For languages such as Pascal or Basic, these meanings are sets of instructions specifying the operations that the computer is to perform in order to solve a particular problem. Such languages are referred to as **procedural**. Prolog, however, is an example of a non-procedural or **declarative** language. That is, a Prolog clause is interpreted as a *declaration* that a relation holds between its arguments providing all the conditions of the clause are met. Take the definition of member:

```
member(Element, [Element|_]).

member(Element, [_|Tail]) :-
     member(Element, Tail).
```

The declarative meaning of these two clauses is that something is a member of a list if either it is the head of the list or a member of the tail.

A declarative interpretation provides no indication about *how* to decide whether a particular relationship holds or not. However, a Prolog program must have a procedural interpretation otherwise it would not do anything. This interpretation is provided by reference to the Prolog interpreter which uses the program in order to solve particular problems. In these terms, the member predicate is thought of as saying; to find out if something is a member of a list check whether it is the head of the list or, if not, check whether it is a member of the ·tail. In addition, the procedural interpretation specifies how to satisfy a goal, in which order compound goals are to be tried, the order in which the program clauses are to be searched, what to do if a goal fails, and so on.

One of the regularly quoted advantages of Prolog is that the procedural interpretation can be largely disregarded since it is automatically handled by the interpreter. The assertion is that this allows the programmer to concentrate solely on the logical specification of the problem, something that is supposed to be more 'human oriented' compared with the writing of machine operations. Whatever the merits of this latter claim, the procedural interpretation of a Prolog program cannot, in fact, be ignored.

In the first place, even for fairly simple procedures, the procedural interpretation often has to be taken into account in order to prevent unexpected results. Consider the definition of dominates from the previous chapter:

```
dominates(Node, Node1) :-
    immediately_dominates(Node, Node1).

dominates(Node1, Node3) :-
    immediately_dominates(Node1, Node2),
    dominates(Node2, Node3).
```

Declaratively, it would be possible to swap the goals of the body of the recursive rule; after all, 'Node1 dominates Node3 if Node1 immediately dominates Node2 and Node2 dominates Node3' means the same as 'Node1 dominates Node3 if Node2 dominates Node3 and Node1 immediately dominates Node2'. However, changing the definition in this way radically changes the procedural interpretation. In fact, with the rule:

```
dominates(Node1, Node3) :-
    dominates(Node2, Node3),
    immediately_dominates(Node1, Node2).
```

the program will no longer work in the intended way. To see why, reconsider the question:

```
?- dominates(s, mountain).
```

from chapter 5.2.3. This goal will initially match with the head of the (terminating) rule. However, the resulting subgoal, immediately_dominates(s, mountain), is not satisfiable. Prolog next attempts a match with the head of the recursive rule. This succeeds, resulting in the two subgoals:

```
dominates(_234, mountain)
immediately_dominates(s, _234)
```

Trying to solve the first of these subgoals produces, for the same reasons as the original goal, the two new subgoals:

```
dominates(_725, mountain)
immediately_dominates(_234, _725)
```

Which again will spawn the two subgoals:

```
dominates(_916, mountain)
immediately_dominates(_725, _916)
```

Already, the pattern should be clear; each dominates subgoal is resulting in another call to dominates which is, variable names aside, identical to the previous goal. The satisfaction process is essentially standing still, stuck in a loop, calling the same goal over and over again, never getting any closer to satisfying the initial goal. The reason for the success of the original definition lies in calling immediately_dominates before dominates. The result is that when the latter is evaluated, the variable in the first argument position has become instantiated to some value so that the dominates subgoal differs from the dominates goal which invoked it.

The other aspect to procedurally interpreting Prolog clauses is that often they are easier to understand this way. Reconsider the definition of member:

```
member(Element, [Element|_]).
member(Element, [_|Tail]) :-
      member(Element, Tail).
```

The declarative reading is obviously true but, especially for the beginner, it is hard to see why it might *work*. However, thinking of the definition procedurally as stripping off item after item until the relevant one pops to the top makes it much clearer.

The real advantage of Prolog is not that it has a declarative interpretation but that a program has both a declarative *and* procedural meaning. The result is that the programmer can usually approach a problem from both angles, swapping between them, each aiding the other, until a solution is reached. Frequently, the best approach is to think procedurally when initially trying to devise a definition and then check its declarative meaning once it has been written. However, there is no hard and fast rule except that Prolog programming is always a blend of procedural and declarative thought.

6.2 Designing Programs

As in all creative processes, it is not possible to provide a formula for how to arrive at a good program. This can only be discovered through experience and practice. However, all programmers are agreed that the most important stage in programming is the pre-coding phase when the structure of the problem is the main concern. Care and consideration spent during this time will greatly facilitate the eventual writing of the program. Crucially, the initial stages should involve thinking about the problem area as a whole. Usually this involves thinking at quite a high level of abstraction. Once the overall structure of the task is clear, it becomes easier to address the more detailed level of specification required for actual programming.

One of the most crucial decisions to be taken in the early stages of program design is the form of the data structures to be used. There are many different ways of representing the same information and the eventual choice may have repercussions throughout the rest of the program. For example, two different ways of representing `spoken_in` facts have been used in previous chapters.

```
spoken_in(spanish, peru).
spoken_in(quechua, peru).
spoken_in(piro, peru).

spoken_in([spanish, quechua, piro], peru).
```

As was seen, the choice of representation determined the form of the definition of the predicate `language`.

```
language(Language) :-
    spoken_in(Language, Country).

language(Language) :-
    spoken_in(LangList, Country),
    member(Language, LangList).
```

Procedurally, the first definition of `language` is the more efficient of the two since it only involves a simple match with a `spoken_in` fact whilst the second requires the use of `member` to get inside the language list, a process of some computational complexity. However, this efficiency is gained at the cost of the number of individual `spoken_in` facts that must be coded up. The trade-offs between the amount of program code required and computational efficiency may not matter very much for this simple example, but may become more pressing for much larger programs.

In a general checklist of design criteria, the programmer should first and foremost be concerned with the correctness of the program; in other words, does the program do what it is designed to do? After that, other questions may be addressed; is the program wasteful of computational resources?; does it crash when confronted with unexpected input?; can it be easily modified and extended to more complex cases and so on. The particular weight attached to each individual question will often vary from application to application but at all times the program must work correctly.

It is a useful practice to develop **modular** programs. A module is an independently defined unit which can function as a separate entity. The actual modules used will usually be a consequence of the logical analysis. As such, the modular approach is a way of breaking a complex problem down into its simpler constituent parts. There are other advantages. For example, the same module may appear in more than one program without further modification. It is also possible to refine modules without necessitating drastic changes to the rest of the program. Modularity also often aids the finding and correcting of mistakes by allowing the programmer to focus on smaller, well-defined units.

Prolog has a degree of in-built modularity since most procedures are independently defined. For example, the definition of member is self-contained, its definition not depending upon any other predicate. As a result, it may easily be incorporated into the specification of other predicates. Indeed, this is usually the case with 'utility' predicates such as member and concat which are defined mainly with this ubiquitous role in mind.

6.3 Laying out Programs

Little has been said about the layout of a program file. As programs become more complex, it is important that certain typographical conventions be observed. Good layout will not make a program perform any better but it will considerably aid the programmer's understanding of it and the process of error correction discussed in section 6.7.

Take a simple example. It makes no difference to the Prolog interpreter whether facts and rules are placed on separate lines or not since the full-stop indicates where each ends. Accordingly, the program used in the last chapter could be laid out as follows.

```
spoken_in([english],uk).spoken_in([eng-
lish],usa).spoken_in([english],australia).
spoken_in([spanish,quechua,piro],piro).
language(Language):-spoken_in(LangList,
Country),member(Language,LangList).member
(Element,[Element|_]).member(Element,
[_|Tail]):- member(Element, Tail).
```

This is almost totally opaque. As a result, it is extremely difficult to determine the structure of the program. It is hard even to determine what it is designed to do. The spotting of errors is virtually impossible; indeed, one of the clauses in the above has been deliberately corrupted; can you see which?

In general, layout conventions have as their primary goal the readability of the program. It is good practice to place each new fact or rule on a new line. All clauses defining the same predicate are best kept together. Further, if the procedure includes facts and rules, the former are best placed first. It usually aids legibility if blank lines separate the different procedures.

When laying out rules, it usually makes the structure of the rule clearer if each goal of the body is placed on a separate, indented line. Whatever indentation conventions are chosen will be a matter of personal choice but should be used consistently throughout the program.

In general, it is best to place all the main predicates at the beginning of the file with subsidiary predicates following. The 'utility' predicates such as member and concat are usually placed together at the end of the file.

As already discussed in chapter 3, it is best to choose names for functors and arguments which give a reasonable indication of their intended meaning. The following conventions are usually adopted for multi-word names; constants are joined together using the underscore – spoken_in – whilst variables are combined together but with each name starting with a capital – LangList.

Although the structure of Prolog programs is often clearer than their equivalents in other programming languages, they are still not always easy to follow. Such problems grow as programs increase in complexity. Even your own program returned to after some months of neglect may no longer be comprehensible! It is important, then, to include comments in the layout which will guide the user through the program.

There are two ways of commenting in a program. One method is to place the comments between the special brackets /* (open) and */ (closed). Anything placed between them is not treated by Prolog as part of the program definition. The brackets may be separated by any number of lines. Do remember, however, if using this format to include the closing bracket. The alternative is to use the percentage sign, %. In this case, everything after the sign to the end of the line is ignored.

```
% Prolog ignores everything after this sign
% but only up to the end of the line.

/* However, Prolog ignores everything after
   this bracket until the closing bracket
   (which may be some lines away). */
```

There are as many different commenting conventions as programmers but it is best to try to keep a balance between informativeness and comprehension. Sometimes, to over-comment is as unhelpful as to under-comment; in some programs it is hard to find the Prolog code amongst the commentary! Usually, some header comment giving the name of the program, perhaps, with a brief description of what the program does and the form of question expected, should be included. Descriptions of any predicate whose meaning or purpose is not clear should also be freely inserted. Some programmers like to include information about which of a predicate's arguments are instantiated at run time. For example, the comment:

```
% member(+,+).
```

indicates that both arguments will be instantiated when member is called. On the other hand:

```
% concat(-,-,+).
```

shows that in this particular program when concat is invoked only its third argument will have a value.

The following is an example of what a program file might look like.

```
/* ********************************************

FILE NAME:   EXAMPLE.PL

DESCRIPTION:   A simple database of languages and the
               countries in which they are spoken.

********************************************* */

% The database of information

    spoken_in([english], uk).
    spoken_in([english], usa).
    spoken_in([english], australia).
    spoken_in([spanish,quechua,piro], peru).


% Definition of the property of being a language

    language(Language) :-
        spoken_in(LangList, Country),
        member(Language, LangList).
```

```
% Definition of membership relation; checks whether
% first argument is a member of the list given as second
% argument

   member(Element, [Element|_]).
   member(Element, [_|Tail]) :-
           member(Element, Tail).
```

/* *** */

6.4 Search Trees

In the last chapter proof trees were introduced as a graphical means of showing the satisfaction relationships holding between the various goals involved in the proof of a main goal. A proof tree is not an exact record of the computational process since it does not include those goals that were tried but turned out to be dead ends or any alternative proofs that might exist. It is useful to be able to extend the proof tree notation to include such cases. The resulting trees are called **search trees**.

A search tree represents the total computational space from which the interpreter attempts to find a solution to a specific goal given a particular program. To illustrate the notion, consider the following program.

```
understood_in(Person, Country) :-
     speaks(Person, Language),
     spoken_in(Language, Country).

understood_in(Person, Country) :-
     speaks(Person, Language),
     world_language(Language).

spoken_in(english, uk).
spoken_in(french, belgium)
speaks(john, english).

world_language(english).
```

The definition of understood_in is a slight extension of that used in section 4.1. The combination of rules state that someone is understood in a country if they either speak the language of that country or if they speak a world language (which is assumed to be understood in all countries). The following represents the search tree for the question:

```
?- understood_in(john, belgium).
```

relative to this program.

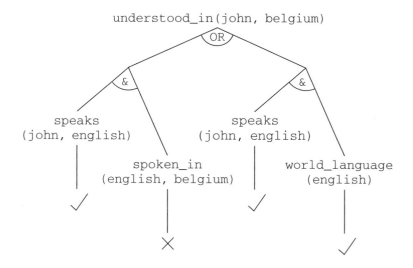

The root of the tree is the initial goal. Alternative solutions to a goal are indicated by an **OR-node** represented by a curved arc spanning the branches leading to the alternatives and labelled with *OR*. Compound goals are represented by an **&-node** as in a proof tree. The tree shows that there are two possible ways to proceed to satisfy the goal understood_in(john, belgium); either that speaks(john, english) and spoken_in(english, belgium) or that speaks(john, english) (again) and world_language (english) are satisfiable. The left-to-right order of the daughters of the *OR*-node reflects the top-to-bottom ordering of clauses in the program. Similarly, the left-to-right ordering of the &-node mirrors the order of the goals within the body of the rule. As in a proof tree, a goal that successfully matches with a fact is shown by a tick; failure to match is indicated with a cross.

Whether understood_in(john, belgium) follows from the program or not depends on whether the search tree contains a **solution tree**. This is a subtree whose root is the root of the search tree, and where for any node in the tree, if it is an *OR*-node just one of its subgoals is satisfied, or if it is an &-node all of its subgoals are satisfied. understood_in(john, belgium) does follow from this particular tree as shown by the indicated solution tree.

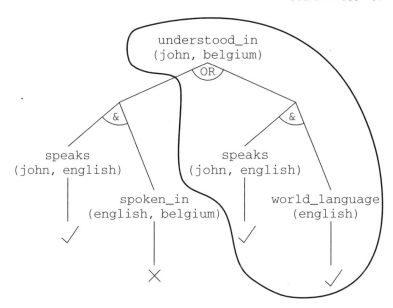

Removing the extraneous *OR*-branch would result in what was previously called a proof tree.

A search tree may contain more than one solution tree. Consider the following tree for the goal ?- member(Item, [spanish, quechua, piro]).

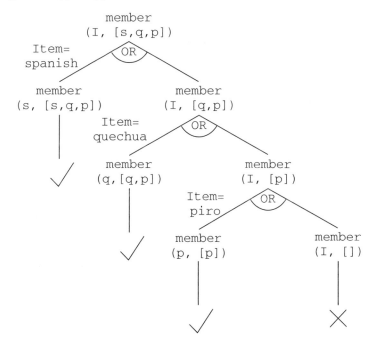

This contains three solution trees corresponding to the three different ways that the goal can be satisfied.

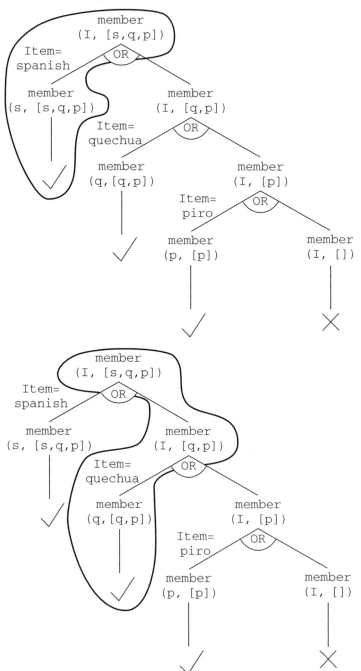

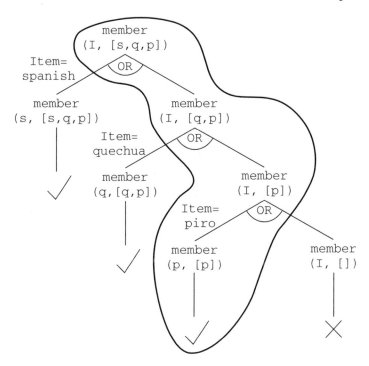

6.5 Search Strategies

A search tree, just like a Prolog program, can be interpreted both declaratively and procedurally. For example, the &-tree:

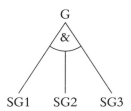

can be read declaratively as saying "goal G is true if each of the subgoals SG1, SG2 and SG3 are true" or procedurally as "to solve G, solve each of SG1, SG2 and SG3". Similarly, the *OR*-tree:

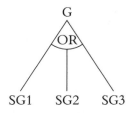

has the declarative reading "G is true if either SG1 or SG2 or SG3 is true" and the procedural reading "to solve G, solve either SG1 or SG2 or SG3".

It is useful to think of the procedural interpretation of Prolog in terms of exploring a search tree in an attempt to find a solution tree. Note though that Prolog does not construct a search tree and then go through it. Rather, the interpreter can be thought of as *constructing* the tree during the proof procedure. However, it is a useful deceit to imagine the interpreter as moving through the search tree in an attempt to locate a solution tree.

The process by which the tree is searched is called a **search strategy** (or, sometimes, a **control strategy**). In principle, there are various ways that this could be done. The actual strategy that Prolog uses is referred to as a **top-down**, **depth-first**, **left-to-right** strategy with **backtracking**. To see what this means, consider how Prolog would attempt to solve the problem ?- understood _in(john, belgium) with respect to the program of the previous section.

Given understood_in(john, belgium) as a goal, the interpreter matches with the head of the first rule producing the two subgoals speaks(john, english) and spoken_in(english, belgium). The speaks-subgoal is tried first and succeeds but the spoken_in-subgoal, which is tried next, fails. Therefore, the conjunction of subgoals fails. However, since there is an alternative way of satisfying the main goal, the interpreter backtracks and tries matching with the head of the second rule. This again succeeds producing the two subgoals speaks(john, english) and world_language(english). The speaks-subgoal is processed first, followed by the world_language-subgoal, and this time both succeed. Accordingly, so does the dependent main goal.

A trace of the route of this progress through the search tree looks as follows.

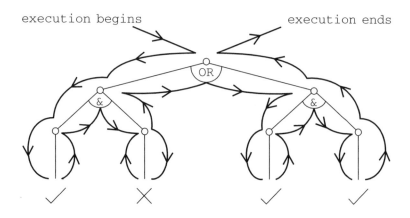

execution begins   execution ends

This diagram graphically indicates at least three of the properties of the Prolog search strategy. First, the search proceeds from the top of the tree downwards; hence, the term *top-down strategy*. Secondly, given a choice of subgoals to solve, the leftmost is always chosen first. This results in a *left-to-right* strategy. Thirdly, if a computation does not work, the interpreter backs up to the last encountered *OR*-node with alternatives still left untried and attempts the (leftmost) of these. Thus the strategy involves *backtracking*.

The Prolog control strategy, chosen mainly on grounds of efficiency, is just one amongst a number of alternatives for exploring search trees. For example, rather than top-down, the strategy could be **bottom-up**. In this case, as the name suggests, the tree is searched from the leaves of the tree upwards. For example, given the two facts speaks(john, english) and world_language(english) and the second understood_in-rule, it is possible to reach the desired conclusion that understood_in(john, belgium).

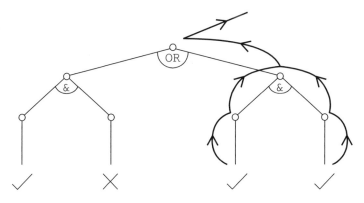

Notice how, since this approach only proceeds from knowns, that the left-hand side of the search tree is not explored. This would appear more efficient compared with the top-down strategy. The problems with bottom-up search only become apparent with larger search trees. In these cases, there may be many derivable conclusions which do not contribute to the desired conclusion. Without some means of constraining the growth of these accumulating conclusions through directed search, memory limitations can quickly be reached. Top-down search does not face these problems since it is a goal-directed strategy.

The previous diagrams have not shown the *depth-first* nature of the search. Given a choice between a number of different goals to explore, a depth-first strategy tries the deepest one in the tree first. As a result, a single branch is pursued to its conclusion before the other goals are tried. In certain cases, this can cause problems. Consider the following reordering of the previous definition of dominates.

```
dominates(Node1, Node3) :-
    dominates(Node2, Node3),
    immediately_dominates(Node1, Node2).
dominates(Node, Node1) :-
    immediately_dominates(Node, Node1).
```

Here the terminating definition has been placed after the recursive rule in addition to the goals of the latter also having been swapped over. The following is (part of) the search tree for the goal dominates(s, vp) with the Prolog search path for this goal indicated.

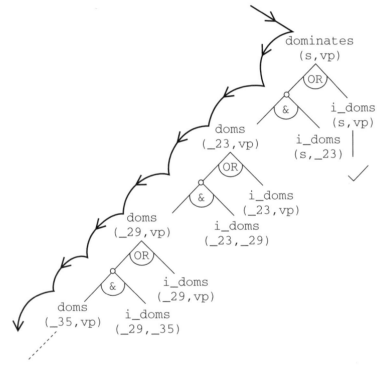

As can be seen, the depth-first strategy (in conjunction with the left-to-right strategy) sends the interpreter down an infinitely long path. Since the interpreter will never reach a point where it will be able to backtrack, it will never find the answer that is so tantalisingly close if only the right branch of the top-most OR-node could be tried.

An alternative strategy to the depth-first search which would find an answer in this case is a **breadth-first** search. Unlike a depth-first search this strategy explores all the nodes of the search tree at the same level before going down to the next level.

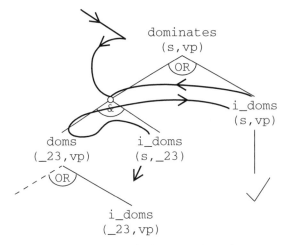

The main problem with breadth-first search is the excessive computational (notably memory) resources it requires, especially if the tree contains numerous 'bushy' nodes.

Search is an important issue for any problem-solving system faced with choice. As will be seen in later chapters, parsing a sentence is no exception. As a result, it is possible to classify parsing strategies along the same dimensions as search strategies; top-down vs. bottom-up, depth-first vs. breadth-first and so on. Chapter 12 will also show how it is possible to simulate, say, a bottom-up parsing strategy using Prolog's top-down control strategy.

6.6 Tracing a Proof

Earlier discussions about the procedural interpretation of Prolog have been illustrated by what might be called 'hand' or 'desk-top' simulations of Prolog's computations. Most implementations of Prolog also provide a facility whereby the system itself supplies information about what it is doing as a proof proceeds. This information is called a **trace**.

The use of the trace facility is an important skill to learn. In the first place, it provides a useful pedagogic aid to understanding how complex procedures work, allowing, as it does, the user to watch them 'in action'. This is the way that tracing will be used in this book. However, the main use of the trace is when a program behaves in an unexpected way. A trace can be used to follow through Prolog's execution of the goal to see where it breaks down. With this information an attempt at fixing the program can then be made. Because programming errors are commonly referred to as **bugs**, this process of correction is called **debugging**.

In order to understand the information generated during a trace, it is necessary to describe the **procedure box** model of computation.

Imagine that each procedure is enclosed within a box. This box may be entered and left via various points called **ports**.

The initial entry port into any box is the **CALL port**. This is used when Prolog first starts trying to satisfy a goal. The box is left via the **EXIT port** if the goal has been satisfied. If a goal fails, however, the box is exited through the **FAIL port**. The final port is used for re-entry into a box caused by backtracking and is called the **REDO port**. Attempting to satisfy a goal can be thought of in terms of the interpreter moving in and out, via their ports, of the procedure boxes associated with the various goals invoked during the proof.

The following diagram shows this flow of control for the simple question ?- speaks(jacques, french) evaluated against the program that was introduced in chapter 3.

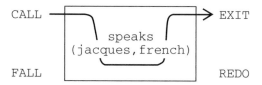

The procedure box is entered through the CALL port and, since the goal is satisfied through a simple match with a fact, is immediately left via the EXIT port.

A slightly more complex flow of control is exhibited with the query ?- understood_in(john, australia).

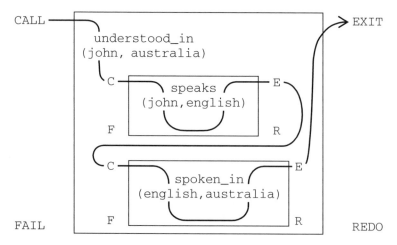

Since understood_in is defined as a rule, before exiting from the procedure box the flow of control must pass through two sub-boxes corresponding to the predicates of the body of the rule. These boxes stand side by side since they represent a conjunction of subgoals. Note how the EXIT port of the first subgoal is linked to the CALL port of the second.

The trace facility provides feedback about the progress of the interpreter through the various procedure boxes as it attempts to find an answer to a query. This information takes the form of a sequence of lines of the form:

```
(Num) Depth Port: Goal
```

The number, Num, uniquely identifies a particular goal throughout the proof. This is particularly important for recursive calls to the same procedure. The numbering is sequential in the order of the invocation. Port names which of the four ports is involved whilst Goal displays the goal in question. Depth can be thought of as the degree of nesting of the procedure box within other boxes. For example, the procedure box of the main goal is at depth 0, its sub-procedures are at depth 1, theirs at depth 2 and so on.

The trace facility is switched on with the special predicate trace.

```
?- trace.
   yes
```

Tracing is switched off with the predicate notrace. Once the tracing facility is switched on, any query to Prolog will result in trace information being written to the screen, line by line. Pressing the RETURN key moves the trace to the next line of information. The following presents a complete trace for an earlier example.

```
?- understood_in(john, belgium).

(1)   0 CALL: understood_in(john,belgium)?
(2)   1 CALL: speaks(john, _286)?
(2)   1 EXIT: speaks(john,english)?
(3)   1 CALL: spoken_in(english, belgium)?
(3)   1 FAIL: spoken_in(english, belgium)?
(2)   1 REDO: speaks(john,english)?
(2)   1 FAIL: speaks(john,english)?
(4)   1 CALL: speaks(john, _286)?
(4)   1 EXIT: speaks(john,english)?
(5)   1 CALL: world_language(english)?
(5)   1 EXIT: world_language(english)?
(1)   0 EXIT: understood_in(john,belgium)?

yes
```

As the third line of this trace shows, any variables that have become instantiated during the invocation of a procedure are replaced with these values on exiting the procedure. Although not relevant in this case, re-entering a procedure through the REDO port has the effect of resetting any variables to the values they had immediately prior to the procedure box which caused the failure.

The procedure box diagram that goes with the above trace is shown below for comparison. Also reproduced for comparative purposes is the search tree for this example.

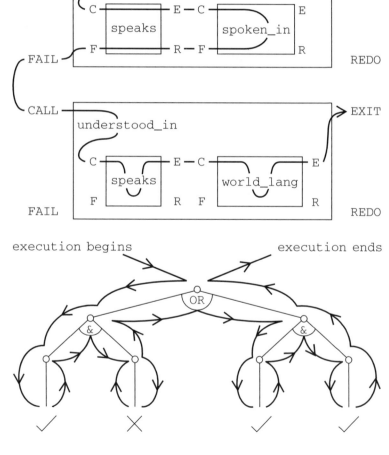

It is also useful to trace Prolog's use of a recursive predicate. The following repeats a previous example.

```
?- member(piro, [spanish,quechua,piro]).
(1)   0 CALL: member(piro, [spanish,quechua,
      piro]?
(2)   1 CALL: member(piro, [quechua,piro])?
(3)   2 CALL: member(piro, [piro])?
(3)   2 EXIT: member(piro, [piro])?
(2)   1 EXIT: member(piro, [quechua,piro])?
(1)   0 EXIT: member(piro, [spanish,quechua,
      piro])?

yes
```

Note the nesting of procedure boxes that this predicate induces.

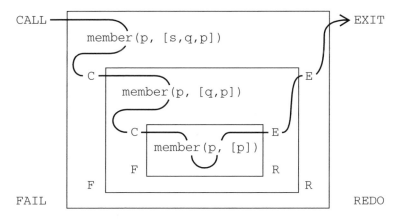

Most implementations of Prolog allow varying degrees of control over the tracing process. For example, typing a at the end of a line will abort the trace once the RETURN key has been pressed. Since the exact details of which tracing predicates are supported by a particular implementation vary, the reader is referred to the relevant manuals for further information. However, one other predicate will be briefly mentioned. With large programs a full trace is often too detailed for the programmer's needs. In these cases, it may be more helpful to skip over those parts of the program that are known to be working properly and concentrate only on those predicates that are suspect. Such localised tracing is possible due to the modular nature of Prolog programs. The command spy(P) places a **spy-point** on the predicate P. For example:

```
?- spy(spoken_in).
```

will cause the trace only to report on any action involving the spoken_in predicate. spy may take a list of predicates as argument if more than one procedures is to be traced. nospy(P) removes the spy points.

6.7 Some Common Programming Errors

The trace facility is usually invoked when a program performs in an expected way; perhaps, Prolog reports yes instead of no, or the variables are instantiated to the wrong values, or the program does not produce any answer at all having been caught in an endless loop of computation. Tracing such a proof enables the programmer to locate the point in the process where things start to go wrong. How easy it is to correct the problem will depend upon its cause.

Luckily, many errors are simply due to 'slips of the keyboard' and are quickly remedied once spotted. For example, it is an easy matter to forget to add the full stop at the end of a clause or a comma between conjoined goals. Alternatively, in some cases it is hard to keep track of bracketing, the result usually being too many or too few closing brackets, or matching brackets of the wrong sort. As an example of how difficult this may become, try and complete the bracketing at the end of the following complex term.

```
uto_aztecan([corachol([cora,huichol]),
      aztecan([nahuatl([nahuatl,pipil]),
          pochutec([pochutec
```

Errors of this sort will be picked up by the interpreter on loading the file. Depending on the implementation, the location of the error will be indicated along with a brief gloss of the problem.

There are other typographical errors, however, which the interpreter will not flag. For example, misspelling the name of a predicate or function will result in expressions which are syntactically permissible but which will not match up with the rest of the procedure. If the error is in the head of a rule, this will create a new predicate whilst if it is in the body, it will result in an undefined predicate. It is also easy to make case errors, turning constants into variables and variables into constants. For example:

```
speaks(John, English).
```

means that everybody speaks every language. Errors in the naming of variables can also cause unexpected results. For example, mistyping the second argument in the base clause of the concat definition:

```
concat([], List, List1).
```

will produce incorrect answers:

```
?-  concat([english,welsh],[spanish,quechua],
List).
   List = [english,welsh| _664]
   yes
```

Another common mistake is to make an error in the ordering of arguments to a predicate, especially in the body of a rule:

```
concat([Head|Tail], List, [Head|List1]) :-
     concat(Tail, List1, List).
?- concat([english,welsh], [spanish,quechua],
List).
   no
```

In certain cases, using the wrong punctuation will not lead to faulty syntax but will produce unintended semantics. For instance, in the following a full stop has replaced a comma in the body of a rule turning it into a rule and a fact.

```
understood_in(Person, Country) :-
     speaks(Person, Language).
     spoken_in(Language, Country).
```

whilst in:

```
understood_in(Person, Country) :-
     speaks(Person, Language),
     spoken_in(Language, Country),
speaks(john, english).
```

the full stop at the end of the rule has been mistyped as a comma so turning the rule and fact into a single rule with three subgoals in the body.

Such typological errors aside, the other main cause of faulty behaviour is incorrectly defined predicates. Learning how to compose, say, a recursive definition from scratch is a difficult skill to acquire. However, certain design features are relevant to all recursive procedures. For example, always check that there are terminating conditions in the definition. In addition, make sure that the order of goals will not lead to looping as discussed in section 6.5. It is also worth checking a program file for any duplicate or superseded definitions that may have crept in during the editing process. Quite often the effects of such extraneous clauses will only be felt when all solutions to a problem are being sought through induced backtracking.

As a final aside, it is always worth checking a program even when it is performing as expected since it might turn out that it is doing so for the wrong reasons!

6.8 Further Reading

Search is an important topic in Artificial Intelligence – the use of computers to perform tasks usually associated with human intelligence – and discussed in many introductory textbooks on the subject such as Rich and Knight (1991), Charniak and McDermott (1985) and Winston (1984). Useful summary articles can be found in Barr and Feigenbaum (1981) and various entries in Shapiro (1987). Thornton and du Boulay (1992) is a book-length introduction to the subject which also uses Prolog to illustrate some of the techniques. More theoretical discussion of the control strategies underlying Prolog can be found in Hogger (1984 and 1990) and Kowalski (1979) with a shorter presentation in Kowalski and Hogger (1987).

CHAPTER 7

Built-in Predicates

There are a number of special predicates available in Prolog which do not need definition by the user since they are provided in advance by the designers of the implementation. Such predicates are known as **built-in** predicates. In some cases, common predicates are included so as to save programmers from having to define them themselves. For example, some versions of Prolog come with concat pre-defined. However, the built-in predicates of most interest are those that allow access to facilities that would not be definable using a pure Prolog consisting only of facts and rules. It is these **extra-logical predicates** which, amongst other things, allow a program to interact with the world outside of itself. Consequently, they only admit a procedural interpretation. One example that has already been introduced is the consult predicate which reads a program file into the interpreter.

Which built-in predicates are available varies greatly from system to system. For example, some versions of Prolog have a number of built-in predicates for graphics. These are useful for displaying phrase structure trees but are, as yet, non-standard. This chapter only introduces those predicates which are to be found in most implementations. The reader should consult the relevant manuals for further details of what is available in their own implementation.

7.1 Input and Output

A simple example of a built-in predicate is write. This is a one-place predicate which causes its argument to be displayed on the computer screen. For example:

```
?- write(hello).
   hello yes
```

As well as writing the term, Prolog also outputs a yes to show that the goal has been satisfied. write is typical of extra-logical predicates in that the consequence of satisfying a call to it produces a *side effect*, in this case, writing a term to the screen.

Note that Prolog's yes immediately follows the written term. The built-in predicate nl – standing for 'new line' – causes subsequent output to be displayed on the next line down. nl can be used to separate the printed output from Prolog's report of satisfaction.

```
?- write(hello), nl.
   hello
   yes
```

The following short program uses both write and nl to display each member of a list on a separate line.

```
display_list([]) :- nl.
display_list([Item|Tail]) :-
    write(Item),
    nl,
    display_list(Tail).

?- display_list([spanish,quechua,piro]).
   spanish
   quechua
   piro
   yes
```

The predicate tab(N) can be used to indent a term by N spaces. For example, display_list can be redefined to indent alternate members of a list.

```
display_list([]) :- nl.
display_list([Item|Tail]) :-
    write(Item), nl,
    display_list1(Tail).

display_list1([Item|Tail]) :-
    tab(4),
    write(Item), nl,
    display_list(Tail).

?- display_list([english,welsh,french,german]).
   english
       welsh
   french
       german
   yes
```

If the argument to write is an uninstantiated variable then a suitably named variable will be output.

```
?- write(X), nl.
   _753
   yes
```

If the output contains spaces or upper case letters, the term must be placed in single quotes:

```
?- write('Hello'), nl.
   Hello
   yes

?- write('Which country are you interested in?'),
nl.
   Which country are you interested in?
   yes
```

Paired with write is the built-in predicate read(Term). This takes the next term written at the terminal and instantiates Term to that value. In some implementations read produces a prompt symbol |: on screen after which the user types in their response. The input has to terminate with a full stop.

```
?- read(Term), nl, write(Term), nl.
   |: hello.
   hello
   yes
```

Using these various **input** and **output** predicates it is possible to provide the previous programs with a slightly more user-friendly interface. To do this, a drive predicate go will be defined. A **drive predicate** is one which controls the program by calling the main goals.

```
go :-
    nl,
    write('Which country are you interested
    in?'), nl,
    read(Country), nl,
    spoken_in(Language, Country),
    write(Language), write(' is spoken in '),
    write(Country), nl.
```

Typing go causes the question to be printed on the screen followed by the reading prompt. The user supplies a name which is then passed to the predicate spoken_in which, once satisfied, will result in a value for the first argument being output to the screen. Note the use of nl to separate the various lines and the use of spaces between the quotes in write(' spoken in ') to get the words in the correct place.

```
?- go.
   Which country are you interested in?
   | : peru.
   spanish is spoken in peru
   yes
```

read and write apply to Prolog terms. There are equivalent predicates for handling characters. For example, get0(C) is like read(T) except that it reads in a single character. C then becomes instantiated to the ASCII code of that character. *ASCII* is short for 'American Standard Code for Information Interchange' and is a means of coding characters as numbers. For example, the ASCII code for *a* is 97, *b* is 98, *c* is 99 and so on. Upper case letters have different numbers from their lower case equivalents; so, *a* is 97 whilst *A* is 65. get0 could be used, say, to present a menu of choices.

```
?- go.
   Do you want to search via:
      (a) Languages or
      (b) Countries
   | : b
   Which country are you interested in?
   | : peru
   spanish is spoken in peru
   yes
```

See section 7.6 for some discussion of such a program.

No more will be said about these character handling predicates and the interested reader is referred to the various Prolog textbooks or reference manuals for details. However, a useful program using these predicates is listed at the end of the chapter without comment. The program takes a sentence typed in at the keyboard and converts it into a list. Later programs represent sentences as lists. However, it is usually more user-friendly to be able to input a sentence in its normal format. This is what read_in allows. Its behaviour can be seen in the following interaction.

```
?- read_in(Sentence).
   |: This is an example of a sentence.
   Sentence = [this,is,an,example,of,a,
   sentence,.]
   yes
```

Note that the upper case T of This in the input string is returned as its lower case equivalent in the list and also that the terminating full stop of the input is included in the list.

Question 7.1

Use tab to insert the spaces between is spoken in and the name of the language and country in the definition of go rather than including the spaces in the clause write(' is spoken in ').

Question 7.2

Redefine the predicate translate from question 5.19 into a 1-place predicate which takes a list of numerals and prints the corresponding translation into their corresponding words.

```
?- translate([2,6,4]).
   two six four
   yes
```

Question 7.3

The ASCII code for alphabetic characters runs from 65 to 90 for upper case letters and 97 to 122 for lower case letters. In addition, the integers 0 to 9 are also coded for as are characters such as #, $, %, &, +, *, <, >, /. Using get0(C) and write(C) find out what values are associated with these characters.

Question 7.4

Define the predicate go which presents a menu of choices as illustrated in the text.

7.2 fail

Returning to the interface to the language database, the reader will have noticed that it only outputs one of the languages spoken in Peru. This problem can be overcome with a **failure-driven loop**. This is a technique which makes use of the built-in predicate fail. fail is a predicate which, not surprisingly, fails. It is used to force backtracking. Consider what happens when it is placed at the end of the previous definition of go.

```
go :-
      nl,
      write('Which country are you interested
      in?'), nl,
      read(Country), nl,
      spoken_in(Language, Country),
      write(Language), write(' is spoken in '),
      write(Country), nl,
      fail.
```

The definition works as previously, reading in the name of a country and outputting an answer. However, upon reaching fail, Prolog is forced to backtrack to the last goal that could be resatisfied. The built-in predicates are ignored as far as backtracking is concerned, so that the first subgoal that could be retried is spoken_in. If a new value is found for the Language variable, the interpreter proceeds through the following goals as before, outputting the new solution. fail will be encountered again, whereupon the process is repeated. This continues until no more solutions can be found.

```
?- go.
Which country are you interested in?
| : peru.
spanish is spoken in peru
quechua is spoken in peru
piro is spoken in peru
no
```

The no at the end of this interaction indicates the general failure of the original goal. This, however, is of little importance since the aim of the program is to produce *side-effects* rather than define a logical relation. The program could, however, be tidied up further with an additional go clause:

```
go :-
      write('No (more) answers known'), nl.
```

This needs to be written after the other definition so that it will be invoked upon the (inevitable) failure of the original rule with the result that No (more) answers known is written to the screen after all the answers have been found. This new rule will also be accessed when there are no relevant spoken_in facts which accounts for why more is in brackets.

```
?- go.
   Which country are you interested in?
   |: brazil.
   No (more) answers known
   yes
```

7.3 consult and reconsult

The predicate consult was introduced in chapter 3. Invoking consult(F) has the effect of loading a file F into the interpreter. If another file is consulted later, the clauses of this file are simply added to the end of the current set.

The predicate reconsult(F) is like consult but with one subtle, if important, difference. consult(F) adds all the clauses of file F to the system's database. reconsult(F) similarly reads in F's clauses except for those predicates that are already defined for the interpreter. In this case, reconsult redefines the predicates in question by replacing them with the new versions in file F. reconsult does not affect any predicates which are not defined in F.

Using consult twice on the same file will lead to each clause being duplicated. This will not affect the running of the program if only a single answer is being sought. However, if exhaustive backtracking is used to seek all possible answers to a query, the result will be that each answer is found twice. The use of reconsult avoids any possibility of this happening.

Files can also be consulted and reconsulted using the list notation introduced in chapter 3. Any file to be reconsulted is preceded with a hyphen, -. Those that are not, are consulted. For example, in the following, file1 and file2 are consulted whilst file3 and file4 are reconsulted.

```
?- [file1, file2, -file3, -file4].
```

7.4 Modifying the Database

Once a file has been consulted it is possible to dynamically modify it by adding or retracting clauses whilst the program is being executed. Adding a clause is achieved by using one of two predicates; asserta(C) or assertz(C). The difference between them is in the position the clause is added to the program; asserta(C) adds it to the beginning and assertz(C) to the end. The easiest way to remember this is that a comes at the beginning of the alphabet and z at the end. When asserta(C) or assertz(C) are called, the variable C must be suitably instantiated. That is, the clause may contain variables as arguments as long as the predicate name is instantiated.

Clauses can be removed from the database by using the predicate retract(C). As with asserta and assertz, the argument to retract must be sufficiently instantiated. The predicate retractall(C), as its name suggests, removes all clauses whose head matches with C.

Backtracking does not undo the effects of asserting or retracting clauses. The danger of this is that, if a program using these predicates is run a number of times, it is easy to lose track of just which clauses are in the database at any one time. Added to the fact that these predicates are rather slow in execution, the consequence is that they should be used with a degree of caution.

7.5 Defining Operators

Most of the functors that have been used so far have been placed before their arguments which have been enclosed between round brackets. In some cases it makes for friendlier syntax to use an **infix** notation. For example, in this notation the spoken_in facts would have the form:

```
english spoken_in uk.
```

When predicates are used in this way they are called **operators**.

Operators are declared with a ternary predicate called op.

```
op(P, A, O)
```

The arguments of the predicate express three pieces of information; the precedence of the operator, its position and associativity, and the name of the operator.

To understand the notion of **precedence** consider the following ambiguous arithmetic equation:

$$4 + 8 \div 2 = x$$

The value for x varies depending on which operation is performed first. There are two ways the ambiguity can be resolved. One is to use brackets on all occasions:

$$4 + (8 \div 2) = 8$$
$$(4 + 8) \div 2 = 6$$

The other is to assume a convention about the strengths of the operators. Suppose ÷ is assumed to be stronger than +, then the default reading of the unbracketed equation is the same as the first of the bracketed versions above. To express the other reading brackets are used. It is this second method that is used with Prolog operators where they are assigned a precedence number. The lower the number the stronger the operator. The range of values is usually between 1 and 1200 although this may differ from implementation to implementation.

op allows three types of operator to be defined; **infix**, which go between two arguments, **pre-fix** which precede an argument and **post-fix** which follow an argument. These are characterised using a **specifier**. For example, the specifier xfx is used to define an infix operator. Here f is the operator and x the arguments. Pre- and post-fix operators are specified by fx and xf respectively.

The specifier argument also gives information about the **associativity** of the operator. Although the precedence number determines how operators with different strengths are to read, it says nothing about multiple operators *with the same precedence*. Consider an arithmetic example again.

$$8 \div 4 \div 2 = x$$

The previous precedence conventions do not help in deciding between the two possible bracketings:

$$(8 \div 4) \div 2 = 1$$
$$8 \div (4 \div 2) = 4$$

In such cases, the convention is to take such arithmetic operators as being **left associative**. This means that the first bracketing above is assumed to be the default value. Left associative (infix) operators are defined with the specifier yfx and right associative operators with xfy. The specifier xfx defines a non-associative operator. Pre- and post-fix operators also need classifying in a similar way. A pre-fix operator that can apply to an expression whose main functor is lower in precedence is called **non-iterable** and defined with the specifier fx. One that requires the main functor to have the same precedence is called **iterable** and is expressed by fy. xf and yf are the analogous versions for post-fix operators.

With this discussion in mind, spoken_in can now be defined as an infix operator by the following clause.

```
?- op(400, xfx, spoken_in).
   yes
```

It is usual to declare operators at the beginning of a program. This is done simply by adding the above at the head of the file. Note that the Prolog prompt is included. When the file is read into Prolog, the interpreter will immediately try to satisfy such a goal which, in this case, has the effect of allowing spoken_in to be used as an operator. Accordingly, a file might look as follows. Notice that a fact with an operator still needs terminating with a full stop.

```
/* **********************************************

FILE NAME: EXAMPLE1.PL

DESCRIPTION: To show an operator definition as part
             of a file.

********************************************** */

          ?- op(400, xfx, spoken_in).

          english spoken_in uk.
          english spoken_in usa.
          english spoken_in australia.
          spanish spoken_in peru.
          quechua spoken_in peru.
          piro spoken_in peru.

          language(Language) :-
               Language spoken_in Country.

/* ********************************************** */
```

Question 7.5

Define an infix operator & which can be used to replace the list notation [spanish,quechua,piro]:

    spanish & quechua & piro & end

Note that end is included to mark the end of the list. Redefine the list predicates member and concat to take account of this change of format.

7.6 The 'Cut'

Section 7.1 illustrated a potential use of the predicate get0 through an interface which presented a menu of choices.

```
?- go.
    Do you want to search via
        (a)   Languages or
        (b)   Countries?
```

Suppose go is defined as follows.

```
go :-
    nl,
    write('Do you want to search via:'),
    nl, tab(3),
    write('(a) language or'),
    nl, tab(3),
    write('(b) country?'), nl,
    get0(C),
    do(C).
```

The variable C in do(C) becomes instantiated to the ASCII code number of the user's reply which then determines which clause to call. There will be three definitions of do, depending on whether the user replies with an a (ASCII code 97), b (ASCII code 98) or some other letter.

```
do(97) :-
    nl,
    write('Which language?'), nl,
    read(Lang),
    spoken_in(Lang, Country), nl,
    write(Lang), write('is spoken in'),
            write(Country), nl.
do(98) :-
    nl,
    write('Which country?'), nl,
    read(Country),
    spoken_in(Lang, Country), nl,
    write(Lang), write('is spoken in'),
            write(Country), nl.
do(_) :-
    nl,
    write('Please type either a or b'), nl,
    get0(C),
    do(C).
```

Each clause is designed to handle a single case. Further, invoking one rule should be done at the expense of the other two. For example, once having called do(97) neither do(98) nor do(_)

should be tried later in the execution. However, the program does not quite function like that. The problem occurs when the user asks about a language or country which is *not* in the database. Suppose, having chosen option (a), the user asks about the language Swahili. The interpreter will find no match for the subgoal spoken_in(swahili, Country) in the database and so will backtrack. Since neither write nor nl can be re-satisfied, Prolog will attempt to find another match for do(97). This is possible with the third rule which has the anonymous variable as argument. Accordingly, Prolog will now display the request for the user to type a or b.

```
?- go.
Do you want to search via:
      (a) Language or
      (b) Country?
|: a
Which language?
|: swahili.
Please type a or b
|:
```

Clearly, this is not the behaviour intended of the program.

What is required is some way of ensuring that if either do(97) or do(98) have been called then do(_) will not be attempted at some later stage. Prolog provides a special command called the **cut** which can be used to achieve this. The cut is written with an exclamation mark, !, and is a goal which always succeeds. However, once the cut has been passed, it cannot be re-crossed during backtracking. Consequently, there is no possibility of attempting to re-satisfy any of the clauses to the left of the cut, including the head of the rule. For example, in the following toy rule once the cut has been executed, no alternative solutions for a, b or p can be sought. The cut, however, does not affect backtracking with respect to c or d.

```
p :- a, b, !, c, d.
```

The cut, then, is rather like the funnel-shaped entrance to a lobster pot in that it allows Prolog (the lobster) to pass into the pot, but once in, Prolog cannot back out. In terms of the search tree, the cut has the effect of pruning away all remaining *OR*-branches for the goals which have been isolated by it.

The previous definition of do can now be redefined to include the cut.

```
do(97) :- !,
     nl,
     write('Which language?'), nl,
     read(Lang),
     spoken_in(Lang, Country), nl,
     write(Lang), write('is spoken in'),
               write(Country), nl.
do(98) :- !,
     nl,
     write('Which country?'), nl,
     read(Country),
     spoken_in(Lang, Country), nl,
     write(Lang), write('is spoken in'),
               write(Country), nl.

do(_) :-
     nl,
     write('Please type either a or b'), nl,
     get0(C),
     do(C).
```

Placing the cut as the first subgoal means that as soon as either do(97) or do(98) have been invoked the other two rules are discarded.

Once the cut has been passed, the interpreter is committed to the values of any variables fixed prior to the cut. It does not affect any uninstantiated variables that appear after the cut. For example, the following redefinition of do(97) uses a failure-driven loop to find all answers from the spoken_in database. This is possible since the subgoal spoken_in appears after the cut.

```
do(97) :- !,
     nl,
     write('Which language?'), nl,
     read(Lang),
     spoken_in(Lang, Country), nl,
     write(Lang), write(' is spoken in '),
               write(Country), nl,
     fail.

?- do(97).

Which language?
|: english.
english is spoken in uk
english is spoken in usa
english is spoken in australia
no
```

The cut was used in the previous examples in order to define mutually exclusive clauses. It can also be used to specify that a single solution to a particular predicate will suffice. As an example, imagine a predicate which, at some point, requires that a particular item be a member of some list. Assume, further, that all that matters is that there is at least one instance of this item in the list. In this case, assuming that member(Item, List) has been satisfied once, no useful purpose would be served by attempting to find another solution. To prevent redundant backtracking in this case, the cut can be introduced into the terminating condition of member.

```
member(Item, [Item|_]) :- !
member(Item, [Head|Tail]) :-
    member(Item, Tail).
```

The cut, then, can be usefully used both to define mutually exclusive clauses and improve the efficiency of a program. It should, however, be used with some caution. The problem is that since the cut only admits a procedural interpretation, including it in a definition can partially destroy the declarative interpretation of the predicate. In particular, the cut often reduces the scope of the definition. For example, the original definition of member could be used both to check whether a particular item is an element of a list:

```
?- member(piro, [spanish,quechua,piro]).
   yes
```

or to find all members of a list:

```
?- member(Member, [spanish,quechua,piro]).
   Member = spanish;
   Member = quechua;
   Member -= piro;
   no
```

However, the version of member including the cut cannot be used in this second way since the cut will cause the execution to stop once the first item is found.

```
?- member(Member, [spanish,quechua,piro]).
   Member = spanish;
   no
```

As a consequence, the programmer must be certain that once a cut-version of a predicate is introduced into a program, it is only used to perform the specific tasks for which it was designed.

7.7 Program Listing

The following is the program read_in mentioned in section 7.1.

```
/* ************************************************

FILE NAME: INPUT.PL

DESCRIPTION: Read_in(List) reads in a sentence and
             converts it into a list of words, List.

Taken from Clocksin and Mellish, 1987, pages 101-3

************************************************ */

read_in([Word|Words]) :-
        get0(Char1),
        read_word(Char1, Word, Char2),
        rest_sentence(Word, Char2, Words).

rest_sentence(Word, _,[]) :-
        last_word(Word), !.

rest_sentence(Word1, Char1, [Word2|Words]) :-
        read_word(Char1, Word2, Char2),
        rest_sentence(Word2, Char2, Words).

read_word(Char1, Word, Char2) :-
        single_character(Char1), !,
        name(Word, [Char2]),
        get0(Char1).

read_word(Char1, Word, Char2) :-
        case(Char1, Char3), !,
        get0(Char4),
        rest_word(Char4, Chars, Char2),
        name(Word, [Char3|Chars]).

read_word(Char1, Word, Char2) :-
        get0(Char3),
        read_word(Char3, Word, Char2).

rest_word(Char1, [Char2|Chars], Char3) :-
        case(Char1, Char2), !,
        get0(Char4),
        rest_word(Char4,Chars,Char3).

rest_word(Char, [], Char).

single_character(33).
single_character(44).
single_character(46).
```

```
single_character(58).
single_character(59).
single_character(63).

case(Char, Char) :-
          Char > 96,
          Char < 123.

case(Char1,Char2) :-
          Char1 > 64,
          Char1 < 91,
          Char2 is Char1 + 32.

 case(Char, Char) :-
          Char > 47,
          Char < 58.

case(39, 39).
case(45, 45).

last_word('.').
last_word('!').
last_word('?').
```

```
/* ****************************************** */
```

PART III

Natural Language Processing with Prolog

CHAPTER 8

Finite State Grammars and Sentence Recognition

As was seen in chapter 2, to understand the meaning of an utterance involves being able to determine its syntactic form. Identifying a string of words as syntactically well-formed is a process known as **recognition**. **Parsing**, on the other hand, goes beyond recognition by associating a syntactic structure to those expressions that have been recognised. The two processes are intimately linked since both depend upon the use of the same grammatical information. The present chapter illustrates this from the point of view of a simple grammatical description.

8.1 Sentence Frame Grammars

Perhaps, the simplest recognition procedure imaginable would involve listing all possible sentences and then checking any test string against this list. A string would be a sentence if included in the list and not otherwise. Recognition could be extended to parsing if the listing also included the syntactic structure of the sentence. If this was all there was to recognition (or parsing), it would be easy to express in Prolog; a series of facts, one for each sentence, would suffice.

```
sentence([the,boy,stood,on,the,burning,deck]).
sentence([recognition,is,easy]).
```

The matching process could then be left to the Prolog interpreter.

```
?- sentence([recognition,is,easy]).
   yes
```

There are two obvious problems with this approach. First, as previously noted in section 2.1, there are just too many sentences to be listed. Secondly, even if some suitably large subset were able to be written down, it would be an inefficient form of representation since the same structures would be repeated many times. These problems can be overcome by writing a **grammar** for the language and using this to aid the recognition process. A grammar is a description of the structures that underlie the sentences of a language. There are only a finite number of these structures but they are able to combine and re-combine in such a way as to permit huge numbers of sentences. Armed with such knowledge, a recogniser is able to work out whether a string is well-formed or not by determining whether its structure conforms to one of those permitted by the grammar.

One of the simplest forms of grammatical description is expressed by a **sentence frame grammar**. With such a grammar, each sentence is viewed as an instance of a particular sentential pattern. These patterns are known as **sentence frames**. The following is an example.

Det N Vi

This is read as stating that a string of words which consists of a determiner followed by a noun followed by an intransitive verb is a sentence. The following strings can then be classified as sentences since each is an instance of this particular combination of lexical categories.

The cock crowed
Many buildings collapsed
Two climbers fell

Here are some other sentence frames for English.

Det N Vt Det N
Pn Vi
Det Adj N Vt Pn
Adj N Vi Adv

where *Det* = determiner, *N* = noun, *Pn* = Proper Name, *Adj* = adjective, *Vi* = intransitive verb, *Vt* = transitive verb and *Adv* = adverb. The set of sentences defined by a sentence frame grammar are all those strings which are instances of the sentence frames of the grammar given a particular lexicon.

Question 8.1

Assuming the following lexicon:

Det – *the, a, this, these*
N – *Joshua, box, birds, bacon, queen, king*
V – *put, fly, stole, vanished, saw*

Adj – *large, warm, tall*
Prep – *up, toward, below, into, on*
Conj – *and, or*
Pro – *we, he, us, they, him, I, me*
Adv – *quickly*

and the following sentence frames:

N V Pro
Pro V Det N Conj Det N
Adj N V Det N
Adj N V Adv
Det N V
Det N V Det N

which of the following strings are sentences according to this sentence frame grammar?

(a)   Large birds fly slowly
(b)   The bacon vanished
(c)   Birds saw us
(d)   Warm man put a box
(e)   He saw the king and queen
(f)   The king and the queen vanished
(g)   He put the bacon on the box
(h)   The Joshua stole this bacon
(i)   This box stole the king
(j)   The queen saw he

For those strings which are sentences of English but not covered by the grammar, how would you change the grammar to include them? Are there any ill-formed strings which the grammar would determine as well-formed? How might the grammar be changed to prevent this?

8.2 Parsing and Recognition Using a Sentence Frame Grammar

A grammar is a declarative description of a language. That is, it only states the conditions which must hold for a string of words to be a valid expression of the language. Parsing and recognition, on the other hand, are *processes* which, based upon the grammatical description of the language, determine whether a particular string is a valid expression and, if so, what its associated structure is. It is important conceptually to keep the declarative/procedural distinction between grammars and recognisers/parsers clearly in mind.

The simplicity of a sentence frame grammar suggests an equally simple recognition process. Take the string of words to be recognised. Replace each word by its lexical category. Check whether this transformed string corresponds to one of the sentence frames of the grammar. If it does, then the original string of words is accepted as well-formed, otherwise it is rejected as ill-formed. For example, transforming the string *The small boy bit Felicity* into its lexical categories results in the categorial string *Det Adj N V Pn*. This corresponds to one of the sentence frames listed in section 8.1 and so the original string is accepted as a sentence. On the other hand, *The every small quietly* is rejected since its transform, *Det Det Adj Adv*, is not a sentence frame.

Specifying a sentence frame grammar in Prolog is a simple matter. Sentence frames can be defined using a 1-place predicate, `frame`, which takes a list of lexical categories as its argument.

```
frame([det,n,vi]).
frame([pn,vt,adj,n]).
```

Lexical data, on the other hand, can be expressed through a 2-place predicate `word` where the first argument is a lexical item and the second its lexical category.

```
word(the, det).
word(cock, n).
word(crowed, vi).
```

It will facilitate the development of later programs if the lexical database is placed in a separate file, say `lex.pl`, with the sentence frames in a file called `sf.pl`. These two files constitute the grammar.

The definition of the recognition procedure will be written in a separate file `sfg_rec.pl`. In this way, the distinction between the grammar and the process based upon grammars of that sort will be kept clear. The core of the recognition program is the transformation of the string of words into the corresponding string of lexical categories. To this end a predicate `transform(String, CatString)` needs defining such that `CatString` is the list of lexical categories of the words occurring in `String`. Since both `String` and `CatString` are variables over lists, the definition of `transform` must be recursive. In fact, the relevant procedure has already been defined as the answer to question 5.19 where it went by the name of `translate`. It is repeated here with the relevant modifications.

```
transform([], []).

transform([Word|String], [Cat|CatString]) :-
        word(Word, Cat),
        transform(String, CatString).
```

In other words, the transformation of the empty string is the empty string. This is the boundary clause. For non-empty strings, the word which heads the list of words must match the lexical category which heads the list of categories as determined by the lexical entry for that word and where the tail of the second list is the transform of the tail of the first list.

```
?- transform([the,cock,crowed], CatString).
   CatString = [det,n,vi]
   yes
```

With `transform` defined, the rest of the procedure is simply stated with a drive predicate `recognise`.

```
recognise(String) :-
    transform(String, CatString),
    frame(CatString).
```

That is, a `String` is recognised if its associated transformation into a string of lexical categories corresponds to a sentence frame.

In order to facilitate the consultation of the grammar files, it will be useful to place the following two lines of code at the beginning of the `sfg_rec.pl` file.

```
?- reconsult('lex.pl').
?- reconsult('sf.pl').
```

These have the effect that as the file `sfg_rec.pl` is (re)consulted, the two files `lex.pl` and `sf.pl` are automatically accessed. Note that the Prolog prompt must be included.

With the relevant files loaded, the program can now be used to check whether various strings are sentences or not as defined by the particular sentence frame grammar.

```
?- recognise([the,cock,crowed]).
   yes
?- recognise([crowed,cock,the]).
   no
```

A listing of the file `sfg_rec.pl` is given in section 8.7 along with a sample lexicon, `lex.pl`, and a set of sample sentence frames in the file `sf.pl`.

It is easy to change the recogniser into a parser since the structural information contained in the grammar is expressed through its sentence frames. Therefore, all that has to be reported is the sentence's associated sentence frame which is computed as part of the recognition procedure. The change from recognise to parse is, therefore, minimal.

```
parse(Sentence, Parse) :-
    transform(Sentence, Parse),
    frame(Parse).
```

The resulting simplistic parse only reflects the simplistic notion of syntactic structure that is encoded by a sentence frame grammar.

```
?- parse([the,cock,crowed], Parse).
   Parse = [det,n,vi]
   yes
```

Question 8.2

Assuming you are working with the text with an implementation of Prolog, code the sentence frame grammar given in question 8.1 into two files, one containing the sentence frames and the other the lexical facts. Using these files with sfg_rec.pl, check your original answers to question 8.1 with those given by the program.

Question 8.3

old is ambiguous; it can either be an adjective as in *Old houses take a lot of maintaining* or a noun as in *The old are more militant now*. How will such examples be handled in a sentence frame grammar? Is any alteration to the definition of recognise required?

8.3 An Alternative Notation for Sentence Frame Grammars

It will prove useful in later discussions to introduce an alternative notation for sentence frame grammars. In this notation the sentence frame *Det N Vi* is represented by the following:

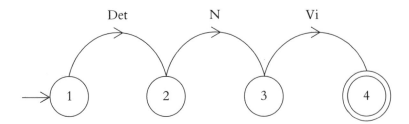

This diagram is a **graph**. A graph consists of a set of **nodes** linked together by **arcs**. Here the nodes are represented by circles and named by the encircled number. The arcs are represented by the lines joining the nodes. In this graph the arcs are **labelled** with the names of lexical categories. Notice that the arrow heads indicate that the arcs are **directed**. It is this direction that imposes a linear ordering on the lexical categories; for example, determiners come before nouns rather than vice versa. The start of the graph is represented by an incoming arrow to node 1 and the end by the doubly circled node 4. Such graphs are referred to as **finite-state transition networks** (FSTN) for reasons that will become apparent in the next section. The resulting grammar is a **finite-state grammar**.

One advantage of adopting the FSTN notation is that it enables more than one sentence frame to be combined into the same network. For instance, this FSTN:

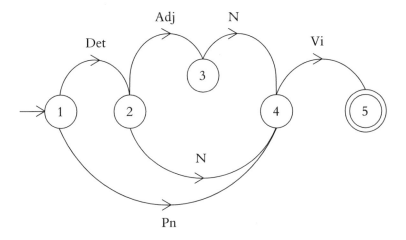

is an amalgamation of the three sentence frames:

Pn Vi	'John smiled'
Det N Vi	'The cobbler disappeared'
Det Adj N Vi	'These new shoes hurt'

Notice how *Det* and *Vi* appear twice and three times, respectively, in the sentence frames but only once in the network.

Question 8.4

Represent the sentence frame grammar in question 8.1 using FSTN notation.

Question 8.5

What are the equivalent sentence frames encoded in the following FSTN?

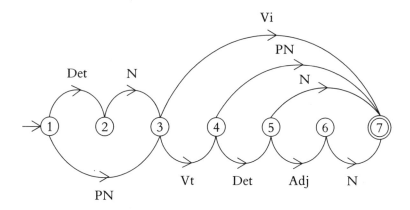

Question 8.6

Choosing one word at random from each of the following columns in turn (taken from Pinker, 1994) will result in an impressive-sounding piece of gobbledygook such as *defunctionalised co-operative interdependence*.

I	II	III
defunctionalised	participatory	interdependence
predicative	aggregating	diffusion
quantitative	simulated	periodicity
synchronous	transfigurative	synthesis
inductive	co-operative	sufficiency
distributive	complementary	equivalence

Write a finite state 'Social Science Jargon' grammar for these expressions.

Question 8.7

The following are some typical examples of a child's utterances at the two-word stage of linguistic development (roughly around the age of 18 to 24 months):

all broke	no bed	more care	other bid	boot off
all buttoned	no down	more cereal	other bread	light off
all clean	no fox	more cookie	other milk	shirt off
all wet	no water	more sing	other shoe	water off
all messy	no mama	more juice	other pocket	pants off

Write a finite state grammar that will define such 'sentences'. What other sentences will be defined and are they all likely to occur? [Do not make the grammar more complicated than necessary. Assume that adult lexical categories are not relevant – for example, do not analyse *broke* as a verb and *cookie* as a noun.]

8.4 A Finite State Grammar-based Recognisor

The change from sentence frames to FSTNs entails a change in the recognition process. The description of the usual procedure is in terms of a device called a **finite-state automaton**. Imagine this as a pointer which can scan an input string one word at a time. At each step, the pointer is in one of a finite number of states, hence, its name. In certain circumstances the pointer may move to scan the next word. Sometimes, as it moves, its state may also change. The following diagram shows the automaton scanning the word *building* whilst in state 2.

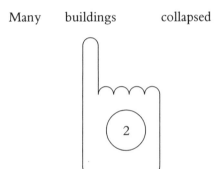

Many   buildings   collapsed

Such a 'snapshot' is called a **configuration** and is defined in terms of the word being scanned and the state of the pointer. The automaton will accept a string of words as a sentence if it manages to scan each word in order from left to right, starting from the **initial** state and ending up in a designated **final** state. The string will be rejected otherwise.

The instructions that allow the automaton to progress from one configuration to another are encoded in the FSTN. In other words, FSTNs can be thought of not only as declarative grammatical descriptions but also as a set of directions for the recognition process. This dual interpretation of FSTNs parallels that of Prolog clauses. The starting state of the device is the same as the name of the initial node of the network. Similarly, the final state corresponds to the name of the final node. The potential transition from one configuration to another is also determined by the FSTN. For example, the previous FSTN (repeated below) can be read as containing the instructions: 'if in state 1 and scanning a determiner, proceed to the next word and change to state 2', 'if in state 2 and scanning a noun, proceed to the next word and change to state 3' and so on.

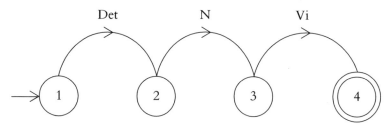

An alternative way of thinking of the recognition procedure is in terms of the pointer 'traversing through the network'. Starting at node 1, it scans the first word and if it is a determiner moves to node 2. From there it scans the next word to check if it is a noun, and so on. A string is recognised as a sentence if the device ends up at the final node having scanned each word in turn.

Producing a Prolog implementation of the procedure is similar to that previously given for sentence frame grammars requiring both a definition of the grammar and of the recognition procedure. An FSTN is simply specified as a series of facts. The predicate arc will encode each individual link in the network; for example:

```
arc(1, det, 2).
```

Whilst the predicates initial and final specify where the network begins and ends.

```
initial(1).
final(4).
```

A full listing of an exemplar FSTN can be found in section 8.7 as the file fstn.pl. As far as the lexicon is concerned, the lexical file, lex.pl, previously used with the sentence frame grammar may be re-used. This was why the lexical facts were originally placed in a separate file.

The main predicate for the recognition process is config. This is a 2-place predicate where the first argument represents the word being scanned and the second the state. As previously, the string will be represented as a list. The head of the list represents the word currently being scanned. For example,

```
config([buildings,collapsed], 2)
```

represents a configuration where buildings is the word being scanned (with collapsed as the next word) whilst the device is in state 2.

The specification of the recognition program must define the starting and end configurations as well as the possible transitions from one configuration to another. The end configuration is defined by the rule:

```
config([], State) :-
        final(State).
```

That is, in the final configuration there are no more words left to scan and the device is in a final state. The recursive part of the definition specifies the possible transitions between configurations:

```
config([Word|Rest], State) :-
        word(Word, Cat),
        arc(State, Cat, State1),
        config(Rest, State1).
```

Note how the call to `config` in the body of the rule is scanning the next word and has changed to the new state as specified by the `arc` fact. Finally, the drive predicate `recognise` ensures that the starting configuration in the sequence is scanning the first word of the input string and in the initial state:

```
recognise(String) :-
        initial(State),
        config(String, State).
```

The listing for this program is given in section 8.7 as the file `fsg_rec.pl`. Note that, like the program `sfg_rec.pl`, `fsg_rec.pl` also automatically reconsults the relevant grammar files.

In fact, it would be possible to make the program slightly more efficient through a process called **partial evaluation**. This involves making changes to the program so that certain computations that would usually be performed during the execution of the rule are built in to the rule itself if the computation will always result in the same value (and this value is known). For example, if we assume that the initial state of any network is always going to be 1, it is a waste of time Prolog attempting to solve the goal `initial(String)` each time simply in order to plug in the value 1 into the the `config` literal. A simpler, and quicker, approach is to replace this goal altogether and build the value 1 directly into `config`.

```
recognise(String) :-
        config(String, 1).
```

Assuming that all networks also had the same final state, it would also be possible to partially evaluate the terminating clause of `config`.

With `fsg_rec.pl` and a suitable lexicon file loaded Prolog can be posed questions such as:

```
?- recognise([some, buildings, collapsed]).
   yes

?- recognise([collapsed, buildings, some]).
   no
```

As usual, it is instructive to follow through a proof of these questions. The following reproduces a trace of the successful satisfaction of the first question with a spy-point placed on `config`.

```
(1)   1 CALL: config([some,buildings,collapsed], 1)?
(2)   2 CALL: config([buildings,collapsed], 2)?
(3)   3 CALL: config([collapsed], 3)?
(4)   4 CALL: config([], 4)?
(4)   4 EXIT: config([], 4)?
(3)   3 EXIT: config([collapsed], 3)?
(2)   2 EXIT: config([buildings, collapsed], 2).
(1)   1 EXIT: config([some,buildings,collapsed], 1).
yes
```

Notice how the series of `config` goals mimics the way the pointer would traverse through the network.

Producing a parse with an FSTN is slightly more complicated than with a sentence frame grammar although the result is the same impoverished notion of syntactic structure.

```
?- parse([the,tall,building,collapsed], Parse).
   Parse = [det,n,adj,vi]
   yes
```

The key to this program is changing `config` into a 3-place predicate with the third argument recording the categorial information of each word as it is processed. The following shows the necessary changes to the definitions.

```
parse(Sentence, Parse) :-
    initial(State),
    config(Sentence, State, Parse).

config([], State, []) :-
    final(State).

config([Word|Rest], State, [Cat|RestCats]) :-
    word(Word, Cat),
    arc(State, Cat, State1),
    config(Rest, State1, RestCats).
```

Question 8.8

Give the Prolog coding for the FSTN used in question 8.5

Question 8.9

The following FSTN is just like that in section 8.3 except that the node names have been changed. Does this matter?

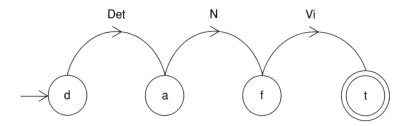

Question 8.10

In the text it was suggested that FSTNs have an advantage over sentence frame grammars in being more compact. Is this advantage carried over to the Prolog coding?

Question 8.11

Assuming that the final state of all FSTNs is 4, partially evaluate the terminating rule of config which was given in the text as:

```
config([], State) :-
      final(State).
```

8.5 Extending the Range of Finite State Grammars

So far it has been assumed that a language such as English consists of a huge number of sentences. In fact, technically there are infinitely many. For example, there is, in principle, no limit to the number of attributive adjectives which may modify a noun:

Two climbers fell
Two small climbers fell
Two small wiry climbers fell
Two small wiry English climbers fell
       . . .

nor how many intensifiers may modify an adjective:

The very famous playwright arrived drunk
The very very famous playwright arrived drunk
The very very very famous playwright arrived drunk
        . . .

The constraints on how many adjectives or intensifiers may actually be used in an utterance are determined not by linguistic properties but the finite resources of our processing mechanisms.

It might be thought that such **iterative** constructions would be problematic for a sentence frame grammar since they would require an infinite number of sentence frames to define them:

Det N Vi
Det Adj N Vi
Det Adj Adj N Vi
Det Adj Adj Adj N Vi
        . . .

To overcome this descriptive problem the **Kleene star** (named after the logician Stephen Kleene) is introduced; the expression $X^\star$ is interpreted as meaning 'a sequence of zero or more instances of X'. Using this notation the first infinite set of sentences can be defined with the single frame:

Det Adj* N Vi

The same iterative effect is achieved in an FSTN through the use of a **loop**. This is an arc that re-enters the same node as it leaves. In the FSTN below the adjective arc is a loop since it leaves and re-enters node 2.

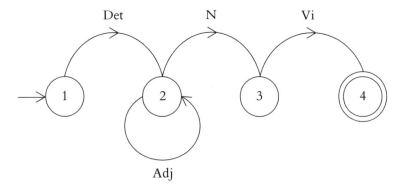

In terms of the finite state grammar recognition procedure, the effect of the adjective loop is that as an adjective is recognised the device moves to the next word *but stays in the same state*. No change is needed to the definition of the recognition process to handle such networks since the information is encoded in the arc definition:

```
arc(2, adj, 2).
```

Other notational conventions allow special ways of handling optional elements. For example, the bracketing in the sentence frame:

Det N Vi (Adv)

is intended to represent that there may be an optional adverb following the verb. One way of capturing optionality in an FSTN is via a **jump** arc. Such arcs will be labelled 'jump'.

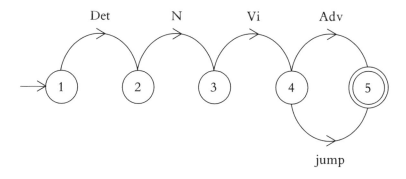

A jump arc leads to a **silent** move in the recognition procedure. That is, it allows a change of state without changing the word being scanned. An additional definition for config is required to handle silent moves. The following does this:

```
config(String, State) :-
            arc(State, jump, State1),
            config(String, State1).
```

Note how the state is changed but not the word being scanned.

A recogniser using the previous FSTN will be presented with a choice of actions when in state 4 and scanning an adverb; it may change to state 5 by taking either the adverb or jump arc. The difference is that with the former move the word being scanned will also change but not with the latter. When a recogniser or parser is faced with a choice about what its next move is to be, the process is said to be **non-deterministic**. If there is no such choice, the process is **deterministic**.

With non-determinism, there is always the chance that the wrong decision will be made at a point of choice. However, no adjustments need to be made to the previous programs to cater for such possibilities since Prolog's backtracking mechanisms will rescue the process in such cases.

There are various benefits to be gained by using finite-state devices. Not least is the fact that they are easy to implement and, especially if deterministic, efficient to run. Various NLP applications have capitalised on these advantages especially in the areas of phonology and morphology. However, finite state techniques are of more limited application within the domain of syntax as discussed in the next chapter.

Question 8.12

It is reported that the birdsong of the black-capped chickadee is made up of four basic elements which may be referred to as A, B, C and D (see Corballis, 1991, pages 139–40 for some discussion). Each call consists of strings of these elements, repeated any number of times but always in the order A-B-C-D. Any element may be omitted altogether from a particular call. Write an FSTN which will describe this language. Code your answer into Prolog and then check that the recogniser accepts strings such as *ABCD, C, ACDD, AABBBCDD* but rejects strings such as *BACD* and *BBDCC.*

Question 8.13

The notion of a loop may be generalised to include an arc which links back to some previous node. Using such a loop, devise an FSTN that will accept sentences with conjunctions such as:

Joshua and Felicity ate the picnic
The dentist and Anne laughed
Bruce and the patient drank the wine
The doctor and the dentist disappeared

Question 8.14

Using a jump arc, write an FSTN that will account for the optional object with such verbs as *eat*:

Ruth ate the pear
Ruth ate

Question 8.15

Revise the sentence frame-based recognition procedure to handle sentence frames including Kleene stars and brackets for optional elements. Note that adj* will not be a suitable Prolog term since it does not decompose into the two parts adj and *.

Question 8.16

The recogniser developed in this chapter will only respond with a no to ill-formed input. However, at the point that the proof blocks there is often enough information available for the system to respond with more helpful feedback. For example, a possible interaction might take the form:

```
?- recognise([the,mary,fell]).
A noun should follow: the.
yes
```

Write a program that will provide such feedback.

8.6 Further Reading

There are a number of other texts treating Prolog and NLP including Pereira and Shieber (1987), Gazdar and Mellish (1989), Gal *et al.* (1991) and Covington (1994).

The description of sentence frame grammars is based on the 'word class grammars' of Baker (1978). Gazdar and Mellish (1989) provides a clear and wide ranging discussion of finite-state techniques and is a good source for further references. Winograd (1983) also provides a short but useful introduction. More formal accounts of the properties of finite state automata can be found in Partee *et al.* (1990), Wall (1972), Minsky (1972), Aho and Ullman (1972) and Hopcroft and Ullman (1979).

Considerable interest has been shown in finite-state devices for phonological and morphological analysis, initially influenced by the research of Koskenniemi (1983). Gazdar (1985) provides a summary and evaluation of this work, whilst Covington (1994) also has a brief discussion in relation to a Prolog implementation. Antworth (1990) provides a book-length tutorial introduction, software and further references.

8.7 Program Listings

(1) sfg_rec.pl

```
/* ************************************************

FILE NAME: sfg_rec.pl

DESCRIPTION: A recogniser based on the sentence frame
grammar notation. Definition of the SFG is defined
in two separate files

************************************************ */
```

```
% Load the lexical and sentence frame files

    ?- reconsult('lex.pl').
    ?- reconsult('sf.pl').

% Drive predicate

    recognise(String) :-
            transform(String, CatString),
            frame(CatString).

% Transform a string of words into a string of lexical
categories

    transform([], []).

    transform([Word|String], [Cat|CatString]) :-
            word(Word, Cat),
            transform(String, CatString).
```

/* ** */

(2) **lex.pl**

/* **

FILE NAME: lex.pl

DESCRIPTION: A sample lexical database giving the
lexical category of each word (roughly based on the
SFG defined in question 6.1)

** */

```
    word(the, det).
    word(a, det).
    word(these, det).

    word(king, n).
    word(queen, n).
    word(bacon, n).
    word(box, n).

    word(left, vi).
    word(put, v).
    word(fly, v).
    word(stole, vt).
    word(saw, vt).
```

```
word(large, adj).
word(warm, adj).

word(slowly, adv).

word(up, prep).
word(on, prep).

word(and, conj).
word(or, conj).

word(he, pro).
word(we, pro).
word(they, pro).
```

/* *** */

(3) sf.pl

/* **

FILE NAME: sf.pl

DESCRIPTION: A list of sentence frames (roughly based
on the SFG defined in question 8.1)

** */

```
frame([det,n,vi]).
frame([n,vt,pro]).
frame([pro,vt,det,n,conj,det,n]).
frame([adj,n,vt,det,n]).
frame([adj,n,vt,adv]).
```

/* *** */

(4) fstn.pl

/* **

FILE NAME: fstn.pl

DESCRIPTION: A Prolog encoding of the FSTN found on
page 129

** */

```
initial(1).
final(5).
```

```
arc(1, det, 2).
arc(1, pn, 4).
arc(2, adj, 3).
arc(2, n, 4).
arc(3, n, 4).
arc(4, vi, 5).
```

```
/* ******************************************* */
```

(5) fsg_rec.pl

```
/* *********************************************
```

FILE NAME: fsg_rec.pl

DESCRIPTION: A recogniser based on the FSTN notation.
Definition of the FSTN is defined in two separate files

```
********************************************* */
```

% Load the lexical and FSTN files.

```
?- reconsult('lex.pl').
?- reconsult('fstn.pl').
```

% Drive predicate which sets up initial configuration.

```
recognise(String) :-
          initial(State),
          config(String, State).
```

% Check whether in final configuration; if not, move to
% next configuration if allowed by network.

```
config([], State) :-
          final(State).
```

```
config([Word|Rest], State) :-
          word(Word, Cat),
          arc(State, Cat, State1),
          config(Rest, State1).
```

```
/* ******************************************* */
```

CHAPTER 9

Recursive Transition Networks

The basic concept behind the grammars of the last chapter is that syntax consists of a set of sequential constraints on word combinations. For example, the FSTN:

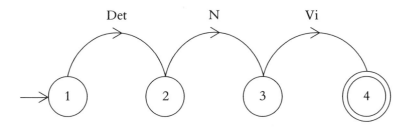

expresses, amongst others, the restrictions that (i) a determiner is the sort of word that may start a sentence and be immediately followed by a noun which, in turn, is followed by an intransitive verb, (ii) that a noun is the sort of word that may be immediately preceded by a determiner and immediately followed by an intransitive verb, and (iii) that an intransitive verb may immediately succeed a noun preceded by a determiner and end a sentence. A string of words is a sentence if each word simultaneously obeys these local restrictions.

Word order facts must be described by a grammar since they vary from language to language. For example, in Kikuyu, a Bantu language of East Africa, nouns come before determiners rather than after them, whilst in Welsh, the verb comes at the beginning of the sentence rather than at the end. However, word order is only part of the syntactic story. This chapter explores the need for an additional level of structural description, how it might be described by a grammar and how a recognisor based on such grammars might be implemented.

9.1 Phrase Structure

Consider the following list of sequences of lexical categories:

Proper Name
Plural common noun
Determiner + Noun
Adjective + Plural common noun
Determiner + Adjective + Noun

Instances of each sequence may occur immediately preceding, say, *frightened the climber* to form a sentence.

$$
\left.\begin{array}{l}
\text{Everest} \\
\text{Couloirs} \\
\text{The cornice} \\
\text{Dark crevasses} \\
\text{Every high serac}
\end{array}\right\} \text{ frightened the climber}
$$

Further, the same sequences pattern together with respect to other sentences.

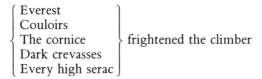

$$
\text{Bad dreams about} \left\{\begin{array}{l}
\text{Everest} \\
\text{couloirs} \\
\text{the cornice} \\
\text{dark crevasses} \\
\text{every high serac}
\end{array}\right\} \text{woke Joe every night}
$$

$$
\text{Joe climbed} \left\{\begin{array}{l}
\text{Everest} \\
\text{couloirs} \\
\text{the cornice} \\
\text{dark crevasses} \\
\text{every high serac}
\end{array}\right\} \text{with great trepidation}
$$

These facts suggest that each expression has some common property in virtue of which they have the same distribution. Since some of the expressions consist of more than one word, this property must be a property of groups of words or **phrases** (where a single word such as *Everest* or *couloirs* is treated as an honorary phrase). In fact, the common element in the above phrases is that each includes a noun. For this reason, they are referred to as **noun phrases** (NPs).

Similar distributional arguments could be marshalled to demonstrate the phrasal identity of the following expressions which, because they crucially include a verb, are referred to as **verb phrases** (VPs).

grimaced
climbed the mountain
gave Simon a fright
knew the game was up

Note that the VP *climbed the mountain* consists not only of a verb, *climbed*, but also an NP, *the mountain*. **Prepositional phrases** (PPs) such as:

> on the mountain
> under every high serac
> behind Siula Grande

also contain an NP along with the obligatory preposition which gives the phrase its name. Other phrasal groupings include **adjectival phrases** (AdjP), such as *very fond of Felicity*, and **adverbial phrases** (AdvP), such as *quite independently of Anne*.

Because phrases may include smaller phrases as constituent parts, phrasal structure is **hierarchical**. The hierarchical structure of a sentence can be graphically represented with a **phrase structure tree** as previously illustrated in section 2.1.

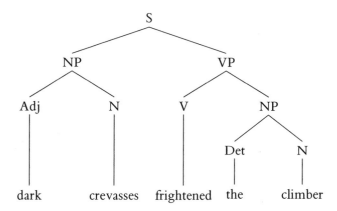

An ability to be able to refer to phrasal categories in the grammar would have two advantages. First, it would result in a more compact form of description since the phrasal name could be used as an abbreviation for the full range of expressions that can appear in a particular position. Secondly, using the same phrasal name in different positions would capture the fact that the same range of syntactic expressions are being referred to each time; for instance, any NP that can occur before a transitive verb can, some exceptions aside, also appear after the verb.

Being able to refer to phrasal categories in the grammar, however, is more than a descriptive nicety. Crucially, the semantics of a sentence are (partially) determined by its phrasal structure. Intuitively this is correct since phrases have a semantic unity that is usually lacking for non-phrases. Compare, for example, the meaning of the phrase *dark crevasses* (which refers to a particular sort of crevasse), with the lack of meaning of the non-phrase *frightened the*.

The ability of phrases to appear in isolation, say as truncated answers to questions, also shows their semantic cohesion.

    A: Is Joe frightened of anything?
    B: Dark crevasses

Further, different phrasal analyses of a string of words can result in different meanings. This was illustrated in section 2.2 by the sentence:

    Joshua hit the boy with the sword

which was associated with the two phrasal structures repeated below.

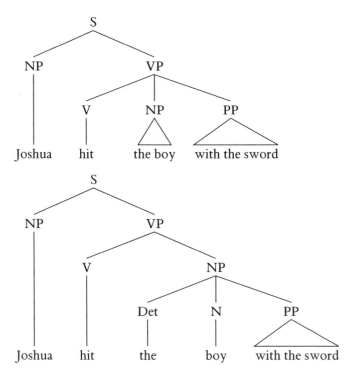

Note the use of the triangles to cover those phrases where the exact internal structure of the phrase is not relevant for present concerns.

For these and other reasons, it is clear that sentential structure goes beyond a set of sequential constraints on word combinations to include a layer of hierarchical phrasal organisation. However, this notion of phrase structure is only implicitly captured in an FSTN. Consider the following example.

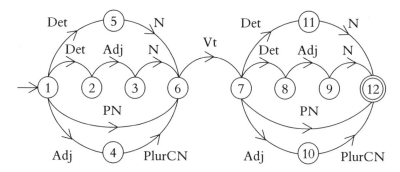

Notice how a bundle of arcs leaves node 1 and converges again on node 6. Similarly, for nodes 7 and 12. In effect, these nodes circumscribe the edges of the NPs on either side of the transitive verb as the following examples show.

$$\left\{ \begin{array}{l} \text{The women} \\ \text{All small children} \\ \text{Batkin} \\ \text{Large players} \end{array} \right\} \text{like(s)} \left\{ \begin{array}{l} \text{the cake} \\ \text{most greasy food} \\ \text{Mog} \\ \text{strong shoes} \end{array} \right\}$$

Further, the two subnetworks are, node names aside, identical, capturing the fact that the same syntactic expressions can appear in both positions. However, it is not possible to explicitly express this fact in an FSTN. This might not seem particularly disastrous since the network as a whole does capture the relevant distributional information. However, this outcome is not dictated by the formalism itself and so is purely fortuitous. It is quite possible, for example, to write an FSTN where, say, the 'subject NP' network includes the full range of NPs but the 'object NP' net only allows *Det Adj N* sequences.

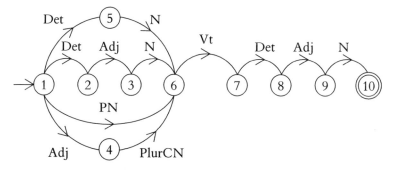

With the FSTN formalism it is just as easy to write the second network as the first. However, given previous observations, the second FSTN describes a situation which should not be possible.

What is required is a representation which is something like the following.

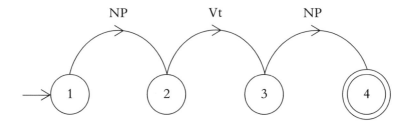

Using the same arc label, *NP*, both before and after the transitive verb, indicates that the same range of expressions is allowed in both positions. The relevant extensions to the graph notation which allows such statements to be made are introduced in the next section.

There is a further problem with FSTNs as a grammar formalism. It was shown in section 8.5 how, through the use of a loop, an FSTN can represent the infinity of sentences that result from the **iteration** of certain expressions. Phrasal structure introduces a different kind of infinity due to the possibility of phrasal categories containing phrases of the same type. For example, a sentence may contain another sentence:

[s Dave thought [s his opponent was beaten]]

or an NP another NP:

[NP The sheep under [NP the bridge]]

and so on. Phrases of this type are called **recursive**. Clearly, if a sentence may contain another sentence, that sentence in turn may contain another sentence, which may also contain another sentence, which . . . and so on. This type of infinity cannot be represented using an FSTN. Intuitively, this should be clear since to represent such an infinity would require an infinity of subnetworks nested inside one another. The extensions to be introduced in the next section are able to overcome this descriptive problem.

Question 9.1

Imagine a species of chickadee like that in question 8.12 but whose calls are only made up of two elements referred to as A and B. Suppose, further, that the language of this bird is $A^n B^n$. That is, each call consists of some number *n* of As followed by the *same number* of Bs. Is it possible to write an FSTN which will correctly define all the 'sentences' of this language?

9.2 Extending the Network Notation

The following FSTN defines a number of different NPs.

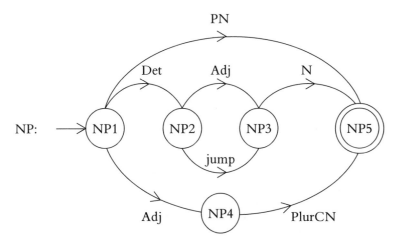

This network is like previous FSTNs except that it is prefixed with a name, *NP*. Although it is not necessary, the node names have also been relativised to the name of the network. Apart from this, the network is interpreted like any other FSTN; a string of words is an NP if it consists of either a proper name, or a plural common noun, or a determiner followed by a noun and so on.

The network formalism can now be extended to allow network names to appear as labels on arcs. For example, a simple VP-network could be defined as follows.

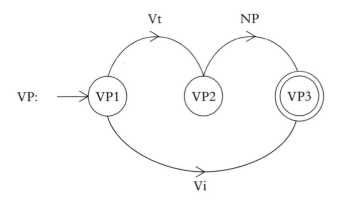

This is interpreted as saying that a string of words is a VP if it consists of an intransitive verb or a transitive verb followed by a string which is an NP. What strings count as NPs are determined by the NP-network.

With both the NP- and VP-networks defined, it is possible to define a sentence as a string consisting of an NP followed by a VP.

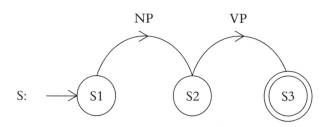

The *NP* label which appears in both the S- and VP-networks refers to the same NP-network on both occasions. This ensures that the same range of expressions may appear in both positions.

Recursion can be simply handled once arc labels refer to other networks. For example, the following two networks jointly make it possible for NPs to appear nested inside other NPs.

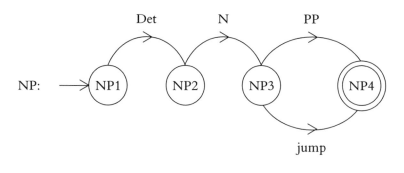

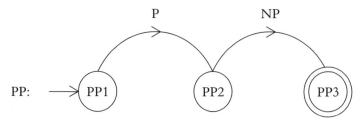

That is, an NP may consist of a determiner, noun and optional PP (note the use of the jump arc). A PP, in turn, consists of a preposition followed by an NP. This NP, of course, may also include an optional PP which will contain an NP which may include an optional PP which . . . and so on. Recursion occurs, then, when an arc label refers to a network which includes the first network name as one of its labels. In the present case, the *NP* label in the PP-network refers to an NP-network which, in turn, contains a *PP* label. Because of this ability to be able to handle recursive structures, the networks introduced in this section are called **Recursive Transition Networks** (RTNs).

Question 9.2

The recursive NP and PP networks include another recursive element apart from NP. What is it?

Question 9.3

Write an RTN-grammar to handle examples such as;

[s Joe said that [s Simon thought that [s he was dead]]]

Question 9.4

Show how RTNs can define the language A^nB^n of question 9.1.

9.3 An RTN-based Recognisor

The recognition procedure developed for FSTNs in chapter 8 can also form the basis for recognition using RTNs. An extension is required, however, to handle those arcs labelled with network names. The basic idea is quite simple. Each network is treated as a set of specialised instructions to recognise phrases of that particular type. Accordingly, when a phrasal label is encountered in a network, control is temporarily passed to the network which specialises in recognising categories of that sort. Using these instructions, an attempt is made to recognise such a phrase. If one is found, control is passed back to the original set of instructions from the point where control was temporarily relinquished.

A worked example will help to clarify this. Suppose that the input string is *The crevasses frightened Joe* and that the processor has access to the following RTNs:

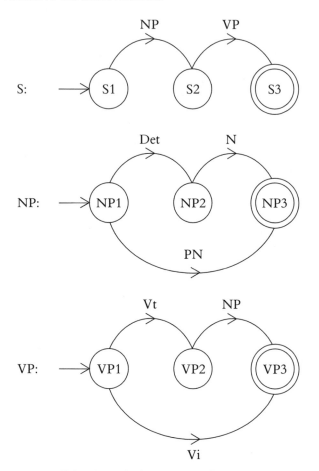

The process will be described in terms of traversing through the various networks.

Since a sentence is being sought, the overall goal of the device will be to move through the S-network. A move from node S1 to S2 is possible if an NP can be found. Since the S-network is not a specialist in recognising such phrases, control is temporarily passed to the NP-network. This is referred to as **pushing** to the new network. The NP-network now has to be traversed. The processor moves through the network by first scanning a determiner and then a noun. At this point, the NP-net has been traversed. In other words, an NP has been recognised. Since this was what was required by the S-network, the device now moves – or **pops** – back to that network. On popping back to the S-network, the device continues from the S2 node.

To proceed further, the process must next push to the VP-network. Here a move from node VP1 to VP2 is possible on recognising *frightened* as a verb. Further progress requires a push to the NP-network. A straight traversal of this network is possible given the input *Joe* being recognised as a proper name. At this point, the device pops back to node VP3 of the VP-network. Since this is the final state of the VP-network, this means that the VP-network has also been successfully crossed. The device can then pop back to the S-network at node S3. At this point, since the S-net has been completely traversed and all of the input string has been accounted for, the recognition process has successfully been completed.

It is quite useful to imagine the flow of control through the various networks visually. For example, the following diagram represents the transition through the networks during the recognition of the sentence *The mountain thrills all climbers.*

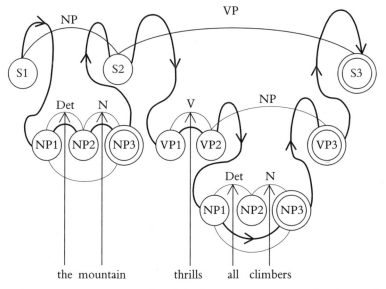

It is important to note that this diagram represents the flow of control passing between the various networks *in a particular computation* rather than a single, expanded-out FSTN.

Compared with the FSTN-based procedure, the RTN-based process requires some means of recording where the processor should pop back to after the successful traversal of a sub-network. A **stack** will be used for this purpose. A stack is a list to which items can only by added or subtracted from the top end. Accordingly, the first item to be taken from the stack is the last item to have been added to it. When a network is pushed to, a record of which network node is to be returned to is placed (or *pushed*) on top of the stack. When popping from a network the processor moves to the network and position as indicated by the record on top of the stack. This record is then removed (or *popped*) from the stack. The following table lists the various configurations during the recognition of the previous example. The top of the stack is to the left.

STRING	STATE	STACK	COMMENT
The crevasses frightened Joe	S1	–	Push to NP-net
The crevasses frightened Joe	NP1	S2	Recognise Det
crevasses frightened Joe	NP2	S2	Recognise N
frightened Joe	NP3	S2	Pop to S-net
frightened Joe	S2	–	Push to VP-net
Joe	VP1	S3	Recognise V
Joe	VP2	S3	Push to NP-net
Joe	NP1	VP3, S3	Recognise PN
–	NP3	VP3, S3	Pop to VP-net
–	VP3	S3	Pop to S-net
–	S3	–	Success

A device which recognises sentences in the way described is often referred to as a **pushdown automaton**.

Question 9.5

With respect to the following RTNs, trace with the aid of a control diagram a pushdown automaton's acceptance of the strings, *Joe ate the cake on the rock*, *The climber on the rock beneath the serac gasped*.

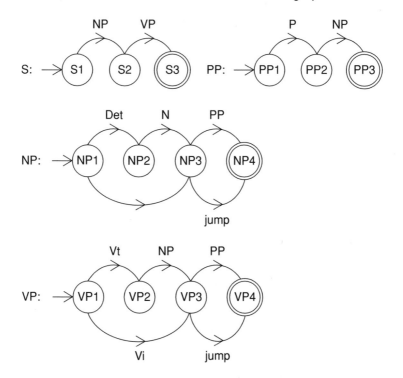

Question 9.6

Using the RTN provided as the answer to question 9.4 and a recognition table as above, trace how the recognition process 'counts' the number of *A*s via the stack so that the same number of *B*s can be checked off.

9.4 Implementing an RTN Recognisor in Prolog

It is a fairly easy matter to implement the recognition procedure described in the last section in Prolog. As far as the network definitions are concerned, the only difference from the FSTN coding of the last chapter is that each predicate must be relativised to a particular network. For example:

```
final(s, 3).
initial(np, 1).
arc(vp, 1, v, 2).
```

are to be read as '3 is a final state of the S-network', '1 is the initial state of the NP-network' and 'in the VP-network there is an arc from node 1 to 2 labelled V', respectively.

The `config` predicate is similar to that used with the finite state recognisor except that a third argument needs adding to represent the stack. This argument is a list. In addition, the state argument of `config` needs relativising to a specific network. To represent this structure the term:

```
Network:State
```

will be used where : is an infix operator defined by the clause:

```
?- op(300, xfx, :).
```

Assuming this declaration, the arguments to `config` take the general form:

```
config(Network:State, String, Stack)
```

The definition of `config` is slightly more complex than the equivalent predicate of the last chapter. The boundary clause handles the case when all of the input string has been scanned. At this point the stack should be empty and the state be the final state of the S-network.

```
config(s:State, [], []) :-
            final(s, State).
```

Traversing lexical arcs is basically the same as that for finite state recognisers.

```
config(Network:State, [Word|String], Stack) :-
        word(Word, Cat),
        arc(Network, State, Cat, State1),
        config(Network:State1, String, Stack).
```

Note that the stack remains unaltered. Additional definitions are required corresponding to the pushing and popping between networks. Pushing is defined by the following rule.

```
config(Network:State, String, Stack) :-
    arc(Network, State, Network1, State1),
    initial(Network1, State2),
    config(Network1:State2,String,
                    [Network:State1|Stack]).
```

In other words, if the transition from State to State1 in the network requires a phrase, take the initial state of the relevant network and proceed from there. At the same time, the old network name and the next state are pushed onto the top of the stack. The 'pop' part of the definition is similar.

```
config(Network:State, String, [Network1:State1
|Stack]) :-
        final(Network, State),
        config(Network1:State, String, Stack).
```

That is, if the state is the final state of the network, then return to the previous network and state as specified by the top of the stack. Note that with both pushing and popping the word being scanned remains the same.

These various definitions can be wrapped together with the drive predicate recognise as follows.

```
recognise(String) :-
    initial(s, State),
    config(s:State, String, []).
```

Notice how the stack is initially empty. The full listing for the program can be found at the end of the chapter as pdr.pl.

As usual it proves useful to follow a trace with a spy point placed on config. The following is the beginning of such a trace.

```
?- recognise([the,crevasses,frightened,joe]).
```

```
(1)    1 CALL: config(s:1, [the,crevasses,frightened,
       joe], [])
(2)    2 CALL: config(np:1, [the,crevasses,frightened,
       joe], [s:2])
(3)    3 CALL: config(np:2, [crevasses,frightened,
       joe], [s:2])
(4)    4 CALL: config(np:3, [frightened,joe], [s:2])
(5)    5 CALL: config(s:2, [frightened,joe], [])
(6)    6 CALL: config(vp:1, [joe], [s:3])
(7)    7 CALL: config(vp:2, [joe], [s:3])
(8)    8 CALL: config(np:1, [joe], [vp:3,s:3])
(9)    9 CALL: config(np:3, [], [vp:3,s:3])
(10)  10 CALL: config(vp:3, [], [s:3])
(11)  11 CALL: config(s:3, [], [])
```

At this point, the call to config matches with the boundary
clause and Prolog backs up through the recursion to report success. Notice how the third argument grows and diminishes in
exactly the same way as the stack in the table at the end of the
last section.

Question 9.7

Partially evaluate the definitions of config so that the calls to final
(s, State) and initial(Network1, State2) are removed. Can the
clause final(Network1, State) also be partially evaluated in the 'pop'
part of the definition?

Question 9.8

Alter the definition of config so as to be able to process networks with
jump arcs.

Question 9.9

If the form of one expression is determined by the form of another, there
is said to be **agreement** between the two expressions. One example in
English is between the head noun of an NP and certain determiners
which agree with respect to number.

this/that man	cf. *these/those man
those/these men	cf. *this/that men
every/*most man	most/*every men

Write an NP-RTN which captures these agreement facts.

9.5 Extending the RTN Notation

Question 9.11 involved agreement within an NP between the determiner and noun. A plausible solution to this problem might seem to be the following RTN.

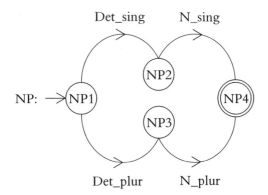

One obvious shortcoming with this approach is the increase in the size of the network due to the addition of the extra arcs. However, from a linguistic point of view there is a more pressing problem; the solution disguises regularities. For example, singular and plural determiners are still determiners. Yet, this rather obvious fact is not represented by the network. The reason for this is because the arc labels have no internal structure. The network specifies, then, that there are things called *Det_sing* and things called *Det_plur* but allows no way of referring to the general class of *Det*s. In this respect, the arc labels are just like the corresponding Prolog atomic terms `det_sing` and `det_plur`. Similar remarks could be made regarding the inability of being able to refer to *N_sing* and *N_plur* as examples of nouns.

The obvious solution to these problems is to introduce arc names with an internal structure. Here it is possible to adopt the syntax of complex Prolog names and treat each category as a predicate which takes a plurality argument.

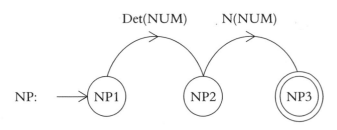

The arguments written in upper case are variables. Using the same variable with both functions ensures that both determiner and noun take the same value. Not only is this network more succinct than the previous one but it also allows reference to common properties; an example of a *Det(sing)* such as *every* has the same function name as *most*, namely *Det(plur)*.

It would seem to be quite easy to encode this network as a set of Prolog facts:

```
arc(np, 1, det(Num), 2).
arc(np, 2, n(Num), 3).
```

with a corresponding extension to the lexical entries:

```
word(every, det(sing)).
word(most, det(plur)).
word(crevasse, n(sing)).
word(crevasses, n(plur)).
```

No adjustments need to be made to the previous definition of the recognition procedure.

However, this will not quite work. The problem lies with the local scope of Prolog variables. That is, although the same agreement variables appear in the two `arc` facts, there is no reason why the Prolog interpreter should assign them the same value. What is required is some way of passing the value of the variable from fact to fact. This can be achieved by making the agreement argument part of the network name:

```
arc(np(Num), 1, det(Num), 2).
arc(np(Num), 2, n(Num), 3).
```

Now, on finding say, a singular determiner, the network argument will also be instantiated to this value. Unifying with the second fact ensures that this value is also passed to n so guaranteeing that only singular nouns will be accepted.

The use of variables in this way is a powerful extension to the formalism. It is possible, for example, to introduce a parse argument to some networks.

```
arc(s(s(NP,VP)), 1, np(NP), 2).
arc(s(s(NP,VP)), 2, vp(VP), 3).
```

Here the network name takes a term representing the parse as its argument with the variables NP and VP representing the parses of the np and vp, respectively, as determined by the NP- and VP-networks. A listing of a complete RTN with an additional parse argument is given in section 9.7 as the file `rtn_parse.pl`. Note that the lexical entries must also have a parse added.

```
word(the, det(det(the))).
word(crevassese, n(n(crevasses))).
```

The only other required change is to the drive predicate and boundary clause of `config`.

```
parse(String, Parse) :-
    initial(s(_), State),
    config(s(Parse):State, String, []).
config(s(_):State,[],[]):-
                final(s(_),State).
```

Using variables in this way is not dissimilar to an extended form of RTN called an **augmented transition network** (ATN). ATNs are like RTNs except that they have associated with each network a set of **registers**. Registers are used to store information. Associated with each arc are a set of conditions and actions which apply to these registers. For example, an NP-ATN might have a DET and NOUN register. It is then possible to specify that a transition from state NP1 to NP2 is possible only if a determiner is recognised and the DET register is set to the value of the determiner's plurality. Similarly, a move from state NP2 to NP3 is only possible if a noun is recognised, the N register is set to the noun's plurality and both the DET and NOUN registers are checked to have the same value. This is the role that variables have been playing in the previous discussion.

ATNs are a very powerful formalism since virtually any kind of condition or action may be specified and for this reason have been widely used in NLP. However, in recent years they have rather fallen out of favour. This is, in part, a result of the general move towards declarative formalisms as discussed in the next chapter. ATNs, with the various operations on registers, tend towards a procedural interpretation.

The expressive power of Prolog means that it is relatively easy to define recognition procedures based on FSTNs or RTNs. However, more concise logical formalisms are possible which are better suited for expression in Prolog as the next two chapters will show.

Question 9.10

Subject NPs agree in number with the head verb of the verb phrase in the present tense.

> The singer sings/*sing well
> The singers sing/*sings well

How can this be expressed using the extended notation of an RTN?

9.6 Further Reading

There are many introductory textbooks on syntax which go into phrase structure in some detail; see, for example, Burton-Roberts (1986), Baker (1995) and Thomas (1993).

RTNs are briefly discussed in Winograd (1983) and Johnson (1983). Gazdar and Mellish (1989) are more detailed in their description and provide an alternative implementation of an RTN-based recognition procedure using the notion of a difference list to be introduced in the next chapter.

There is a large literature on ATNs. Various tutorial introductions with further references can be found in Woods (1987), Bates (1978), Tennant (1981), Winograd (1983) and Allen (1995). Interesting discussion on the psychological implications of an ATN model can be found in Kaplan (1972) and Wanner and Maratsos (1978). Criticism of the procedural nature of ATNs can be found in Pereira and Warren (1980) and Gazdar and Mellish (1989, chapter 3.10).

9.7 Program Listings

(1) **pdr.pl**

```
/* ************************************************

FILE NAME: pdr.pl

DESCRIPTION: A recognisor based on the RTN notation.
Definition of the grammar is in two separate files

************************************************ */

% Define the infix operator for Network:State notation
    ?- op(300, xfx, :).

% Load the lexicon and definition of RTNs
    ?- reconsult('lex.pl').
    ?- reconsult('rtn.pl').

% Drive predicate which sets up initial configuration
    recognise(String) :-
         initial(s, State),
         config(s:State, String, []).

% Final configuration
    config(s:State, [], []) :-
             final(s, State).
```

```
% If in final state for network pop back to previous
% network
    config(Network:State, String,
                    [Network1:State1 |Stack]) :-
        final(Network, State),
        config(Network1:State1, String, Stack).
```

```
% Process next lexical item
    config(Network:State,[Word|String],Stack) :-
            word(Word, Cat),
            arc(Network, State, Cat, State1),
            config(Network:State1, String,
            Stack).
```

```
% If next arc label refers to a network push to it
    config(Network:State, String, Stack) :-
        arc(Network, State, Network1, State1),
        initial(Network1, State2),
        config(Network1:State2, String,
                    [Network:State1|Stack]).
```

```
/* ****************************************** */
```

(2) **rtn.pl**

```
/* *********************************************

FILE NAME: rtn.pl

DESCRIPTION: Definition of set of RTNs

*********************************************** */
```

```
% S-network
    initial(s, 1).
    final(s, 3).

    arc(s, 1, np, 2).
    arc(s, 2, vp, 3).
```

```
% NP-network
    initial(np, 1).
    final(np, 5).

    arc(np, 1, det, 2).
    arc(np, 2, adj, 3).
    arc(np, 3, n, 5).
```

```
    arc(np, 2, n, 5).
    arc(np, 1, pn, 5).
    arc(np, 1, adj, 4).
    arc(np, 4, pcn, 5).
```

% VP-network

```
    initial(vp, 1).
    final(vp, 3).

    arc(vp, 1, vi, 3).
    arc(vp, 1, vt, 2).
    arc(vp, 2, np, 3).
```

```
/* ***************************************** */
```

(3) rtn_parse.pl

```
/* ****************************************

FILE NAME: rtn_parse.pl

DESCRIPTION: Definition of set of RTN which contain
an additional parse argument

*********************************************** */
```

% S-network

```
    initial(s(Parse), 1).
    final(s(Parse), 3).

    arc(s(s(NP,VP)), 1, np(NP), 2).
    arc(s(s(NP,VP)), 2, vp(VP), 3).
```

% NP-network

```
    initial(np(Parse), 1).
    final(np(Parse), 3).

    arc(np(np(DET,N)), 1, det(DET), 2).
    arc(np(np(DET,N)), 2, n(N), 3).
```

% VP-network

```
    initial(vp(Parse), 1).
    final(vp(Parse), 3).

    arc(vp(vp(V,NP)), 1, v(V), 2).
    arc(vp(vp(V,NP)), 2, np(NP), 3).
```

```
/* ***************************************** */
```

CHAPTER 10

Phrase Structure Grammars

It was noted in section 2.1 that the phrasal structure of a language can be expressed by a set of **phrase structure rules** such as:

$$S \rightarrow NP\ VP$$
$$NP \rightarrow Det\ N$$
$$VP \rightarrow V\ NP$$

The arrow is read as 'may consist of'. The first rule, therefore, states that a sentence may consist of a noun phrase followed by a verb phrase, the second that a noun phrase may consist of a determiner followed by a noun and so on. The RTNs of the last chapter can also be interpreted in a similar way. However, there is a significant difference between the two formalisms. RTNs have a natural procedural interpretation (in terms of a pushdown automaton) which phrase structure rules lack. For this reason, RTNs are often referred to as a **procedural** formalism. The process-neutral statements of a phrase structure grammar, on the other hand, are said to be **declarative**.

Since NLP is concerned with processes, the procedural nature of RTNs may appear to give them an advantage over phrase structure grammars. However, it has proved a more fruitful research strategy to factor recognition and parsing processes into two components; a declarative description of *what* is being computed (a grammar) and a specification of *how* the actual computations may be produced (a recognition or parsing procedure). One reason for this is that there must be some process-independent definition of the language as a means of checking the output of the various processes. Another reason for such factorisation is that it is possible to devise a number of alternative procedures, each consistent with the same grammatical description, but with differing properties. Since part of the goal of NLP is to find the optimal solution for the various processing tasks, it is an advantage to be able to keep the grammatical description constant whilst experimenting with different means of computing the properties described by the grammar.

From this perspective, RTNs often blur the distinction between the *what* and *how* due to the close association of the formalism with a particular recognition process. For this reason, RTNs have been replaced with formalisms based upon phrase structure grammars in much NLP research.

Given its declarative semantics, it should come as no surprise to find that Prolog is ideally suited to the task of representing phrase structure grammars. In fact, it turns out that remarkably succinct and elegant grammars can be written in Prolog. This chapter illustrates this point by showing how simple phrase structure grammars may be expressed as Prolog clauses. The discussion provides the foundations for a far more powerful grammar formalism to be introduced in chapter 11.

10.1 Phrase Structure Grammars

Phrase structure rules fulfil two functions. On the one hand, they define the conditions that must hold for a string of words to be of a particular grammatical category and, on the other, they associate with each well-formed expression one or more grammatical structures. For example, the string defining aspect of the rule $S \rightarrow NP\ VP$ can be explicitly spelled out as:

> A string of words, X, has the property of being a sentence if it consists of two substrings, Y and Z, such that:
> (a) string X is the concatenation of Y and Z (in that order) and
> (b) string Y has the property of being an NP and
> (c) string Z has the property of being a VP.

The NP and VP phrase structure rules determine what conditions must hold for a string to be an NP and VP, respectively. Assuming a string X is a sentence as defined by the rule $S \rightarrow NP\ VP$ it will also have associated with it the (partial) phrase structure:

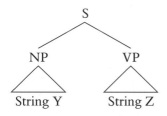

where the internal structure of the NP and VP nodes is determined by the NP and VP phrase structure rules in turn.

Apart from the arrow, phrase structure rules consist of two types of symbol; **non-terminal** and **terminal** symbols. Terminal symbols are the names for either phrasal categories – *S*, *NP*, *VP*, for example – or lexical categories – such as *N*, *V*, *P*. Terminal symbols are the words of the language and will, typically, form the 'leaves' of a phrase structure tree. Each rule is of the form *LHS* → *RHS* where *LHS* is some non-terminal symbol and *RHS* a string of terminal and/or non-terminal symbols. Terminal symbols never appear to the left of the arrow. Rules will usually be either *syntactic* if they define a phrasal category or *lexical* if they define the lexical category of a word. The following are some examples.

Syntactic Rules	Lexical Rules
S → NP VP	Det → *the*
NP → Det N	N → *engineer*
VP → V NP	V → *repaired*

In fact, the lexical rules are somewhat anomalous 'phrase structure' rules since they are not concerned with phrase structure at all but with lexical categorisation. That is, the rule *Det* → *the* does not mean that 'a determiner may consist of *the*' but rather that '*the* is a determiner'. In some cases below, lexical rules will be dispensed with in favour of lexical statements as used in previous chapters.

It is often convenient to adopt certain notational conventions which allow for a more compact statement of the grammar. For example, the force of the following two rules is that an NP may consist of a determiner, an optional adjective and a noun.

NP → Det N
NP → Det Adj N

Optionality can be expressed by placing the optional element inside round brackets. Accordingly, the previous two rules may be collapsed into one.

NP → Det (Adj) N

Also by convention, alternatives may be placed inside curly brackets. This is especially useful for collapsing lexical rules. For instance;

N → {*engineer, boiler, van, spanner, bill*}

replaces the need for five separate lexical rules, one for each word.

It is possible to characterise different types of phrase structure grammar depending upon the form of the rules. The rules used for illustration so far are examples of **context-free** rules since each applies in any context. For example, the rule *NP → Det N* states that any NP anywhere can consist of a determiner followed by a noun. It is also possible to write **context-sensitive** rules. For example, the following rule (for some imaginary language) states that an NP can consist of a determiner followed by a noun if it is preceded by a PP and followed by an AdvP.

PP NP AdvP → PP Det N AdvP

It is more usual to write such rules in the form:

NP → Det N/PP __ AdvP

where the expression to the right of the slash indicates the context in which the rule applies. Given the discussion in section 9.1 such rules might be thought rather suspect and, indeed, their main use is in stating restrictions on lexical items. For instance, the rule:

V → *repaired*/_ NP

licenses the verb *repaired* only if it is followed by an NP. The following discussion solely concentrates on context-free phrase structure grammars.

As previously pointed out, it is possible to devise a number of different recognition and parsing procedures, each consistent with the same (declarative) grammar. In fact, these procedures may vary along the same dimensions as the search strategies discussed in section 6.5. In other words, a recognition process may be classified as top-down or bottom-up, depth-first or breadth-first, left-to-right or right-to-left and so on. The differences result from the variety of ways that a procedure may access and manipulate the phrase structure rules.

By way of illustration, consider the top-down vs. bottom-up classification. This distinction arises depending on whether the procedure identifies a phrase structure rule from its left-hand or right-hand side. Consider the rule *S → NP VP*. A top-down procedure will access this rule initially from its left-hand side because the procedure is seeking an S. Once the rule has been identified in this way, the information to the right of the arrow becomes available, telling the procedure to seek an NP and VP. A bottom-up procedure, on the other hand, would start from the position of already having found an NP and a VP. Accordingly, a match with the right-hand side of the rule is possible. With the rule accessed, the conclusion can be drawn from the left-hand side that an S has also been found.

To see the difference between top-down and bottom-up recognition, consider how the two strategies handle the input string *The engineer repaired the boiler* in relation to the following simple grammar.

S → NP VP
NP → Det N
VP → V NP

It will be assumed that the processor has access to a lexicon containing information about each word's lexical category.

A top-down strategy starts from the position that an S is being sought. To proceed, a rule with *S* as its left-hand symbol is sought. The only example is *S → NP VP*. The right-hand side of this rule supplies the information that the string will be an S if it can be shown to consist of an NP followed by a VP. Attempting to find the NP first, a rule with *NP* as its left-hand symbol is searched for. The only rule fitting this description is *NP → Det N* which directs the processor to find a determiner followed by a noun. The lexicon will inform the processor that *the* is an example of a determiner and *engineer* of a noun. Since both a determiner and a noun have been found, the processor can conclude that it has, indeed, found an NP as initially required by the rule *S → NP VP*. The processor now tries to determine whether the remainder of the string after the initial NP is a VP in the same way that it found the VP. Since the remaining string is a VP, a sentence will be successfully found. The whole process can be summarised as in the following table.

Categories being sought	String still to be accounted for	Action
S	the engineer repaired the boiler	Access rule $S \rightarrow NP\ VP$
NP VP	the engineer repaired the boiler	Access rule $NP \rightarrow Det\ N$
Det N VP	the engineer repaired the boiler	Recognise *the* as a determiner
N VP	engineer repaired the boiler	Recognise *engineer* as a noun
VP	repaired the boiler	Found NP (by rule $NP \rightarrow Det\ N$)
VP	repaired the boiler	Access rule $VP \rightarrow V\ NP$
V NP	repaired the boiler	Recognise *repaired* as a verb
NP	the boiler	Access rule $NP \rightarrow Det\ N$
Det N	the boiler	Recognise *the* as a determiner
N	boiler	Recognise *boiler* as a noun
–	–	Found NP (by rule $NP \rightarrow Det\ N$)
–	–	Found VP (by rule $VP \rightarrow V\ NP$)
–	–	Found S (by rule $S \rightarrow NP\ VP$)

The course of this recognition process is shown in the following phrase structure tree where the arrows indicate the order in which each node of the tree is recognised.

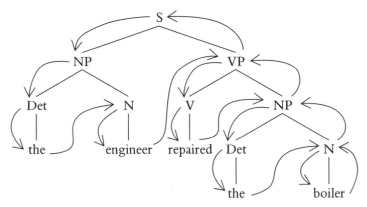

As can be clearly seen, the process starts at the top of the tree and moves downwards, hence the name *top-down*. Note also that the RTN-based recognition procedure of the last chapter follows exactly this same top-down strategy.

A top-down strategy works from the highest phrasal level – i.e. the S – down to the lexical items of the string. A bottom-up strategy works in reverse, starting with the lexical items and placing them into ever more inclusive groups until all can be packaged into an S. So, in the present case, the first words encountered are the determiner *the* and noun *engineer*. Having found a Det and N, a match with the right-hand side of the rule $NP \rightarrow Det\ N$ is possible and the conclusion that an NP has also been found may be drawn. The process continues in this manner until all the words have been assembled together as an S as shown in the following table.

Categories found	String still to be accounted for	Action
	the engineer repaired the boiler	Recognise *the* as a determiner
Det	engineer repaired the boiler	Recognise *engineer* as a noun
Det N	repaired the boiler	Access rule $NP \rightarrow Det\ N$: found NP
NP	repaired the boiler	Recognise *repaired* as a verb
NP V	the boiler	Recognise *the* as a determiner
NP V Det	boiler	Recognise *boiler* as a noun
NP V Det N	–	Access rule $NP \rightarrow Det\ N$: found NP
NP V NP	–	Access rule $VP \rightarrow V\ NP$: found VP
NP VP	–	Access rule $S \rightarrow NP\ VP$: found S
S	–	

Diagrammatically the course of this recognition process can be represented as follows where its bottom-up nature is clearly apparent.

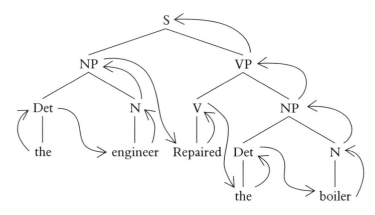

The other dimensions of a recognition strategy – depth-first vs. breadth-first, left-to-right vs. right-to-left – also result as consequences of different ways of utilising the information coded in a phrase structure rule. For example, the top-down strategy just outlined is also a depth-first process because of the decision always to expand the left-most of the categories being sought. If, on the other hand, each were to be expanded in turn before proceeding, the result would be a breadth-first strategy.

The point of these examples is to show that although the recognition procedure may differ, neither the form nor the meaning of the phrase structure rules on which they are based changes. It is in this sense that a phrase structure grammar is said to be process-neutral.

10.2 A Simple Phrase Structure Recognisor

There are various ways of expressing a phrase structure grammar as a set of Prolog facts. As question 5.4 showed, one way is to code a phrase structure rule by a 2-place predicate `rule` where the first argument represents the left-hand side category of the phrase structure rule and the second argument the categories of the right-hand side. Since the right-hand side may consist of more than one category, the second argument must be a list.

```
rule(s, [np, vp]).
```

Rather than use rules for lexical categorisation, the simple lexical definitions of previous chapters will be assumed.

```
word(the, det).
word(boiler, n).
```

This grammatical specification can now be used as a data structure for manipulation by a recognition program. By way of illustration a simple top-down process will be implemented. The procedure employs a stack of grammatical categories recording the categories being sought by the processor. There are two basic moves that can be made. If the category on top of the stack is a lexical category of the same type as the first lexical item in the string, then both the category and word can be removed from their respective structures. Otherwise, if the category on top of the stack matches the left-hand side of some rule, that category is replaced with the categories that make up the right-hand side of the rule. The process starts with the category stack containing S and one or other of the two moves is made in turn until either no words are left to be recognised and the stack is empty – in which case the original string has been successfully recognised – or until no further moves are possible – in which case the string is rejected. In effect, the procedure works by rewriting the various non-terminal symbols in the stack in accordance with the phrase structure rules until lexical categories are produced which can be matched against the particular words of the string.

It is not difficult to define this procedure in Prolog. config will be used as the core binary predicate with both arguments as lists, the first representing the stack of categories and the second the list of words to be recognised. The definition is as follows:

```
recognise(String) :-
    config([s], String).

config([],[]).

config([Cat|RestCats], [Word|String]) :-
    word(Word, Cat),
    config(RestCats, String).

config([Cat|RestCats], String) :-
    rule(Cat, [Cat1, Cat2]),
    config([Cat1, Cat2|RestCats], String).
```

recognise drives the program by setting up the initial configuration. The first clause of the definition for config defines success, the second the matching of lexical items with lexical categories and the third the rewriting of phrasal categories on top of the stack. Note that this third definition assumes that each phrase structure rule consists of a right-hand side with two categories.

Running a trace with a spy point on config for the query:

```
?- recognise([the,engineer,repaired,the,
boiler]).
```

will result in a series of configurations equivalent to those in the top-down table of the previous section.

(1)   1 CALL: config([s], [the,engineer,repaired, the, boiler])
(2)   2 CALL: config([np,vp], [the,engineer,re-paired,the,boiler])
(3)   3 CALL: config([det,n,vp], [the,engineer,re-paired,the,boiler])
(4)   4 CALL: config([n,vp], [engineer,repaired, the,boiler])
(5)   5 CALL: config([vp], [repaired,the,boiler])
(6)   6 CALL: config([v,np], [repaired,the boiler])
(7)   7 CALL: config([np], [the,boiler])
(8)   8 CALL: config([det,n], [the,boiler])
(9)   9 CALL: config([n], [boiler])
(10) 10 CALL: config([], [])

At this point the recursion bottoms out by matching with the 'success' clause for config and, so, exiting through each of the recursive calls to config, Prolog will reply with a yes.

Section 12.3 discusses how a bottom-up recognition process can be defined in Prolog.

Question 10.1

Complete the Prolog listing for the following grammar:

    S → NP VP   Det → PossNP
    NP → Det N   VP → V NP
    NP → Det N PP   PP → P NP

Will the recognition procedure defined in this section work with such a grammar?

Question 10.2

Change the definition of *config* so that it will also allow rules with one or three items on the right-hand side. [Note: there are two types of solution here; either different definitions for each type of rule or a single definition which will apply to any rule.]

10.3 Directly Representing Phrase Structure Grammars in Prolog

Representing the phrase structure rule $S \rightarrow NP\ VP$ by the fact rule(s, [np,vp]) does not explicitly capture the string defining aspect of the rule which was earlier spelled out as:

A string of words, X, has the property of being a sentence if it consists of two substrings, Y and Z, such that:

(a)   string X is the concatenation of Y and Z (in that order) and

(b)   string Y has the property of being an NP and

(c)   string Z has the property of being a VP.

It was only through the workings of the recognition procedure that this meaning was indirectly expressed in the previous section. It is a simple matter, however, to write a Prolog rule which more accurately reflects this interpretation of the rule.

```
s(X) :-
      concat(Y,Z,X),
      np(Y),
      vp(Z).
```

Here s, np and vp are the names of the properties of being a sentence, NP and VP, respectively, properties which are predicated of lists. concat is the concatenation predicate of lists previously defined in section 5.2.2. Lexical definitions will be assumed to take the following form.

```
det([the]).
n([engineer]).
```

Note that because concat is defined over lists, the arguments to the lexical facts must be lists.

At this point, the dual interpretation of Prolog clauses comes into its own since, although the Prolog statement of the phrase structure rule has a declarative interpretation as required, once it is given to the Prolog interpreter, it also takes on a procedural interpretation. That is, the interpreter will take the s-rule as specifying that some list, X, will be a sentence if it can be shown to consist of two concatenated sublists, Y and Z, such that np(Y) and vp(Z) also hold. In other words, once the grammar has been written as a series of Prolog clauses, the Prolog inference engine provides a recognition procedure 'for free'. The procedure it supplies is top-down, depth-first, left-to-right (with backtracking) because that is the interpreter's search strategy. It is important to note, however, that this strategy is a consequence of the logical specification of the grammar being *embedded in Prolog* and not of the specification itself; different proof procedures with the same logical specification will lead to different recognition strategies.

The following proof tree for the query:

```
?- s([the,engineer,repaired,the,boiler]).
```

shows the process by which Prolog recognises the string as a sentence. First, the string is divided into two by concat. The first list of this division, [the,engineer], is then checked as an NP. This involves splitting this sublist again into two by concat and checking that the first list, [the], consists of a determiner and the second, [engineer], of a noun. Since both do, the interpreter concludes that the first list, [the,engineer], is an NP. The process proceeds in the same way by considering whether the second sublist [repaired,the,boiler] is a VP. As can be seen, this is, indeed, the case.

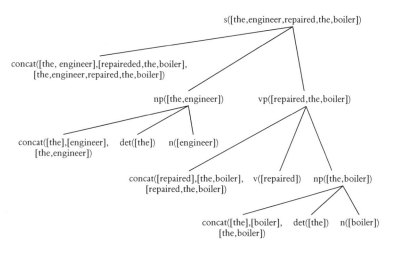

Question 10.3

Using the rule format of this section, complete the listing of the grammar used in question 10.1.

Question 10.4

Does swapping the order of the grammatical predicates in the body of a phrasal rule affect the declarative and/or procedural semantics of the following rule?

```
s(X) :-
        concat(Y, Z, X),
        vp(Z),
        np(Y).
```

10.4 Efficiency

Declaratively, the rule:

```
s(X) :-
      concat(Y,Z,X),
      np(Y),
      vp(Z).
```

is an accurate representation of the string defining side of the phrase structure rule $S \rightarrow NP\ VP$. Further, the procedural interpretation of these rules by the Prolog inference engine produces one of the possible recognition strategies associated with such grammars. However, the resultant strategy is far from efficient.

The problem lies with the definition of concat. As was seen in section 5.2.2, concat is able to decompose a list into all its potential sublists. For the list [the,engineer,repaired,the,boiler] this amounts to six possibilities.

```
[] and [the,engineer,repaired,the,boiler]
[the] and [engineer,repaired,the,boiler]
[the,engineer] and [repaired,the,boiler]
[the,engineer,repaired] and [the,boiler]
[the,engineer,repaired,the] and [boiler]
[the,engineer,repaired,the,boiler] and []
```

Before the proof can proceed to check whether the two sublists are an NP and VP, concat must make a choice from this list. Ideally, this choice should be guided in some way by the NP and/or VP phrasal rules so that divisions are avoided which could never possibly have a chance of success. But this is not the way concat works in this context. Rather, it proceeds systematically, trying each of the possibilities in turn until, the correct one is found. Accordingly, the interpreter will first check whether [] is an NP. Of course, this fails, whereupon, after backtracking, [the] is tried. Failing again, [the,engineer] is tried next which, this time, succeeds.

Although backtracking eventually leads to concat finding the correct division, this blind search leads to a great deal of wasteful computation. This will only increase as the grammar is extended to cover ever more complex phrases. The obvious solution to this problem is to use the phrasal predicates themselves to determine where the divisions may occur. It might be thought that this could be achieved by changing the position of concat in the definition.

```
s(X) :-
     np(Y),
     vp(Z),
     concat(Y, Z, X).
```

Declaratively, this rule is equivalent to the previous definition. However, procedurally the effects are rather different. In the original definition, the effect of concat is to split the list X into two sublists, Y and Z. In the new definition, however, concat is used in reverse, to paste Y and Z together to form X after they have already been determined by the calls to np and vp. In this way, the phrasal rules constrain the composition of the two lists but, it turns out, to no great effect. The problem this time is that the construction of the np and vp lists is not constrained by the input string. In other words, the interpreter will be satisfied with *any* string that can be an np and *any* string that can be a vp. It is only when they are concatenated together that they are actually checked against the input string. If the two candidate lists do not produce the input string, Prolog will backtrack and try again until the right combination is produced. In effect, then, the process works by the recogniser spewing out all the possible sentences of the grammar until one matching the input string is produced. Clearly, this is as inefficient as the previous definition.

Although the definition of concat is correct as far as the logical specification is concerned, procedurally it is problematic. Ideally, what is required is some way of not committing the interpreter too early to the precise division of the input list but that when the decision is made it should be constrained both by the input list and the relevant phrasal rules. It turns out that it is possible to simultaneously satisfy both sides of this equation with a different definition of concatenation.

10.5 Difference Lists

Procedurally, concat works by recursively stripping away each member of the first list until the empty list is reached and a match with the boundary clause is possible. As a result, the longer the first list, the longer it takes to compute concat. It is possible, however, to redefine concat in such a way that it works in *a single step*, no matter how long the lists involved.

The underlying idea is simple. Suppose that the first of the two lists to be concatenated is represented as follows.

```
[a,b| Tail]
```

Tail will be referred to as the **tail variable**. To concatenate a list, say [c,d], on to the end of this list, all that needs doing is to instantiate the tail variable to this second list. Because the length of the first or second list does not affect this process of unification, this technique will always result in concatenation in a single step. Since more items may need to be added later to the resulting concatenated list, it also should contain a tail variable. This is achieved by making the second list also contain a tail variable, say [c,d|Y], which will then become the tail variable of the resulting concatenation, [a,b,c,d|Y].

The problem in defining this new notion of concatenation lies in knowing what the tail variables are inside the various lists. To overcome this, the representation is completed by adding a copy of the tail outside the list. This could be achieved with a functor such as list.

```
list(List, Tail)
```

where Tail is the tail variable of the list List. However, it is more common to use - as an infix operator connecting the two lists.

```
List-Tail
```

Here List is referred to as the **head** of the structure and Tail as the **tail**. Note that - is already pre-defined in Prolog as an infix operator where, when between two integers, it is used for arithmetic subtraction. Since lists rather than integers are involved in the present case, it is possible to hijack this infix property of - to be used as a kind of punctuation mark.

Lists in the form List-Tail are referred to as **difference lists**. The reason for this can be appreciated by considering the standard representation of the list [a, b] and its difference list equivalent [a,b|Tail]-Tail. If the tail of the difference list were to be taken away from the head, then the resulting *difference* would just be the original list. As such, a list has any number of different representations using difference lists, including:

```
[a,b,c,d]-[c,d]
[a,b,c,d,e,f,g]-[c,d,e,f,g]
[a,b,c|Tail]-[c|Tail]
```

The representation [a,b|Tail]-Tail is the most general difference list for the list in question.

Although, [a,b] and [a,b|Tail]-Tail are not notational variants of one another, being completely different terms, note that the head of the difference list will be identical to the standard list if Tail is instantiated to the empty list []. The empty list itself is represented by Tail-Tail in the difference list notation.

Question 10.5

Using the standard list notation, what lists are represented by the following difference lists?

(1) `[the,rain,swept,over,the,mountain]-[rain,swept, over,the,mountain]`
(2) `[the|X]-X`
(3) `[walks, slowly|Y]-[slowly|Y]`
(4) `[walks, slowly|Y]-Y`
(5) `[the,trees,bent,in,the,wind]-[the,trees,bent,in, the,wind]`
(6) `[simon,cut,the,rope]-[]`
(7) `[]-[]`

It is a simple matter to redefine `concat` using the difference list notation. The new version will be called `concat_dl`.

```
concat_dl(A-B, B-C, A-C).
```

That is it! Notice how the head of the second list, `B`, is the same as the tail of the first list. This ensures that once the head of the second list is instantiated to some value it will be automatically passed into the head of the first list via the tail variable. The tail variable of the resulting list will be the same as the tail of the second list, namely `C`. The following shows the definition in action.

```
?- concat_dl([a,b|X]-X, [c,d|Y]-Y, Result).
X = [c,d|Y]
Result = [a,b,c,d|Y]-Y
yes
```

This is equivalent to the result produced by `concat`.

```
?- concat([a,b], [c,d], Result).
Result = [a,b,c,d]
yes
```

Although `concat` and `concat_dl` produce equivalent answers in the above example this is not always case. One of the most important differences is that whilst the former is non-deterministic, the latter is **deterministic**. This can be most clearly seen when the two predicates are used to split a list into two. The list [a,b,c,d] can be partitioned into five different combinations of sublist. The following table shows these in both standard and difference list format.

Standard list notation	Difference list notation
(1) `L1 = []` `L2 = [a,b,c,d]`	`[a,b,c,d|Tail]-[a,b,c,d|Tail]` `[a,b,c,d|Tail]-Tail`
(2) `L1 = [a]` `L2 = [b,c,d]`	`[a,b,c,d|Tail]-[b,c,d|Tail]` `[b,c,d|Tail]-Tail`
(3) `L1 = [a,b]` `L2 = [c,d]`	`[a,b,c,d|Tail]-[c,d|Tail]` `[c,d|Tail]-Tail`
(4) `L1 = [a,b,c]` `L2 = [d]`	`[a,b,c,d|Tail]-[d|Tail]` `[d|Tail]-Tail`
(5) `L1 = [a,b,c,d]` `L2 = []`	`[a,b,c,d|Tail]-Tail` `Tail-Tail`

As previously discussed, concat will (with induced backtracking) decompose the list into all these possible sublists. This is why the definition is said to be non-deterministic. With concat_dl, however, only one answer is ever returned.

```
?- concat_dl(L1, L2, [a,b,c,d|Tail]-Tail).

    L1 = [a,b,c,d|Tail]-_234
    L2 = _234-Tail;
    no
```

Notice, however, that the returned values for L1 and L2 are the most general representation of *all* the actual pairs in the previous table. In other words, the definition does not commit the system to one particular value or another. Of course, once the tail variable, _234, of the first list becomes instantiated to some value, the list L2 will also become fixed to a particular value. It is this 'non-committal' property that overcomes the original problems with the procedural interpretation of the previous phrase structure rules.

Re-defining a phrase structure grammar with concat_dl rather than concat is a simple matter. Syntactic rules will be like the following example.

```
np(A-C) :-
     concat_dl(A-B, B-C, A-C),
     det(A-B),
     n(B-C).
```

whilst lexical definitions are exemplified by:

```
det([the|Tail]-Tail).
n([engineer|Tail]-Tail).
```

To see the general effect of this change in the procedural interpretation of the grammar, consider the following query.

```
?- np([the,engineer]-[]).
```

Here the target string has been represented as a difference list with the tail being the empty list. Recall that this means that the head list is equivalent to the simple list [the,engineer].

This initial goal matches with the head of the np-rule which then invokes the following call to concat_dl.

```
concat_dl(L1, L2, [the,engineer]-[])
```

As just seen, satisfying such a call results in the two most general difference lists for these sublists.

```
L1 = [the,engineer]-_234
L2 = _234-[]
```

It is the first of these difference lists that is passed to the det-rule. The goal:

```
det([the,engineer]-_234)
```

is satisfied through a match with the lexical fact for det with the result that the tail variable, _234, now becomes instantiated to the value [engineer]. This now means that the call to n becomes:

```
n([engineer]-[])
```

This is also satisfied through a simple match with the lexical fact. Accordingly, np([the,engineer]-[]) has been satisfied.

The general effect of this new account should now be apparent. The np-rule requires a partition of the list into two. concat-dl does this but without committing the proof to the exact point of cleavage. This is only determined after the call to det has been satisfied. Once the determiner has been found, the division becomes fixed. In this way, the new definition gets the best of all worlds. The difference list handed to det, although not precisely fixed, is constrained by the target list given to np. However, the exact division is dependent upon the lexical predicates in the body of the phrase structure rule. This pattern is repeated with all the rules. For example, with the s-rule:

```
s(A-C) :-
       concat_dl(A-B, B-C, A-C),
       np(A-B),
       vp(B-C).
```

it is only after an NP has been found (as determined by the np-rule) that the exact division of the list is fixed and the second half of the original list is passed over to the vp-rule.

The phrasal rules can be stated more succinctly. Note that concat_dl works solely by relying upon the unification properties of Prolog to compute the relations between the three arguments. As such, the predicate name concat_dl plays no role apart from being a means of bundling the arguments together. But notice that these same arguments are also spread amongst the grammatical categories of the rules. Consequently, nothing is gained by including concat_dl in the definition and it can be dispensed with altogether. The result is a rather elegant formulation of a phrase structure rule.

```
s(A-C) :-
        np(A-B),
        vp(B-C).
```

The lexical definitions remain the same.

Although the role of difference lists in the phrasal definitions is to express the concatenation of lists, it may be easier to think of them in a slightly different way. Consider the difference pairs that form the arguments to the following three predicates.

```
s([the,engineer,repaired,the,boiler] - [])
np([the,engineer,repaired,the,boiler] -
[repaired,the,boiler])
vp([repaired,the,boiler] - [])
```

In each case, the tail of the difference list is the remains of the head list when a phrase of the relevant kind has been removed from its front. So, removing an S from [the,engineer,repaired, the,boiler] leaves the empty list; removing an NP from [the,engineer,repaired,the,boiler] leaves [repaired, the,boiler] and so on. In these terms, the various calls to the phrasal predicates can be thought of as taking a list, removing the relevant phrase from the list and passing the remainder on to the next rule.

Question 10.6

Define concat_dl to concatenate three lists together.

Question 10.7

Recast the rules in question 10.1 into the difference list format of this section.

Question 10.8

Construct a proof tree for the question:

```
?- s([the,engineer,repaired,the,boiler]-[]).
```

10.6 The Grammar Rule Notation

The rule:

```
s(A-C) :-
      np(A-B),
      vp(B-C).
```

would be very close in form to the equivalent phrase structure rule *S → NP VP* if the difference list variables were suppressed. In fact, many implementations of Prolog support a notation which allows this. This is referred to as the **grammar rule notation**. Further, the notation replaces the Prolog operator :- with the operator --> so that the previous rule would be written in the form:

```
 s --> np, vp.
```

Note that standard Prolog syntactic conventions are retained; the grammar symbols are in lower case, separated by commas on the right-hand side, and terminated with a full stop. Lexical rules in this notation take the form:

```
det --> [the].
```

Optional phrases can also be represented in this notation. For example, the following allows for an optional PP:

```
pp --> [].
```

and is equivalent to the Prolog clause:

```
pp(List, List).
```

The grammar rule notation is only a piece of 'syntactic sugar', introduced as an aid to user-friendliness. The Prolog interpreter still functions with rules in the standard form. This is achieved by a special translation program which automatically converts the shorthand of the grammar rule notation into the equivalent Prolog clauses. If your own version of Prolog does not support this notation, it is possible to write a Prolog program which performs the

8

translation. A listing for such a program is given in section 10.8. It
should be noted, however, that the resulting translation is slightly
different from that used in this chapter since the infix operator –
used previously to represent difference lists is suppressed (for reasons
of efficiency) and the head and tail lists simply represented as two
separate arguments. As a result, queries to the program must take
the form:

```
?- s([the,engineer,repaired,the,boiler], []).
```

rather than:

```
?- s([the,engineer,repaired,the,boiler]-[]).
```

The grammar formalism that has been developed in this chapter
looks like a simple notational variant of a standard (context free)
phrase structure grammar. However, the formalism allows for a
number of powerful extensions which form the subject matter of
the following chapter.

Question 10.9

What are the full Prolog translations of the following grammar rules?

```
np --> det, n.
vp --> v, np, pp.
n --> [mountain].
rel_clause --> [that], vp.
```

Recall that the difference list connector – should not be included.

10.7 Further Reading

Good overviews of phrase structure grammars can be found in
Joshi (1987), Wall (1972) and Partee *et al.* (1990) with more technical discussion of their formal properties in Hopcroft and Ullman
(1979) and Perrault (1984). See also Gazdar and Pullum (1985).
See references in the next chapter for particular phrase structure
analyses of English.

10.8 Program Listings

The following is the program listing for a simple grammar rule
compiler given in Clocksin and Mellish (1987, pp. 250–1). A more
general translation program to handle the extensions to be introduced in chapter 11 is included in the listings for that chapter.

```
/* **********************************************

NAME: g_rule_trans.pl

DESCRIPTION: Translate(Rule, Clause) takes a grammar
rule Rule (such as s --> np, vp.) translates it into
its corresponding Prolog clause with difference lists

*********************************************** */

?- op(1199, xfx,  -->).

translate((P1 --> P2), (G1 :- G2)) :-
           left_hand_side(P1, S0, S, G1),
           right_hand_side(P2, S0, S, G2).

left_hand_side(P0, S0, S, G) :-
           nonvar(P0),
           tag(P0, S0, S, G).

right_hand_side((P1, P2), S0, S, G) :-
           !,
           right_hand_side(P1, S0, S1, G1),
           right_hand_side(P2, S1, S, G2),
           and(G1, G2, G).

right_hand_side(P, S0, S, true) :-
           islist(P),
           !,
           concat(P, S, S0).

right_hand_side(P, S0, S, G) :-
           tag(P, S0, S, G).

tag(P, S0, S, G) :-
           atom(P),
           G =.. [P, S0, S].

and(true, G, G) :- !.
and(G, true, G) :- !.
and(G1, G2, (G1, G2)).

islist([]) :- !.
islist([_|_]).

concat([], X, X).
concat([A|B], C, [A|D]) :-
           concat(B, C, D).

/* ********************************************* */
```

CHAPTER 11

Definite Clause Grammars

The notation for representing phrase structure rules introduced in the last chapter is not ideally suited for treating some important aspects of the grammars of natural languages such as English. However, it can be extended in two simple ways by (i) treating grammar symbols as complex terms and (ii) allowing the inclusion of procedure calls into the body of the rule. Since the grammar formalism is expressed as a series of Prolog facts and rules and since such expressions are sometimes referred to as 'definite clauses', grammars of this sort are known as **definite clause grammars** (DCGs). The result is a powerful and flexible grammar formalism, well-suited to describing a wide range of syntactic constructions. The hope is that the reader will be inspired to use the various techniques described in this chapter to write grammar fragments for areas of English syntax not covered in this chapter as well as applying them to languages other than English.

11.1 Grammar Symbols as Complex Terms

A grammar rule's symbols are either **terminal** or **non-terminal**. Terminal symbols represent lexical items, are written as lists and only occur on the right-hand side of the rule. Non-terminal symbols represent syntactic categories and may occur on either side of the arrow and are written as logical terms (other than lists).

Logical terms in Prolog, as was seen in section 4.3, may be arbitrarily complex and DCGs also allow such compound terms as non-terminal symbols. The inclusion of (arbitrarily complex) terms as arguments to the grammatical category allows various pieces of linguistic information to be easily encoded within the grammatical rules as the following sections will illustrate.

The rules of a DCG will be expressed using the grammar rule notation introduced in the previous chapter. For example, a rule might take the form:

```
cat1(Term1, Term2) --> cat2(Term3), cat3(Term4,
Term5).
```

where `Term1` to `Term5` represent (possibly complex) arguments to the predicates `cat1`, `cat2` and `cat3`. As with the rules of the previous chapter, difference lists are suppressed so that the above rule would be translated into the Prolog rule:

```
cat1(Term1, Term2, L1, L3) :- cat2(Term3, L1, L2),
                        cat3(Term4, Term5, L2, L3).
```

where `L1`, `L2` and `L3` are the various lists encoding the difference pairs. Any implementation of Prolog which supports the grammar rule notation will automatically translate DCG rules into the relevant Prolog form. If your own implementation does not provide the notation, a listing of a translation program for DCGs into Prolog clauses is given in section 11.4.

11.1.1 Number Agreement

A simple use for complex grammar symbols is to ensure number agreement between various elements within a sentence. For example, the determiner *every* requires a singular noun, whilst *most* requires a plural noun.

> Every student   (cf. *every students)
> Most students   (cf. *most student)

This constraint could be captured via two np-rules with a suitably adjusted lexicon.

```
np --> det_sing, n_sing.
np --> det_plur, n_plur.

det_sing --> [every].
n_sing --> [student].
```

It was noted in section 9.5, however, where a similar approach was considered with respect to recursive transition networks, that such an approach is problematic since it not only increases the size of the grammar but also fails to capture the generalisations that `det_sing` and `det_plur` are both examples of determiners and `n_sing` and `n_plur` examples of nouns. These problems can be overcome through the use of a predicate which includes an argument position for number. For example, the lexical rules for determiners might take the form:

```
det(sing) --> [every].
det(plur) --> [most].
```

These rules capture the fact that *every* and *most* are of the same broad lexical category since both are associated with the same predicate name, det. Similarly for nouns.

```
n(sing) --> [student].
n(plur) --> [students].
```

As a consequence of these changes, the two previous np-rules can be collapsed into one.

```
np --> det(Num), n(Num).
```

Using the same variable argument Num for both predicates imposes the relevant agreement constraint.

In fact, this rule needs amending slightly in order that subject-verb (number) agreement can also be accommodated. That is, singular subject NPs require the verb to be in its singular form (in the present tense), whilst plural subject NPs require the verb to be in its plural form.

> The student likes/*like this course
> The students like/*likes this course

The number of an NP as a whole is the same as its head noun. So, *the student* is singular because *student* is singular. Similarly, for a VP; its number is the same as its head verb. These facts can be captured by including a number argument for the relevant phrasal categories.

```
np(Num) --> det(Num), n(Num).
vp(Num) --> v(Num), np(Num1).
```

Each verb's lexical entry needs to be suitably amended to include number information. Subject-verb agreement can now be simply stated.

```
s --> np(Num), vp(Num).
```

Question 11.1

Translate the following DCG rules:

```
s --> np(Num), vp(Num).
np(Num) --> det(Num), n(Num).
v(plur) --> [likes].
```

into their corresponding Prolog clauses.

Question 11.2

What, if anything, is wrong with the rule?

```
vp(Num) --> v(Num) , np(Num) .
```

Question 11.3

Assuming the argument to the predicate represents information about number, explain the following lexical rule:

```
det(_) --> [the] .
```

Question 11.4

The verb *be* not only agrees in number with the subject when in the present tense but also in **person** if the subject is a pronoun:

I am . . .	(first person, singular)
We are . . .	(first person, plural)
You are . . .	(second person, singular and plural)
he/she/it is . . .	(third person, singular)
they are . . .	(third person, plural)

Write the relevant rules to handle sentences such as *I am happy* and *He is sad*.

Question 11.5

French nouns are classified as being either *masculine* or *feminine*. The reason for drawing this **gender** distinction is that the noun's gender determines the form of certain determiners and adjectives. For example, masculine nouns such as *timbre* ('stamp') require the definite article to be in the form *le* ('the') and the indefinite article to be in the form *un* ('a') whilst feminine nouns such as *porte* ('door') require these articles to be *la* and *une*, respectively.

> le/un timbre   *la/*une timbre
> la/une porte   *le/*un porte

In addition, certain adjectives take a different form depending upon whether they are modifying a masculine or feminine noun:

> un timbre *gris*   'a grey stamp'
> une porte *grise*   'a grey door'
>
> un *beau* timbre   'a beautiful stamp'
> une *belle* porte   'a beautiful door'

Write the relevant phrasal and lexical rules which will ensure such agreement for the above examples. Note that you will have to distinguish between two types of adjective – those that immediately precede (e.g. *beau/belle*) and those that immediately follow the noun (e.g. *gris/grise*).

Question 11.6

Verbs like *be* and *became* may take a **predicate nominal**, an NP which, rather than referring to an object, refers to a property of the subject.

That woman is [a doctor]
Those women became [doctors]

Predicate nominals agree in number with the subject NP:

*That woman is doctors
*Those women became a doctor

Extend the grammar to cover such constructions.

Question 11.7

English personal pronouns take on different forms depending upon whether they are in subject or object position:

He likes Taurey   Katkin likes him
*Him likes Taurey   *Katkin likes he

Subject pronouns (e.g. *he*) are said to take the **nominative case** and object pronouns (e.g. *him*) the **accusative case**. Extend the grammar to handle the different case forms of the pronoun: *I, you, he, she, we, they*.

11.1.2 The Verb Phrase

The grammars in previous chapters have been restricted to VPs equivalent to the rules:

```
vp --> v.
vp --> v, np.
v --> [fell].
v --> [saw].
```

The present section shows how complex terms may be used to extend the coverage of VP structure.

11.1.2.1 Subcategorisation

fall is an example of an intransitive verb, a verb which requires no following complements. *see*, on the other hand, is a transitive verb, a verb which requires a following object NP. The previous rules, however, do not distinguish between these different **subcategories** of verb. Consequently, the grammar defines as well-formed both of the following since there is no constraint on intransitive verbs appearing in transitive environments or transitive verbs occurring in intransitive environments.

The cat fell the tree
The eagle saw

The grammar needs to ensure, then, that *fell* is a possible v for the first vp-rule but not for second and *vice versa* for *saw*. There are various ways of achieving this. The simplest is to add a subcategorisation argument to each verbal entry which is then associated with a particular vp-rule. For example:

```
vp --> v(intrans).
vp --> v(trans), np.

v(intrans) --> [fell].
v(trans) --> [saw].
```

Accordingly, only verbs classified as v(intrans) will be licensed to appear in the environment [$_{VP}$ ____] and those as v(trans) in the environment [$_{VP}$ ____ NP], where ____ indicates the position of the verb.

Question 11.8

Rewrite the simple grammar:

```
s --> np, vp.
np --> det, n.
vp --> v.
vp --> v, np.
```

(with suitable lexical entries) to combine both agreement and subcategorisation information.

Question 11.9

Extend the lexical and phrasal definitions of the grammar so that VPs containing the following verbs will be accepted.

eat, put, defer, detract, abide, insist, realise, claim, tell, become, be

It may prove easier to refer to the different subcategories of verb with a numeral rather than a name – e.g. v(1) rather than v(intrans). Note that in some cases a verb may occur in more than one context and so will require more than one lexical entry.

Question 11.10

Verbs such as *give* or *catch* may be followed by an NP and PP:

gave the book to Mary
caught the fish for the woman

Note, however, that the PP cannot be headed by just any preposition; *give* requires *to* whilst *catch* requires *for*. How can this subcategorisation requirement be handled?

Question 11.11

There are many different subcategories of verb in English. This results in a correspondingly large number of vp-rules when writing a more complete grammar. A more compact notation would be achieved if there were a single vp-rule stating that a VP consists of a verb followed by its complements where those complements are determined by the verb's lexical entry. Assume that the lexical entry for a verb includes a list of its complements.

```
v([np,pp]) --> [give].
v([]) --> [fell].
```

Alter the grammar to handle this information as indicated. [Hint: write a DCG version of a recursive predicate comps which checks off each complement from the complement list.]

Question 11.12

The subcategorisation requirements of a verb might determine that the verb be followed by an NP. However, in some cases there are also **selectional restrictions** on the type of NP which are imposed in virtue of a verb's meaning. For example, *frighten* subcategorises for a following NP but that NP must also refer to an animate object – i.e. the type of thing that can be frightened.

John frightened the cat
?John frightened the picture

Note that there is no restriction on what the subject of frighten may be, however.

The picture frightened the cat

The reverse holds with *admire*.

John admired the picture/cat
?The picture admired the cat

Using features such as *animate, human, female,* etc. devise a series of rules which will ensure that selectional restrictions are respected for sentences containing verbs and adjectives such as: *frighten, admire, marry, pray, pregnant, dead*. Provide a sample of nouns, correctly classified, which may combine with these predicates. Note that the nouns may have more than one semantic feature associated with them – e.g. something which is human will also be animate.

11.1.2.2 Tense

In the examples used so far, all verbs have either been in the past or present tense although no distinction has been made between the two different forms. It is a simple matter to specify this information through the use of an extra argument to each verb's lexical entry, fin(Value), where Value may be either past or pres:

```
v(fin(pres),sing) --> [likes].
v(fin(pres),plur) --> [like].
v(fin(past),_) --> [liked].
```

Note that for the past tense the anonymous variable is used for the agreement value since there is no number distinction in the past tense.

When other verb forms are introduced in the next section it will be important to ensure that the VP of the main sentence is finite.

The eagle saw the rabbit
★The eagle seeing/see/seen the rabbit

The following amendment ensures this requirement.

```
s --> np(Num), vp(fin(Value),Num).
vp(Tense, Num)--> v(Tense, Num), np(Num1).
```

Notice how the first argument to the vp predicate introduces the finite value which is then passed down to the verb which heads the VP via the vp-rule. Because the argument to fin is a variable, the only commitment the rule makes is that the VP will be either past or present.

Question 11.13

Provide the various lexical entries for the tensed forms of the following verbs: *take, want, can, have, be.*

11.1.2.3 Auxiliary Verbs

The final extension to the coverage of the VP to be discussed is the introduction of auxiliary verbs. The main auxiliary verbs in English are *do, be* and *have*, the modal verbs (*can, may, will, might, should* and *must*) and the form of *be* used in the passive. At first glance, the sequence of auxiliary verbs that appear in a VP seems to be haphazard both in form and order.

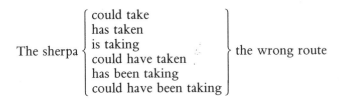

The sherpa { could take / has taken / is taking / could have taken / has been taking / could have been taking } the wrong route

However, there is a strict and fairly simple structure to such VPs. Before describing this structure some traditional terminology distinguishing between the different forms of the verbs will be useful.

take/takes	Present tense
took	Past tense
taking	Present participle
taken	Past participle
take	Base (or Stem)

The main observation regarding the form of the verbs in the sequences above is that each is determined by the *preceding* verb. For example, verbs preceded by a modal appear in the base form.

The sherpa could take/*took/*taking/*taken the wrong route

In contrast, verbs immediately following *have* take the past participle form,

The sherpa has taken/*takes/*took/*taking the wrong route

whilst a verb appears in the present participle form if preceded by *be*.

The sherpa is taking/*takes/*took/*taken the wrong route

These restrictions equally apply if the following verb is a main or auxiliary verb. Note also that the first verb of the group is always finite.

The ordering of the auxiliaries is fairly simple and can be expressed as:

(Modal) (Have) (Be)

That is, each auxiliary is optional as indicated by the brackets but modals always precede *have* and *be*, and *have* always precedes *be*. This ordering can be seen as a consequence of the range of forms that are available to the different auxiliaries. For example, the modals only have finite forms. Since the first verb of the verbal group is finite, the upshot is that modals may only appear first in the sequence. They cannot occur after either *have* or *be* since this would require them to be in the past participle or present participle forms, respectively, forms which they do not possess. On the other hand, *have* has not only finite forms, which means it can appear in the initial position, but also a base form which entails it can follow a modal. However, it does not possess a present participle form, from which it follows that *have* cannot follow *be*.

Verbal sequences, then, can be thought of as a chain of agreement relations where two adjacent verbs agree in the sense that the
one to the right is of the form required by the verb to the left. To
capture this idea with a DCG, requires lexical entries for auxiliary
and main verbs to be of the following form.

```
aux(fin(past)-base) --> [could].
aux(base-past_part) --> [have].
v(past_part) --> [taken].
```

The argument to the predicate aux is a complex term using the
infix operator – that has already been used for difference pairs. The
term to the left of the operator represents the form of the lexical
item whilst that to the right represents the required form of the
verb that will occur to its immediate left. The first rule, then, says
that *could* is the past tense form and requires a base form to its
right.

Turning to the vp-rules, the form of a VP will be the same as its
head verb. For a VP without an auxiliary the requisite rules will be
of the following form.

```
vp(Form) --> v(Form).
vp(Form) --> v(Form), np.
```

For example, *taken the wrong route* will be a past participle VP since
this is the form of the head verb *taken*. As far as combining an auxiliary with the rest of the verbal group is concerned, this is achieved
by the rule:

```
vp(Form) --> aux(Form-Require), vp(Require).
```

In other words, an auxiliary can be combined with another VP as
long as the VP is of the required form and where the resulting
combined phrase is of the same form as the auxiliary. For example,
the past participle VP *taken the wrong route* can combine with *have*
since that is a past participle VP as required by *have* with the result
that *have taken the wrong route* is a base VP because *have* is the base
form. This, in turn, can combine with *could* with the result that
could have taken the wrong route is a finite VP. Recall that the initial
verb in the sequence is required to be finite by the sentential rule:

```
s --> np, vp(fin(Value)).
```

The structure, then, of this VP is as represented by the following
phrase structure tree.

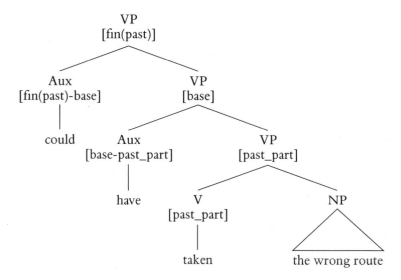

One form of the verb that still needs to be considered is the infinitive form as it appears in a sentence such as

The violinist wants [to play after lunch]

There is some debate amongst linguists as to the constituency of the phrase *to play after lunch*. The analysis adopted here treats *to* as a highly irregular auxiliary verb which combines with a base VP to form an infinitival VP. Such VPs may be introduced by the vp-rule:

```
vp(Form) --> v(Form), vp(infinitival).
```

where the sorts of verb that can appear as the head of such VPs are *wants*, *tends*, *seems*, *forgot* and so on. With the lexical entries:

```
aux(infinitival-base) --> [to].
v(fin(pres)) --> [wants].
```

the grammar defines the string *wants to play after lunch* as a present tense VP which consists of *wants* concatenated with the infinitival string *to play after lunch*.

Question 11.14

Give all the lexical entries for the different forms – past, present, past and present participle and base – of the verbs *will, have, be, bake* and *sleep* using the following two rules as exemplars.

```
aux(fin(pres)-base) --> [can].
v(pres_part) --> [taking].
```

Question 11.15

Verbs and adjectives differ in the forms of sentential complement they may take. For example, some verbs/adjectives may take a following tensed S:

> We believe [the girl has won]
> Bill is confident [the girl has won]

Others may take a following base *that*-clause – i.e. the VP of the subordinate clause is in the base or stem form:

> The rules require [that the girl win]
> Bill is insistent [that the girl win]

Note that the clause is introduced by the complementiser *that*. Other verbs and adjectives take a *for*-infinitival clause:

> The duke prefers [for the butler to open the wine]
> The duke is eager [for the butler to open the wine]

These last examples may also appear with just an infinitival VP:

> The duke prefers [to open the wine]
> The duke is eager [to open the wine]

Write a DCG to handle such verbs and adjectives.

Question: 11.16

Extend a DCG to handle passive VPs. This requires consideration of two aspects. First, passive VPs must contain *be*. This is different from the *be* used for the present participle as the form of the verb following passive-*be* shows:

> He *was* (present participle) hitting Mary
> He *was* (past (or passive) participle) hit

The full sequence of auxiliaries can now be expressed as:

> (Modal)-(*Have*)-(*Be*: present participle)-(*Be*: past participle)-Main Verb

Provide, then, the relevant lexical entries for the past participle *be*. The additional complication lies in the VP containing the main verb. In the above example this consists of a transitive verb but with no following object. Note that an intransitive verb cannot appear here – *He was smiled*. Extend the VP rules so as to allow a transitive verb in the environment vp --> v as long as the vp is passive (this being required by the presence of the immediately preceding passive auxiliary).

11.1.3 Parsing

The same technique that was used in section 9.5 to represent the parse of a recursive transition network can also be used with DCGs. For example, the rule:

```
s(s(NP,VP)) --> np(NP), vp(VP).
```

specifies that the parse of the sentence will have the structure s(NP, VP) where NP and VP are the parses of the NP and VP, respectively, as determined by the np- and vp-rules. The parse arguments for these rules are determined in an analogous way to that for s.

```
np(np(Det,N)) --> det(Det), n(N).
vp(vp(V,NP)) --> v(V), np(NP).
```

The categorial structure associated with lexical items is introduced as an argument in the lexical definitions.

```
det(det(the)) --> [the].
n(n(climber)) --> [climber].
```

A DCG such as this embedded under Prolog results in a parser.

```
?- s(Parse,[the,climber,saw,the,mountain],[]).
   Parse = s(np(det(the), n(climber)), vp(v(saw),
               np(det(the), n(mountain))))
```

Question 11.17

Add a parse argument to the following DCG fragment.

```
s --> np, vp.
np --> pn.
np --> det, adj, n.
vp --> v, np.
vp --> v, np, pp.
vp --> v, s.
pp --> p, np.

pn --> [john].
adj --> [small].
p --> [under].
```

Question 11.18

Because of the categorial ambiguity of various lexical items, the following sentence is ambiguous:

They can fish

Write a grammar with parse arguments which will associate two different parses to this sentence.

Question 11.19

The following sentences are each structurally ambiguous:

> Simon saw the sherpa with the telescope
> Joe saw the sherpa on the hill with the telescope
> We gave her wet dog biscuits

Write a DCG (with parse arguments) which will provide the relevant analyses.

11.1.4 Empty Categories

In section 2.1 the notion of an **empty category** was briefly introduced. This section expands this discussion and shows how they may be handled in a DCG.

11.1.4.1 Indirect Questions

Some verbs subcategorise for an indirect question as indicated by the following bracketing.

> Felicity knows [who took the cake]
> Simon forgot [who ate the sandwich]

In these examples, an indirect question looks rather like a simple sentence except that the subject NP is the wh-pronoun *who*. Assuming this to be correct, the following rules will handle such examples.

```
vp --> v(ind_ques), ind_ques.

ind_ques --> wh_pro, vp.

wh_pro --> [who].
v(ind_ques) --> [knows].
```

The difficulty comes with indirect questions of the form:

> Joshua forgot [who Simon saw]
> Chris told Richard [who David beat]

As before, the indirect question starts with a wh-pronoun. However, the phrases which follow are a little hard to describe. At first glance, they look like simple sentences consisting of a subject NP followed by a VP but this VP is rather strange. In section 11.1.2.1

saw was listed as a transitive verb and was subcategorised in such a way as to only occur in environments with a following NP object. In this case, however, *saw* appears with no following object. Indeed, it must not be so followed.

★Joshua forgot [who Simon saw the actor]

As a further puzzle, the environment is that usually associated with intransitive verbs – i.e. there is no following object NP – but replacing the transitive verb with an intransitive verb also leads to an ill-formed example:

★Joshua forgot [who Simon smiled]

These examples could be explained if it was assumed that in such constructions the verb is followed by a special kind of object NP. This would account for why a transitive verb can occur – since they require objects – but not an intransitive – since they do not occur with objects. Such an object NP would be special in the sense that although it has syntactic properties – fulfilling subcategorisation requirements in this case – it does not have any lexical content. Such 'missing' NPs are referred to as **empty categories** or **gaps**. Using this notion, it is possible to say that in *Joshua forgot who Simon saw* the phrase *saw* is a VP consisting of a verb and empty NP category which combines with *Simon* to form an S with an NP gap, *Simon saw*.

It is important to ensure that if empty categories are to be allowed by the grammar, they are not able to occur just anywhere. For example, without any constraints it would be possible to define as well-formed:

Simon saw

on the assumption that the relevant structure contains an empty NP object, so licensing the appearance of the transitive verb. To rule out such cases, empty categories will only be allowed when there is some other phrase which can 'stand for', or be associated with, the gap. These items are sometimes referred to as **fillers**. In the example:

Joshua forgot [who Simon saw ec]

the filler for the missing object – represented as *ec* – is the wh-pronoun *who* which fronts the indirect question. The example:

Simon saw ec

is ruled out because the empty category cannot be associated with a filler.

Such constructions can be represented with a DCG through the use of an argument carrying the relevant gap information. Two sorts of argument are required to express this: nogap will be used if there is no gap and gap(Phrase) if there is a gap of the type Phrase. Using this, the indirect question rule can be expressed as follows:

```
ind_ques --> wh_pro, s(gap(np)).
```

That is, an indirect question consists of a wh-pronoun followed by a sentence which contains an empty NP category. The gap that appears in the S is licensed by the presence of the wh-pronoun. The gap information now introduced into the s-clause in turn must be passed down to the vp-rule and this is achieved with the rule:

```
s(GapInfo) --> np(nogap), vp(GapInfo).
```

Note that the subject NP does not contain a gap. The vp-rule now becomes:

```
vp(Gapinfo) --> v, np(Gapinfo).
```

where the gap information is passed down to the object NP. There are two possibilities regarding the np-rule. If there is no gap, then the NP is 'normal'; for example:

```
np(nogap) --> det, n.
```

On the other hand, an NP with an NP-gap should cover nothing. This is expressed by the rule:

```
np(gap(np)) --> [].
```

Gaps are only introduced if there is a filler; in the case of indirect questions it is the wh-pronoun that fulfils this role. The s-rule introducing root sentences should not, then, introduce a gap.

```
s --> s(nogap).
```

The following tree diagram indicates the overall structure for the sentence *Joshua forgot who Simon saw.*

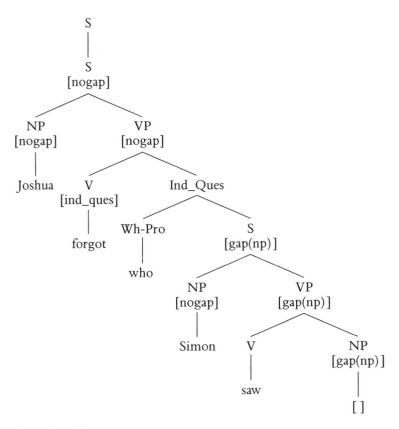

Question 11.20

Once the gap-information argument is included into the grammar, the first rule for indirect questions previously given as:

```
ind_ques --> wh_pro, vp.
```

needs adjusting. Do this.

Question 11.21

Extend the definition of wh-phrase to include full forms rather than just a wh-pronoun.

Joe knows [*which mountain* Simon saw]
Simon wonders [*which sherpas that Joe likes* upset the cart]

Question 11.22

NP gaps may also occur in PP complements:

Joe knows who Simon gave the rucksack to

Provide the rule to account for such an example.

Question 11.23

The gap in an indirect question may be any distance away from the relative pronoun:

Joe knows [who Simon saw ___]
Joe knows [who Bill said [Simon saw ___]]
Joe knows [who Fred thought [Bill said [Simon saw ___]]]

Make sure your grammar handles such cases.

Question 11.24

In the text it was assumed that an indirect question such as:

The engineer knows [who repaired the boiler]

consists of a wh-pronoun followed by a VP whilst the indirect question in:

The father knows who the child upset

consists of a wh-pronoun followed by an S with an NP gap in object position. An alternative analysis would view both indirect questions as consisting of a wh-pronoun followed by a gapped S; the difference being whether the gap is realised as a subject (in the first) or an object (in the second). Express this analysis with a DCG.

Question 11.25

Relative clauses such as those bracketed:

The climber [who saw the sherpa]
The sherpa [who Simon likes]

are similar in structure to indirect questions. Write the DCG rules to introduce these constructions.

11.1.4.2 Questions

Wh-questions are another canonical example of a 'gapped' construction. Wh-questions are typically a request for information regarding the identity of some object and are so-called because they involve an interrogative word typically beginning *wh-*; for example, *who, what, why, when, where, which* – but also *how*. The following are some examples:

Who cooked the breakfast?
Where is the rehearsal?
When is Sim expected to arrive?
How will Jim ever finish the pipes in time?

Before seeing how to handle such constructions, it will be helpful to consider the analysis of **yes-no questions**. As their name suggests, these are questions for which either a 'yes' or 'no' is an appropriate reply as in the following examples.

Could Anne have eaten the chocolate?
Is David bringing the ice-cream?

Syntactically, yes-no questions are just like declarative sentences except that the first auxiliary of the verbal group precedes the subject NP. This is known as **subject-auxiliary inversion**. Note that it must be an auxiliary that is inverted rather than a main verb.

*Eaten Anne have the chocolate?

The following DCG rule handle such clauses.

```
s_inv --> aux(fin(Value)-Required),
          np, vp(Required).
```

where s_inv represents the category of inverted sentence. Because the inverted auxiliary is the first element of the verbal group it will, as seen previously, be tensed and this fact is built into the rule. Following the subject NP is the VP minus its first auxiliary which is now in the initial position. However, the required form of the VP is still determined by the displaced auxiliary in the same way as if it were still part of the VP; hence, the variable Required.

Returning to wh-questions, questions such as:

Who will see Claude?
Who has Nicole seen?

are similar to the indirect questions of the last section. The first example can be considered to consist of a wh-pronoun *who* followed by a VP and is described by the following rule:

```
question --> wh_pro, vp(fin(Value)).
```

The second example is also like an indirect question in that it has an empty object NP which is licensed by the wh-pronoun filler. The difference is that the gapped sentence also has subject-auxiliary inversion. Accordingly, the following rules are required:

```
question --> wh_pro,
             s_inv(fin(Value), gap(np)).
s_inv(Form, Gapinfo) --> aux(Form-Require),
                         np(nogap),
                         vp(Require, Gapinfo).
```

Question 11.26

Subject-verb inversion also occurs when a 'negative' adverb appears in initial position:

> Rarely/seldom has Joe written a better book
> > cf. *Rarely/seldom Joe has written a better book
> Nowhere will Joe see a bigger mountain
> > cf. *Nowhere Joe will see a bigger mountain

Provide the DCG rules to handle such cases.

11.1.4.3 Gap Threading

The approach to gap-filler constructions outlined above has two problems. First, it can result in a proliferation of rules if a gap appears in more than one constituent. For example, consider dative VPs. A dative verb is one taking a following NP and PP as in:

> Jiff bought [NP the drop spindle] [PP for Bess]

In a gapped construction an NP gap may occur in either the NP or PP position.

> Pat knows what Jiff bought ec for Bess
> Pat knows who Jiff bought the drop spindle for ec

Accordingly, two versions of the same basic rule will be required.

```
vp(GapInfo) --> v, np(GapInfo), pp(nogap).
vp(GapInfo) --> v, np(nogap), pp(GapInfo).
```

As a consequence, a dative VP containing no gap – as in *bought the drop spindle for Bess* – will have two essentially identical analyses since GapInfo in either rule may be instantiated to the value nogap.

One solution to these problems is a technique known as **gap threading**. This works by associating with each relevant phrase a pair of lists; the first 'gaps in' list represents the gaps that might appear in the construction and the second, 'gaps out', those gaps that remain after any gaps that occur in the construction have been removed. For example, the 'gaps in' list associated with the VP *bought for Bess* might be [np] whilst the 'gaps out' list will be [] since the VP contains a gap.

The two gap lists will be represented as a difference pair argument to the categorial predicate; for example:

```
s(GapsIn-GapsOut) --> np(GapsIn-RestGaps),
                      vp(RestGaps-GapsOut).

np(GapsIn-GapsIn) --> det, n.

vp(GapsIn-GapsOut) --> v,
                       np(GapsIn-GapsOut).
```

Those rules which introduce fillers will push the relevant gap onto the 'gaps in' list as in the following for indirect questions.

```
ind_ques(GapsIn-GapsIn) --> wh_pro,
                    s([gap(np)|GapsIn]-GapsIn).
```

The rule for NP-gaps will pop gap(np) off the 'gaps in' list:

```
np([gap(np)|GapsOut]-GapsOut) --> [].
```

Since the difference lists are passed or 'threaded' from constituent to constituent, only a single dative VP rule is required which overcomes the previously outlined problems.

```
vp(GapsIn-GapsOut) --> v,
                    np(GapsIn-GapsRest),
                    pp(GapsRest-GapsOut).
```

The resulting analysis of the sentence *Pat knows who Ruth gave the guide to* may be represented by the following tree.

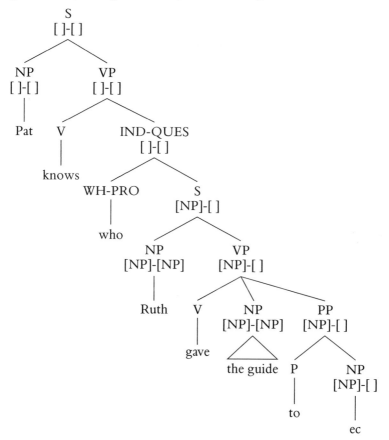

Questions to Prolog will take the form:

```
?- s([]-[], [pat,knows,who,ruth,gave,the,guide,
to],[]).
   yes
```

The next section introduces the other major extension of DCGs over simple phrase structure grammars, the inclusion of procedure calls.

11.2 Procedure Calls

The appearance of the same variable in different grammar symbols of a DCG rule places certain conditions – namely that of identity – on the terms that appear in these positions. However, the DCG notation also includes the possibility of stating much stronger conditions by allowing *any* definable predicate to appear to the right of the arrow. These predicates are referred to as **procedure calls**.

In order to distinguish procedure calls from the grammar symbols, they are placed between braces { }. Any number of predicates may appear between the braces as long as they are separated by commas just as with standard Prolog predicates. In the next three sections a number of examples are given to indicate some of the uses to which procedure calls may be put.

11.2.1 Simplifying the Lexicon

Lexical entries have so far been handled by sets of rules such as:

```
n --> [climber].
n --> [mountain].
n --> [serac].
```

If DCGs are considered from a linguistic perspective – i.e. as statements about linguistic structure – a body of such rules is slightly odd. Grammars make general statements. For example, the rule $S \rightarrow NP\ VP$ states that 'a sentence can consist of an NP followed by a VP'. The assertion is not made with regard to specific NPs and VPs but to *any* NP and *any* VP. Lexical rules, however, are highly specific since particular lexical items are mentioned on the right-hand side of the rule. A more general statement might be something like: 'the grammar symbol n may describe any word as long as that word is a noun'. This can be expressed by the following DCG rule:

```
n --> [Word], {n(Word)}.
```

Here the requirement that the word be a noun is imposed by the call to the predicate n(Word) which, by assumption, is a well-defined predicate describing the nouns of the language.

```
n(climber).
n(mountain).
n(serac).
```

Although conceptually neater, it is not immediately clear that this approach has any great benefit. However, the approach starts to come into its own as lexical entries become more complex since it can lead to more concise statements. For example, imagine that rather than specifying number information as two separate facts as in:

```
n(climber, sing).
n(climbers, plur).
```

single entries are used to represent the information as a kind of table.

```
n(climber, climbers).
```

A procedure call could be used to pick out the relevant information.

```
n(sing) --> [Word], {n(Word, _)}.
n(plur) --> [Word], {n(_, Word)}.
```

Question 11.27

Lexical entries for nouns could be reduced to a single entry:

```
n(dog, dogs).
```

along with a change in the rules which identify lexical items:

```
n(sing) --> [Word], {n(Word, _)}.
n(plur) --> [Word], {n(_, Word)}.
```

Produce similar entries for the personal pronouns distinguishing their different case forms as well as the relevant lexical rules.

Question 11.28

Representing verbal entries in the general format:

```
v(Pres_sing, Pres_plur, Past, Past_part, Pres_part,
Base).
```

make the corresponding adjustments to the grammar rules to pick out the relevant item in each table. Give the entries for the verbs *take*, *bake*, *put*, *sleep* and *try*.

11.2.2 An Alternative Approach to Agreement

So far nouns and verbs have been distinguished with respect to number in order to determine various agreement relations. However, at least as far as subject-verb agreement is concerned, **person** is also relevant. Person is used to indicate the nature of the participants in a situation. In English there is a three-way distinction which most clearly shows up in the pronominal system:

> First person: *I, we*
>> – referring to a group which includes the speaker
>
> Second person: *you*
>> – referring to a group which includes the person or persons being addressed by the speaker
>
> Third person: *he, she, it, they*
>> – referring to a group that does not include the speaker or addressee(s)

In each case, the group may include one or more members which means that each pronoun can be distinguished with respect to number and person. For example, *I* is first person singular and *they*, third person plural; *you* does service for both singular and plural forms of the second person. All non-pronominal nouns are third person (either singular or plural).

In terms of agreement (in the present tense), a verb form such as *likes* agrees with a third person singular subject whilst *like* agrees with the rest – first and second person singular and all the plurals.

> He/she/it/the sherpa likes Joe
> *He/she/it like Joe
> I/you/we/they/the sherpas like Joe
> *I/you/we/they/the sherpas likes Joe

Rather than capturing this requirement through the introduction of an additional person-argument, an alternative approach will be illustrated. This works by associating with each verb a list of the types of subject that the verb may appear with. For example, the rule:

```
v([sing(3)]) --> [likes].
```

states that *likes* may occur with a third person singular subject, whilst:

```
v([sing(1),sing(2),plur(1),plur(2),plur(3)])
-->[like].
```

indicates that *like* may occur with any of the other possible forms. Person and number for the pronouns can be specified similarly.

```
pronoun([sing(1)]) --> [i].
pronoun([plur(1)]) --> [we].
pronoun([sing(2),plur(2)]) --> [you].
```

whilst non-pronominal nouns will take the form:

```
n([sing(3)]) --> [sherpa].
n([plur(3)]) --> [sherpas].
n([sing(3),plur(3)]) --> [sheep].
```

The agreement list for an NP and VP will be the same as for the head noun and verb, respectively.

```
np(Agr) --> det, n(Agr).
vp(Agr) --> v(Agr), np(Agr1).
```

With agreement features expressed as lists, the previous means of expressing subject-verb agreement:

```
s --> np(Agr), vp(Agr).
```

will no longer work since the two lists will not usually be identical. However, the two phrases will agree if they contain at least one feature in common; in other words, if the intersection of the two lists is not empty.

The climbers   like the mountain
‾‾‾‾‾‾   ‾‾‾‾‾‾‾‾‾‾‾‾   Intersection = [p3]
[p3]   [s1, s2, p1, p2, p3]

The climber   like the mountain
‾‾‾‾‾   ‾‾‾‾‾‾‾‾‾‾‾‾   Intersection = []
[s3]   [s1, s2, p1, p2, p3]

This intersection test may be applied through a procedure call to a predicate intersect which defines the list of common elements to two other lists. The requirement is that the intersection of the two lists should not be empty.

```
s --> np(Agr), vp(Agr1),
      {intersect(Agr, Agr1, Int),
      not(Int = [])}.
```

intersect may be defined as follows.

```
intersect([], X, []).

intersect([X|R], Y, [X|Z]) :-
      member(X, Y), !,
      intersect(R, Y, Z).

intersect([X|R], Y, Z) :-
      intersect(R, Y, Z).
```

Question 11.29

The usual order for describing a noun is *Person + Number* – for example 'third person singular' – but in the text we reversed this to, say, sing(3). Why cannot we use the form 3(sing)?

Question 11.30

Using the ideas of this section, capture the agreement relation previously expressed by the rule:

```
np --> det(Num), n(Num).
```

Is there any need for using intersection since won't each item only be associated with a single value? What should the value for the np as a whole be?

11.2.3 Providing Feedback

The previous two uses of procedure calls in the body of a DCG rule have been used as conditions on grammatical statements. However, since the call may be to *any* Prolog procedure, there is no requirement that this be so. The following is a simple use of a call to a predicate which is used for extra-grammatical purposes.

Imagine a very simple program designed to provide feedback to a learner of English. For example, the student might type in a sentence and if it is well-formed, the system would respond with a 'Well done'. This can be achieved with a procedure call to write, the built-in predicate introduced in section 7.1.

```
s --> np, vp,
      {write('Well done'), nl}.
```

Of course, a learner is likely to make various errors and it would be even more useful if the system could also provide some feedback in these cases. For example, a typical mistake of French learners of English is to place attributive adjectives such as *difficult* after the noun:

This is a book difficult

since this is their usual position in French. One way of providing feedback for such ill-formed input is to add special rules to the program to pick up the ill-formed cases. For example:

```
np --> det, n, adj,
       {write('You have got the adjective in the wrong
place'), nl,
       write('In English they always precede the noun'),
nl}.
```

From a grammatical point of view, rules of this type are rather suspect. For example, what language would a DCG containing such rules be a grammar of? It cannot be English since it should not include rules of the form *NP → Det N Adj*. Indeed, this particular rule has been included in the program just because it is *not* a rule of English. Note also how calls to extra-logical predicates such as `write` destroy the declarative nature of the formalism. As a general approach to parsing ill-formed input for large applications, this solution suffers from the further problem that it can lead to a huge increase in the size of the program if all possible interference errors are to be covered. The potential result is a program which is too inefficient for practical purposes. Consequently, this type of approach to handling ill-formed input is best thought of as merely illustrating the potential use of procedure calls, rather than providing a serious solution to this particular problem.

Question 11.31

Write a program which will provide feedback on agreement errors in English such as *Every men will read this book* and *The student like this section*.

11.3 Further Reading

DCGs were originally introduced in Pereira and Warren (1980) as a simplification of the metamorphosis grammars (MGs) of Colmerauer (1978). Pereira and Shieber (1987), Gazdar and Mellish (1989), Gal *et al.* (1991) and Coelho (1987) provide tutorial introductions.

Covington (1994) and Allen (1995) present brief overviews of English phrase structure. More detail is provided in Burton-Roberts (1986) and Thomas (1993). Baker (1995) is especially valuable and it would be a worthwhile exercise attempting to work through this text and coding up the material (and answers to the questions) into a DCG format after having completed this book.

The DCG formalism is just one of a group of formalisms which are jointly referred to as **Logic Grammars**. The other formalisms have been developed in order to rectify some of the shortcomings of DCGs (often related to problems involving gap-filler constructions). Some of the more important logic grammars are, Extraposition Grammars (Pereira 1981), Slot Grammars (McCord, 1980), Modifier Structure Grammars (Dahl and McCord, 1983), Gapping Grammars (Dahl and Abramson, 1984), Definite Clause Translation Grammars (Abramson, 1984) and Restriction Grammars (Hirschman and Puder, 1988). Saint-Dizier and Szpakowicz (1990a) provides a brief overview to some of this work. A much fuller introduction can be found in Abramson and Dahl (1989). Comprehensive collections of research papers on logic grammars may be found in

Saint-Dizier and Szpakowicz (1990), Dahl and Saint-Dizier (1985 and 1988) and Brown and Koch (1991).

Logic grammars are examples from a general class of grammar formalism referred to as *unification-based*. Shieber (1986) and Carlson and Linden (1987) provide tutorial introductions to this work. Both Gazdar and Mellish (1989, chapter 7) and Covington (1994, chapter 5) include further discussion as well as providing implementations of the PATR formalism outlined in Shieber (1986).

11.4 Program Listings

The following program is a compiler for DCGs as given in Clocksin and Mellish (1987, pp. 251–253).

```
/* **********************************************

NAME: dcg_trans.pl

DESCRIPTION: A DCG compiler

********************************************** */
?- op(1101, fx, '{').
?- op(1100, xf, '}').
?- op(1199, xfx, -->).

translate((P0 --> Q0), (P :- Q)) :-
    left_hand_side(P0, S0, S, P),
    right_hand_side(Q0, S0, S, Q1),
    flatten(Q1, Q).

left_hand_side((NT, Ts), S0, S, P) :- !,
    nonvar(NT),
    islist(Ts),
    tag(NT, S0, S1, P),
    concat(Ts, S, S1).

left_hand_side(NT, S0, S, P) :-
    nonvar(NT),
    tag(NT, S0, S, P).

right_hand_side((X1, X2), S0, S, P) :- !,
    right_hand_side(X1, S0, S1, P1),
    right_hand_side(X2, S1, S, P2),
    and(P1, P2, P).

right_hand_side((X1;X2), S0, S, (P1;P2)) :- !,
    or(X1, S0, S, P1),
    or(X2, S0, S, P2).
```

```
right_hand_side({P}, S, S, P) :- !.
right_hand_side(!, S, S, !) :- !.
right_hand_side(Ts, S0, S, true) :-
    islist(Ts),
    !,          .
    concat(Ts, S, S0).
right_hand_side(X, S0, S, P) :-
    tag(X, S0, S, P).

or(X, S0, S, P) :-
    right_hand_side(X, S0a, S, Pa),
    (var(S0a), S0a \== S, !,
        S0=S0a, P=Pa, P=(S0=S0a, Pa)).

tag(X, S0, S, P) :-
    X =.. [F|A],
    concat(A, [S0, S], AX),
    P =.. [F|AX].

and(true, P, P) :- !.
and(P, true, P) :- !.
and(P, Q, (P, Q)).

flatten(A, A) :- var(A), !.
flatten((A, B), C) :- !,
    flatten1(A, C, R),
    flatten(B, R).
flatten(A, A).

flatten1(A, (A, R), R) :-
    var(A), !.
flatten1((A, B), C, R) :- !,
    flatten1(A, C, R1),
    flatten1(B, R1, R).
flatten1(A, (A, R), R).

islist([]) :- !.
islist([_|_]).

concat([], X, X).
concat([A|B], C, [A|D]) :-
    concat(B, C, D).

/* ****************************************** */
```

CHAPTER 12

Alternative Parsing Strategies

The recognition and parsing procedures described and implemented in previous chapters have all been versions of a top-down, depth-first, left-to-right strategy (with backtracking). With regards to the phrase structure grammars of chapter 10 and the DCGs of chapter 11, these strategies were seen to be a consequence of the in-built proof procedure of Prolog. However, as noted in section 10.1, a context-free phrase structure grammar (and, by extension, a DCG) is compatible with a number of different procedural interpretations. If Prolog were only suitable for expressing the one strategy, this would severely restrict its usefulness as a tool for NLP research. However, one of the strengths of Prolog is the ease with which it is possible to devise other control strategies. This is the subject matter of the present chapter.

A word of caution before proceeding. In order to be able to give a reasonably broad coverage of material and still keep the text to a manageable length, the presentation is much more compact than in previous chapters. The reader, however, should now have reached a sufficient level of expertise where careful reading will overcome any initial problems.

12.1 A Top-down Interpreter

Before examining some alternative strategies, it will prove useful to consider another way of producing a top-down, depth-first, left-to-right strategy for a DCG. For this purpose, the rules of the grammar will be expressed in a slightly different form from that used previously as shown below.

```
s ==> [np, vp].
np ==> [det, n].
```

The arrow is specified by the following declaration:

```
?- op(1200, xfx, ==>).
```

Using the infix operator ==> rather than --> is necessary in order
to prevent the rules being automatically transformed into their
equivalent Prolog clauses by the DCG translation program. Using
a list for the right-hand side of the rule rather than a conjunction of
literals is adopted for programming convenience. To simplify the
discussion it will be assumed that the rules contain no procedure
calls via the brace notation. Lexical rules will be dispensed with in
favour of the predicate word as used on a number of occasions in
previous chapters.

DCGs in the last chapter were **compiled**. That is, the rules of
the grammar were initially translated into Prolog clauses which
were then directly executed. The approach adopted here is for the
DCG rules to form a *database* for another program to access and
manipulate during its execution as needs be. Programs which
manipulate other programs in this way are called **interpreters**. It
is because the same DCG rules can be used by different interpreters
that different parsing strategies are possible.

In fact, an interpreter has already been introduced in section 10.2
for a basic context-free phrase grammar. The following interpreter
is similar except that rules are cast in the form s ==> [np,vp]
rather than the format rule(s, [np,vp]) and difference lists will
be used to encode string positions. The predicate recognise(Cat,
String-Tail) is used to state that the string coded by the difference pair String-Tail is of the category Cat. If Cat is a lexical
category, then the first word of the input list must be an example
of that category.

```
recognise(Cat, [Word|String]-String) :-
     word(Word, Cat).
```

Otherwise, if Cat is a phrasal category, a rule should be located
with this category as the left-hand side category and then the con-
stituents specified by the right-hand side recognised in turn.

```
recognise(Cat, String-String1) :-
     (Cat ==> CatList),
     recognise_list(CatList, String-String1).
```

Because the right-hand side of a phrasal rule is a list, the definition
of recognise_list is recursive. If the list is empty, then,
recognise_list succeeds immediately. Otherwise, the first
category of the list should be recognised and then the operation
repeated with the remainder of the list.

```
recognise_list([], String-String).

recognise_list([Cat|RestCats], String-String1):-
      recognise(Cat, String-String2),
      recognise_list(RestCats, String2-String1).
```

Queries to this program take the form:

```
?- recognise(s, [every,child,booed,the,villain]
-[]).
```

A spy placed on `recognise` shows that, indeed, the sentence is recognised with the familiar top-down, depth-first, left-to-right strategy.

The crucial point to note regarding this example is how the rules of the DCG are accessed by the recognition program at various points during execution in order to provide information about how to proceed – in particular, which categories to look for next – but that the recognition strategy itself is determined by the definition of `recognise`. That is, the process is top-down because the grammar rules are identified by their left-hand symbol, depth-first because the strategy always pursues the 'deepest' category first, and left-to-right because the categories on the right-hand side of the arrow are recognised in that order. Note how both the top-down and left-to-right aspects of the procedure are consequences of the way the program has been written whilst the depth-first aspect is due to the program being executed in Prolog which pursues goals depth-first.

Question 12.1

How must the program be altered in order to ensure subject-verb agreement?

Question 12.2

Change the program from a recognisor to a parser.

Question 12.3

How could the recognition procedure be changed from a left-to-right strategy to a right-to-left strategy?

12.2 Problems with Top-down Parsing

Different processing strategies have different strengths and weaknesses. The major difficulty for the top-down strategy of the previous section is caused by certain types of recursive rule. A rule is **recursive** if the category being defined on the left-hand side of the rule also appears as one of the right-hand side categories. A rule is **left-recursive** if the recursive element is the left-most category of the right-hand side. Each of the following rules is left-recursive.

```
np ==> [np, pp].
np ==> [np, conj, np].
vp ==> [vp, pp].
```

As was seen in section 6.5, left-recursive rules can cause the Prolog search strategy to enter into an infinite loop of computation and the same applies to a recognition or parsing procedure based on the same type of control structure.

Depending on which rules a grammar contains and their order of listing, looping need not necessarily occur with a top-down interpreter containing a left-recursive rule. For example, a grammar containing the following rules would not cause the previous query to abort.

```
np ==> [det, n].
np ==> [np, conj, np].
```

However, if the processor attempts to find all possible parses for the string – say, through enforced backtracking – looping will inevitably occur since the left-recursive rule will eventually be used as a potential alternative analysis.

```
?- np(Parse, [every child]-[]).
   Parse = np(det(every),n(child));

Stack area overflow
Execution aborted
```

One way of preventing looping is to rewrite the grammar in such a way as to remove the left-recursion. For example, the left-recursive rule np ==> [np, pp] can be converted into the following set of rules.

```
np ==> [det, n, preps].
preps ==> [pp].
preps ==> [pp, preps].
```

It might appear that although both the recursive and non-recursive definitions describe exactly the same set of strings they differ on the constituent structure that they assign to a phrase such as *most children at the party*. This conclusion, however, overlooks the possibility of utilising variables to manipulate the various structures into the desired parse. For example, the following rules will produce the same parse as the original left-recursive version.

```
np(Preps) ==> [det(Det),
          n(N),
          preps(np(det(Det),n(N)),Preps)].
preps(NP, np(NP,PP)) ==> [pp(PP)].
preps(NP, Preps) ==> [pp(PP),
          preps(np(NP,PP),Preps)].
```

Another solution to the left-recursion problem is to retain the left-recursive rules but change the control strategy to one which is not troubled by them. One possibility is to use a bottom-up strategy.

12.3 A Bottom-up Interpreter

A simple bottom-up procedure was described in section 10.1 showing how, starting from the string's words, the strategy works by reducing categories into ever more inclusive units until all the words can be combined into the single category S. The particular process illustrated in that section is often referred to as a **shift-reduce** recognisor since the process consists of a sequence of two types of move, a 'shift' move and a 'reduce' move. A **shift** consists of removing the first word of the input string and placing its lexical category on the top of a category stack. A **reduce** move replaces a sequence of category symbols at the top of the category stack which match the right-hand side of some rule with the symbol on the left-hand side of the rule. For example, *Det* and *N* may be replaced by *NP* following a match with the rule $NP \rightarrow Det\ N$. The process starts with an empty category stack and the input is recognised if all of the words in the input string have been shifted and the category stack's only symbol is *S*. The following table traces a shift-reduce recognisor processing the string *The snow blocked the road*. The top of the category stack is to the right.

Category Stack	Input String	Action
–	the snow blocked the road	Shift
Det	snow blocked the road	Shift
Det N	blocked the road	Reduce ($NP \rightarrow Det\ N$)
NP	blocked the road	Shift
NP V	the road	Shift
NP V Det	road	Shift
NP V Det N	–	Reduce ($NP \rightarrow Det\ N$)
NP V NP	–	Reduce ($VP \rightarrow V\ NP$)
NP VP	–	Reduce ($S \rightarrow NP\ VP$)
S	–	Success

Implementing a shift-reduce recognisor for a DCG in Prolog is a fairly simple matter. The main predicate will be `recognise` as with the top-down procedure of section 12.1 but this time the first argument will be a list of categories representing the category stack. The input string will be represented by a difference pair. The boundary condition for `recognise` handles the case where all the input string has been shifted and the category stack contains the single item s.

```
recognise([s], []-[]).
```

The 'shift' move is simply stated.

```
recognise(Stack, [Word| String]-String1) :-
        word(Word, Cat),
        recognise([Cat|Stack], String-
        String1).
```

Notice that because items are pushed onto the top of a Prolog list, the categories will be represented in reverse order of their discovery. This has to be taken into account in the 'reduce' move where the categories Cat2 and Cat1 on top of the stack are swapped back into their correct order Cat1, Cat2 in the call to the rule. Once a rule has been identified, the categories on top of the stack are reduced to the left-hand side symbol.

```
recognise([Cat2, Cat1|Stack], String-String1):-
        (Cat ==> [Cat1, Cat2]),
        recognise([Cat|Stack], String-
        String1).
```

The complete listing of the program is in the file shift.pl in section 12.8 which includes a 1-place version of recognise as the drive predicate setting up the initial state of the recognisor.

It might be thought that the only adjustments needed to change a shift-reduce recognisor into a parser would be to add parse arguments to the DCG rules and lexical definitions:

```
s(s(NP,VP)) ==> [np(NP), vp(VP)].
det(the, det(det(the))).
```

rename recognise as parse and suitably modify the boundary clause:

```
parse([s(Parse)], []-[]).
```

However, this will not quite work. If the reader traces a proof with a spy point placed on parse, it will be seen that as the above boundary clause is satisfied the parse argument is, indeed, correctly instantiated to the parse of the sentence. The problem is that this value is lost as the interpreter returns through the recursion since Parse is not included in the initial call to parse. The trick in this situation is to introduce a **result** variable which can be used to record the parse at the bottom of the recursion and, then, pass it back up to the initial call. This can be achieved by redefining the boundary clause as:

```
parse([s(Parse)], Parse, []-[]).
```

where the second argument is the result variable. The other definitions also need modifying to include this extra argument.

```
parse(Stack, Parse, [Word|String]-String1) :-
          word(Word, Cat),
          parse([Cat|Stack], Parse, String-
          String1).
parse([Cat2, Cat1|Stack], Parse, String-
String1):-
          (Cat ==> [Cat1, Cat2]),
          parse([Cat|Stack], Parse, String-
          String1).
```

The drive predicate can now take the form:

```
parse(Parse, String) :-
      parse([], Parse, String-[]).
```

The variable Parse will be passed down through the recursion,
uninstantiated, acting as a kind of place holder until the boundary
clause is satisfied, when it will become bound to the value of the
parse that has been built up during the proof.

```
?- parse(Parse, [the,snow,blocked,the,road]).
 Parse = s(np(det(the),n(snow)),vp(v(blocked),
 np(det(the),n(road))))
 yes
```

Question 12.4

Extend the previous program so that it will handle grammar rules with one
and three categories on the right-hand side of the grammar rule.

Question 12.5

Alter the program so that the categories appear on the stack in the same
order as they appear on the right-hand side of the grammar rules with the
result that the categories in the reduce move do not need swapping over:

```
recognise([Cat1, Cat2|Stack], String-String1):-
      (Cat ==> [Cat1, Cat2]),
      recognise([Cat|Stack], String-String1).
```

12.4 A Left-corner Interpreter

One of the problems with top-down parsing is that the processor
commits itself to a particular analysis before attempting to connect
up with the words of the input string. Incorrect guesses may be

recovered through backtracking but this process can involve a great deal of futile computation as structures are pursued which could never be supported by the data. Bottom-up parsing, being data driven, does not get misled in this way. However, a bottom-up strategy can also result in much fruitless processing if analyses are attempted which could never be true *in that particular context*. Ambiguous words can lead to this problem since the decision as to which of the possible interpretations to choose is made independently of what has been previously recognised even though this information may rule out certain impossible interpretations. For example, a word such as *can* may be either a noun or a verb (auxiliary or main) and yet when found immediately following a determiner such as *every*, it could only ever be a noun, there being no rules which contain the sequence . . . *Det V* . . . as part of their right-hand side. In this situation, pursuing an analysis where *can* is classified as a verb must lead to a dead-end.

It is possible to temper a blind bottom-up strategy with a degree of top-down control using a method called *left-corner* processing. The **left-corner** of a phrase is its left-most constituent. In the following tree, for example, the *NP* is the left-corner of the *S*.

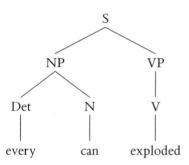

By extension, both *Det* and *S* will be referred to as left-corners of *S* although the *NP* is *the* left-corner. The left-corner of a phrase structure *rule* is the first element of its right-hand side.

Left-corner parsing proceeds by building the analysis from the left-most corner of the sentence in standard bottom-up fashion. Once a left-corner has been established, this information is used to identify a rule by matching this found category with the left-corner of a rule. Once identified in this way, the processor attempts to find the remaining categories which follow the left-corner of the rule. Establishing each of these categories proceeds bottom-up as before. Once all of the right-hand side of the rule has been satisfied, the left-hand symbol can be used to identify the next rule by matching with another left-corner, whereupon the process is repeated.

To see how this works, consider the example *The can exploded*. Starting from the left-most position, the processor initially recognises *the* as a determiner. This information is now used to identify the rule np ==> [det n]. The processor must now establish that a noun follows the determiner. This is demonstrated by showing that the next item is a left-corner of a noun. Since the next word, *can*, can be analysed as a noun and since any category is its own left-corner, the processor will successfully establish that a noun follows. Notice that this conclusion would not be possible if *can* was assumed to be a verb. As a result, the further conclusion that an np has been identified as the left-corner of the input string may be drawn. This result can now be used to key the rule s ==> [np, vp] through its left-corner. Showing that the left-most element of the remaining string, *exploded*, is a left-corner of a vp is quickly established. First, *exploded* is recognised as a verb which then allows the identification of the rule vp ==> [v]. Since there are no categories beyond this left-corner, it can also be concluded that a vp has been successfully located. This completes the recognition of the right-hand side of the s-rule. Accordingly, a sentence has been successfully recognised. The following diagram indicates the processor's discovery path through this example.

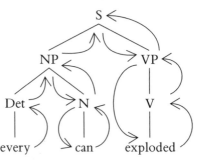

There are various ways of implementing a left-corner recognisor. The following is one solution. The predicate recognise(Cat, String-String1) will be used to state that the string represented by the difference pair String-String1 is of the category Cat. This will be true if the first word of the string is found to be of some category, say Cat1, and that Cat1 is a left-corner of the string. One way of expressing this is shown below.

```
recognise(Cat, [Word|String]-String1) :-
        word(Word, Cat1),
        left_corner(Cat1, Cat, String-
        String1).
```

However, this is not quite enough. The problem is that there is no guarantee that the chosen category Cat1 for the lexical item Word *is* a potential left-corner of Cat. It is important that this be so since there will be no savings in efficiency otherwise. The potential left-corners of a particular phrase can be easily deduced from the rules of the grammar. For example, given the rules:

```
s ==> [np, vp].
np ==> [det, n].
vp ==> [v, np].
```

the potential left-corners of the various phrases are expressed by the following facts:

```
link(np, s).
link(det, np).
link(det, s).
link(v, vp).
link(Cat, Cat).
```

The last definition says that any category is a left-corner of itself. With such a set of definitions, the additional requirement that Cat1 be a potential left-corner of Cat can be included in the definition of recognise.

```
recognise(Cat, [Word|String]-String1) :-
    word(Word, Cat1),
    link(Cat1, Cat),
    left_category(Cat1, Cat, String-String1).
```

Notice how the string represented as the third argument to left_category is the initial string minus the first word. It is this remainder, to the right of the left corner Cat1, which provides the potential continuation of Cat1. As the left-corner is extended right-wards, so the input string diminishes. The boundary condition on left_category is based on the observation that everything is its own left-corner.

```
left_category(Cat, Cat, String-String).
```

In this case, none of the string is consumed. The recursive element of left_category involves matching up with the left-corner of a grammar rule, recognising the rest of the right-hand side and then checking whether the resultant category is a left-corner of the relevant category of the remaining string.

```
left_category(Cat1, Cat, String-String1) :-
    (Phrase ==> [Cat1|Rest]),
    recognise_list(Rest, String-String2),
    left_category(Phrase, Cat, String2-String1).
```

The definition of recognise_list is a simple recursive definition:

```
recognise_list([], String-String).

recognise_list([Cat|Rest], String-String1) :-
        recognise(Cat, String-String2),
        recognise_list(Rest, String2-String1).
```

The complete program is listed as lc.pl at the end of the chapter. Queries to the program take the form:

```
?- recognise(s, [the,minstrel,played,the,
bagpipes]-[]).
     yes
```

It is possible to greatly increase the efficiency of this left-corner technique by compiling the grammar rules into a suitable format for direct left-corner recognition rather than relying on an interpreter. This is achieved by expressing a rule such as:

```
np ==> [det, n].
```

by the clause:

```
left_corner(det, Cat, String1-String) :-
        recognise(n, String1-String2),
        left_corner(np, Cat, String2-String).
```

Expressing the rule in this way removes the need for the processor to identify a rule and then recursively recognise the remainder of its right-hand side through a call to recognise_list. A listing of a left-corner parser in this format is given as the file bup.pl in section 12.8.

Question 12.6

Provide the set of link facts for the following grammar:

```
S → NP VP
NP → Det N PP
VP → V NP
VP → AdvP V
AdvP → Adv
AdvP → Intensifier Adv
PP → P NP
```

Question 12.7

Translate the following grammar rules into their equivalent `bup.pl` format.

NP → PN
NP → Det N PP

Question 12.8

Check whether a left-corner recogniser accepts left-recursive rules without entering into a loop.

Question 12.9

Modify `lc.pl` so as to change the program into a parser.

Question 12.10

Modify `bup.pl` so as to change the program into a parser.

Question 12.11

Compare how both `lc.pl` and `bup.pl` recognise a string such as *The minstrel played the bagpipes.*

12.5 Deterministic Parsing

In section 2.3 the notion of local ambiguity – temporary ambiguity that arises as part of the parsing process – was introduced. Each of the strategies presented so far – top-down, shift-reduce and left-corner – handle local ambiguity by arbitrarily choosing one of the options available and relying upon backtracking to rescue the situation if subsequent material shows the decision to have been misguided. For example, a shift-reduce parser with access to the rules:

```
np ==> [adj, n].
np ==> [det, adj, n].
```

and with the symbols det, adj, n . . . on top of the stack may reduce either to det np . . . or np . . . depending upon whether the first or second rule is chosen. Alternatively, a left-corner parser equipped with the rules:

```
np ==> [det, n].
np ==> [det, adj, n].
```

and having just recognised a determiner may key either rule and so set up expectations for either an immediately following noun or adjective depending upon which is chosen. Since in both cases only one rule will be the correct choice, backtracking must be available to allow the processor to try the alternatives if the wrong rule is initially selected.

The previous parsing strategies are non-deterministic in the sense used in section 8.5 which is why they have to rely on backtracking. However, as previously noted in section 2.3, backtracking can be costly in computational terms and a number of techniques have been developed which permit deterministic parsing. The particular technique to be introduced in this section allows a shift-reduce parser to be guided by top-down information, rather like a left-corner parser, but in such a way that the process is not committed to a particular rule until enough disambiguating material has been processed. It is this delay in the decision making which makes the process deterministic for certain classes of grammar.

The technique works by providing the parser access to an **oracle** which determines not only whether to shift or reduce in a particular situation but also, if directed to reduce, which rule to use. Oracles are represented as finite state networks. The following network represents the oracle for the immediately preceding grammar.

```
s ==> [np, vp]
np ==> [det, n].
np ==> [det, adj, n].
vp ==> [v, np].
```

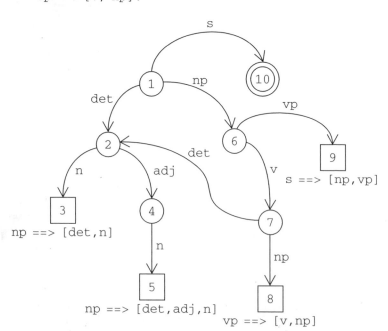

The network indicates when to shift and when to reduce. If the recognisor is in a state which corresponds to a node with a lexical arc leaving it, and the next word in the input string is an example of that category, then it is removed and the recognisor adds the state at the end of the arc to a state stack. For example, if in state 1 a determiner has been recognised, then state 2 is added to the state stack. If the recognisor ends up in a state which corresponds to one of the square nodes, then a reduce move is made. Such nodes in the network are annotated with the particular rule to be used for the reduction. Reduction involves removing the same number of states from the top of the stack as there are categories on the right-hand side of the rule. This will reveal some state. The corresponding node in the network will have an arc leaving it labelled with the same category as the left-hand side of the rule. It is the state at the end of this arc that is pushed onto the top of the state stack. For example, suppose the stack consists of the states *1, 2, 4, 5* (with the top of the stack to the right). Since *5* is a reduction state annotated with the rule np ==> [det,adj,n], the last three states are removed – there being three categories on the right-hand side of the arrow – revealing *1*. Since there is an arc from node *1* to *6* labelled np, state *6* is pushed on to the stack, which now becomes *1, 6*. The process continues until all the words of the string have been shifted and the recognisor ends up in the final state, *10*. The following table traces this process for the input string *Most good musicians play the piano* (with the top of the stack to the right).

Stack	Input	Action
1	most good musicians play the piano	Shift
1 2	good musicians play the piano	Shift
1 2 4	musicians play the piano	Shift
1 2 4 5	play the piano	Reduce (*NP → Det Adj N*)
1 6	play the piano	Shift
1 6 7	the piano	Shift
1 6 7 2	piano	Shift
1 6 7 2 3	–	Reduce (*NP → Det N*)
1 6 7 8	–	Reduce (*VP → V NP*)
1 6 9	–	Reduce (*S → NP VP*)
1 10	–	Success

As with a left-corner parser, a shift-reduce parser with oracle is a bottom-up parser guided by top-down information. However, as already seen, the shift-reduce version does not commit itself to which rule it is pursuing until sufficient information has been gathered. This is due to the structure of the oracle. Consider, for example, the arc leaving state 1. The path from this arc will either terminate at state 3 or 5, corresponding to the rules np ==> [det, n] and np ==>[det, adj, n], respectively. But on recognising a determiner, the processor will change to state 2 which is consistent with ultimately reaching *either* state 3 or 5. In other words, the processor is committed to finding an np but is hedging its bets as to its exact form. However, if the next word is, say, an adjective, the processor will change to state 4, after which it is committed to finding an np of the structure np ==>[det, adj, n].

Oracles are constructed using **dotted rules**. A dotted rule is a normal phrase structure rule but with a dot included somewhere in its right-hand side. The following are all the dotted versions of the rule np ==>[det, adj, n].

```
np ==> [•, det, adj, n]
np ==> [det, •, adj, n]
np ==> [det, adj, •, n]
np ==> [det, adj, n, •]
```

Dotted rules can be understood as indicating how much of a particular rule has been found. For example, the rule np ==> [det, •, adj, n] shows that a determiner has been found with a possible continuation of an adjective followed by a noun. A rule with the dot as the right-most element is said to be **completed**.

The states of the oracle can be thought of as representing the complete set of dotted rules that are appropriate at that stage of the parse. Take state 1. This will include the dotted rule:

```
s ==> [•, np, vp]
```

which says that in this state an s is being sought, although nothing has so far been found, and that an np is expected next. Because an np is predicted next, the various dotted rules for an np also need adding to the state. Since there are only two such rules the complete set for state 1 is:

State 1:
```
        s ==> [•, np, vp]
        np ==> [•, det, n]
        np ==> [•, det, adj, n]
```

This state can now be read as saying that an np is being sought in order to build an s and a determiner in order to build the np.

Transitions to other states are the result of locating the items immediately following the dots. These may be calculated by moving the dot one category to the right for each rule in the set and using this 'seed' rule to derive a new state. For example, doing this to the first dotted rule in state 1 will result in the following state.

State 6:
```
s ==> [np,•, vp]
vp ==> [•, v, np]
```

Note how the dotted vp-rule has been added to the 'seed' rule since the dotted s-rule shows that a vp is a possible continuation of the previously found np. The arc from state 1 to state 6 is labelled with name of the category over which the dot has moved, namely np.

Since both the second and third rules in state 1 have det as the category next to the dot, they are both placed into the same state:

State 2:
```
np ==> [det,•, n]
np ==> [det,•, adj, n]
```

No more dotted rules need adding to this state since there are no phrasal rules with either n or adj as their left-hand side. It is important to note that this state represents a delayed commitment to a particular np-rule. Having found only a determiner, both rules are possible candidates for application. It is only after either a noun or adjective is found next that the relevant states reflect the commitment to one rule or the other.

State 3:
```
np ==> [det, n, •]
```
State 4:
```
np ==> [det, adj, •, n]
```

Note also that, in the completed oracle, the arc from node 7 labelled det also goes to state 2 since the result of moving the dot over det in the rule set of state 7 results in the identical rule set.

Continuing this process of constructing rule sets will eventually result in states which just contain a single completed rule, as in state 3 above. It is these nodes which are represented in the network by square nodes and annotated with the completed rule (minus the dot). Once this process has been reiterated until all possible continuations are completed a final arc is added from the initial node to a final state and labelled with s.

To code the oracle into Prolog the basic predicate action will be used. This takes two forms depending upon whether the action is a shift or reduce move. A shift move will take the general form:

```
action(State, shift, Cat, NewState)
```

where State is the current state, Cat the lexical category to be recognised and NewState the corresponding changed state. Two examples from the exemplar network are shown below.

```
action(1, shift, det, 2).
action(2, shift, n, 3).
```

Reduce moves are coded by facts of the general form:

```
action(State, reduce, Rule)
```

where `State` is the current state and `Rule` the relevant rule for the reduction; for example:

```
action(3, reduce, np ==> [det, n]).
action(5, reduce, np ==> [det, adj, n]).
```

In addition, the new state after the reduction needs specifying. These correspond to those arcs labelled with phrasal categories and will be represented with the predicate `arc`.

```
arc(1, np, 6).
arc(6, vp, 9).
```

To complete the specification, the final state of the network needs declaring.

```
final(10).
```

Since the recognition process is basically a shift-reduce parser, the definitions will follow those used in section 12.3. The two main differences are that before making a move the oracle must be consulted in order to determine the requisite move and the stack is a list of states. The boundary clause for `recognise` checks that all the words of the input have been shifted and the top-most state on the stack is a final state.

```
recognise([State|Stack], []-[]) :-
            final(State).
```

Shift moves are as before except that first `action` is consulted to check that a shift is, indeed, required. If so, the next word is removed if it is of the correct category and then the new state pushed onto the top of the stack.

```
recognise([State|Stack],[Word|String]
String1):-
        action(State, shift, Cat, NewState),
        word(Word, Cat),
        recognise([NewState, State|Stack],
        String-String1).
```

Reduce moves also check the oracle first, which not only indicates that such a move is required but also which rule is to be used for the reduction. The number of categories on the right-hand side of the rule then determines how many states from the top of the stack are to be removed. It is the newly revealed top-most state which is used to check for an arc starting at that state and labelled with the category of the left-hand side of the rule. It is the new state at the end of the phrasal arc which is pushed on to the stack. Separate rules will be used depending on how many categories appear on the right-hand side of the rule.

```
recognise([State1,State|Stack], String-
String1):-
      action(State1, reduce, Cat ==> [Cat1]),
      arc(State, Cat, NewState),
      recognise([NewState,State|Stack], String-
      String1).

recognise([State1,State2,State|Stack], String-
String1) :-
      action(State1, reduce, Cat ==> [Cat1,
      Cat2]),
      arc(State, Cat, NewState),
      recognise([NewState,State|Stack], String-
      String1).

recognise([State1,State2,State3,State|Stack],String-
String1) :-
      action(State1, reduce, Cat ==> [Cat1, Cat2,
      Cat3]),
      arc(State, Cat, NewState),
      recognise([NewState,State|Stack],
      String-String1).
```

Queries to the program, which is listed as shift_or.pl in section 12.8, take the form:

```
?- recognise([1], [most,good,musicians,play,the,
piano]-[]).
   yes
```

Deterministic oracles can only be constructed for unambiguous grammars. For example, a grammar containing the two rules:

```
np ==> [det, n].
np ==> [det, n, pp].
```

would result in a state consisting of the following dotted-rule set:

```
np ==> [det, n, •].
np ==> [det, n, •, pp].
pp ==> [•, p, np].
```

which is both a reduce state (because of the completed rule np ==> [det, n, •]) and a shift state (looking for a p). Besides *shift-reduce* conflicts of this sort, other grammars can give rise to *reduce-reduce* conflicts where the state contains two completed rules.

One way of maintaining determinism in the shift-reduce conflict is to allow the parser to look at the next word of the input before making its decision. In the previous case, if the next word is a preposition, then the parser should perform a shift whilst if something other than a preposition follows, a reduce move is in order. Introducing a **lookahead** facility certainly increases the power of the recognition process but it has its limits. Consider the following grammar which allows structural ambiguity in conjunction with an input sentence such as *The boy hit the soldier with the sword*.

```
s ==> [np, vp].
np ==> [det, n].
np ==> [det, n, pp].
vp ==> [v, np].
vp ==> [v, np, pp].
```

Imagine that the parser has just recognised *soldier* as a noun. At this point, should the parser reduce *the soldier* to an NP and then attach the following PP to the VP or should it shift the rest of the input so that the PP will form a constituent of the NP? Lookahead will be of little use in resolving the shift-reduce conflict in this case.

It might be argued that the shift-reduce conflict should, in fact, not be resolved in the previous example since the sentence is structurally ambiguous. However, it has been claimed that heuristically resolving shift-reduce conflicts in favour of shifting has, at least, one interesting consequence. Take an example from chapter 2.4, *Nicole said Claude left yesterday* and imagine that the parser has just processed *left*. At this point, the parser may either reduce the v to vp (ultimately combining the resulting np *Claude* and vp into an s before attaching the adverb to the vp *said Claude left*), or shift the adverb on to the stack where it will be attached to the vp *left*. Now recall that in chapter 2.4 it was claimed that, in a neutral context, the favoured interpretation of such an utterance is with *yesterday* associated with *left* rather than *said*. It is this parsing preference that is automatically achieved in this case by preferring to shift rather than reduce. Further, in the case of reduce-reduce conflicts it has also been suggested that choosing the rule which uses up the most symbols from the stack results in the same parsing preference illustrated in chapter 2.4 with respect to the example *Richard wanted the necklace for Ruth* where hearers are inclined to attach the pp *for Ruth* to the vp rather than the np. That is, assuming all the string has been scanned and that the stack corresponds to the categories np v np pp, then the parser may either reduce the v np and pp to vp (the preferred reading) or the np and pp to np. Since the former uses up more symbols from the stack, the proposed heuristic will deliver up the preferred reading.

Considerations such as those raised in the previous paragraph are only the beginnings of the development of parsing techniques which will mesh more closely with the human parser. This is of some importance since NLP systems must assign the interpretation of an utterance intended by the user and taking account of parsing preferences is part of this process. At present, this work is still in its infancy although some advances have been made on this front. However, the subject area is fraught with difficulties since parsing preferences are just that, preferences, and various factors may lead to them being over-ridden. In these cases, parsing appears to be a complicated interaction between syntactic, semantic and pragmatic considerations.

Question 12.12

How could we ensure that any shift-reduce conflicts are resolved in favour of shifting?

12.6 Chart Parsing

One of the problems with relying on backtracking to recover from errors in non-deterministic parsing is that the parser forgets everything it has found between the backtracking points. In many cases, investigating other possible rules results in the processor rediscovering previously recognised lexical items or phrases. For example, a top-down recognisor equipped with the following rules:

```
vp ==> [v, np, pp].
vp ==> [v, np, np].
```

might attempt to show that the string *awarded the group a substantial grant* is a vp by using the first rule and recognising *awarded* as a verb and *the group* as an np. However, since *a substantial grant* cannot be analysed as a pp, the processor will be forced to backtrack and attempt to use the second vp-rule. In doing so, the previous results are undone so that the recognisor will be obliged to rediscover that *awarded* is a verb and *the group* an np before finding that *a substantial grant* is an np. As grammars become more complex, such reduplication of effort can become considerable.

One solution to this problem is for the processor to keep a record of any word or phrase it finds so that, if backtracking occurs, a check can be made to ensure that some previously recognised item is not rediscovered. This record is usually referred to as a **chart**. A common way of thinking about a chart is as a network where the nodes (usually referred to as **vertices** in this context) represent the gaps between the words and the arcs (referred to as **edges**) the lexical or phrasal categories of the words spanned by the edge. The following is an example of a chart.

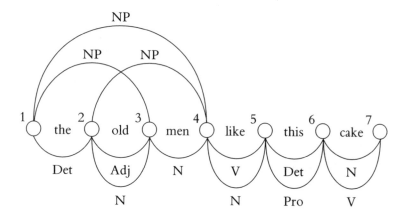

A couple of points are worth making about charts. First, they allow a simple representation of alternative analyses. So, since *old* may be either a noun or an adjective there are two arcs spanning the vertices 2 and 3 labelled *Adj* and *N*, respectively. Similarly, the string of words *the old men* between vertices 1 and 3 may be analysed as constituting an NP or a Det followed by an NP or an NP followed by an N. Secondly, a chart may be used to represent a partial analysis of a string. That is, the previous chart does not represent all the structural information that may be associated with the sentence *The old men like this cake.* As such, charts may be used to represent intermediate analyses during the parsing process. They are also potentially useful for handling ill-formed input such as *This sentence no verb* which cannot be assigned a conventional phrase structure tree but can be associated with a chart.

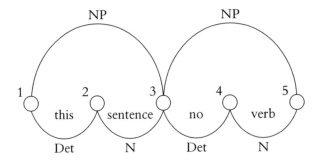

The kind of structural information available from this chart may be sufficient to enable a semantic or pragmatic component to construct some form of interpretation for the string, or, if it is a tutoring program, remedial advice to a learner of English.

The first chart above is unclear on at least one important question: is the edge labelled *NP* that spans *the old men* licensed in virtue of the string consisting of a det-adj-n sequence, an np-n sequence or a det-np sequence? In order to clarify this, edges will be labelled with the rule used to justify the particular analysis. However, rather than use standard phrase structure rules for such labelling, it will prove useful for this purpose to employ completed dotted rules as introduced in the previous section.

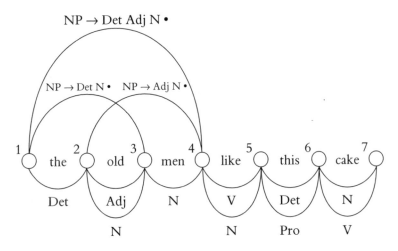

Capitalising on the use of dotted rules, incomplete rules may also be introduced into the chart to represent hypotheses. For example, the following (simplified) chart indicates that the processor has hypothesised that there may be a sentence starting from vertex 1 consisting of an NP followed by a VP, and that an NP has been found between vertices 1 and 4 and that there may be a VP consisting of a verb followed by an NP commencing at vertex 4.

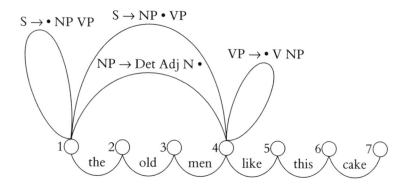

A distinction will be made between **inactive edges** which represent completed analyses – and are labelled with completed dotted rules – and **active edges**, labelled with incomplete dotted rules, which represent incomplete hypotheses. Rules with the dot as the left-most element of the right-hand side are called **empty rules**.

Processing using a chart involves an interaction between active and inactive edges, an interaction which leads to the introduction of a new edge into the chart. These new edges are determined by the **fundamental rule** of chart parsing. Suppose that an active edge spanning vertices i to j meets an inactive edge spanning vertices j to k and that the inactive edge is of the same category as that which occurs immediately to the right of the dot in the dotted rule of the active edge. In such circumstances, the fundamental rule allows the construction of a new edge from point i to k labelled with the previous dotted rule but with the dot moved rightwards over the next category of the right-hand side. For example, consider the following chart.

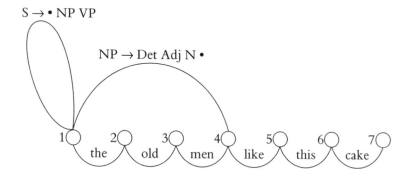

The active edge labelled $S \rightarrow \bullet NP\ VP$ meets the inactive edge labelled $NP \rightarrow Det\ Adj\ N \bullet$ at vertex 1. Consequently, the fundamental rule permits the addition of a new edge from vertex 1 to 4 labelled $S \rightarrow NP \bullet VP$.

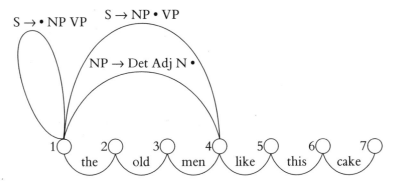

Note that a completely new edge labelled $S \rightarrow NP \bullet VP$ is *added* to the chart rather than relabelling the $NP \rightarrow Det\ Adj\ N \bullet$ arc. This is important since the information that there is an NP between vertices 1 and 4 may be of some use at a later stage in the process if backtracking occurs.

A chart must contain a number of edges before the fundamental rule may apply. An initial set of edges is provided by looking up the lexical category of each word in the input string and adding a completed edge to the chart for each. This process is known as **initialisation**. If a word is ambiguous more than one edge will be added. The following represents the chart after the initialisation of the input string *The old men like this cake*.

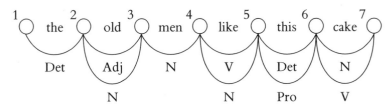

Initialisation is not sufficient to invoke the fundamental rule since it only results in entering inactive edges into the chart. However, active edges can now be added to the chart by keying rules via their left-corner. That is, once an inactive edge has been added to the chart for some category, all rules with that category as the left-corner may be added into the chart as active edges labelled with the relevant empty rule. In these cases, since none of the right-hand side of the rule has been located, the edge will start and finish at the same vertex.

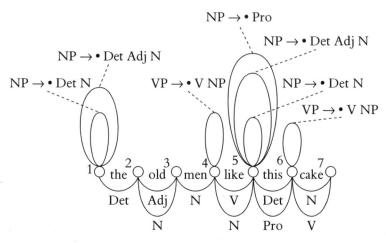

There are now enough active and inactive edges to enable the fundamental rule to be applied. Each time an active edge becomes an inactive edge, new empty active edges are added to the chart if the newly found category is the left-corner of any rule. This process continues until no more edges can be added to the chart. If, at the conclusion, there is an inactive edge for an S spanning the first and last vertices, then a sentence has been successfully recognised.

In order to implement a chart parser in Prolog, edges will be represented by the predicate:

```
edge(Start, End, Cat, Found, ToFind)
```

where Start and End are integers representing the beginning and end of the edge, respectively, Cat the left-hand side category of a rule, Found the categories of the right-hand side of the rule found so far and ToFind the categories still to be found. Found and ToFind are both lists. The following give some examples of the predicate.

```
edge(1, 2, det, [], []).
edge(1, 4, np, [n, det], []).
edge(1, 1, s, [], [np, vp]).
edge(1, 4, s, [np], [vp]).
```

The first and second facts both represent inactive edges; the empty list as fifth argument shows that no more categories are needed for the completion of the category. The first of these inactive edges, since it only identifies a lexical category, also has an empty list as fourth argument since its completion was not dependent upon any intermediate categories. This is not the case with the second inactive edge. Here the extension of the edge is a consequence of there being a determiner followed by a noun between vertices 1 and 4 as indicated. Note that the order of the categories is the reverse of their actual order in the chart. This is a consequence of the way the list is built up during the execution of the program. The third fact is an example of an empty rule where all the categories of the right-hand side of the rule $S \rightarrow NP\ VP$ still need to be found. The fourth fact is an inactive edge equivalent to the dotted rule $S \rightarrow NP \bullet VP$; an NP has been found and a hypothesised VP remains to be dis-covered. As edges are discovered during the recognition process they will be asserted into the Prolog database using the built-in predicate `asserta` introduced in chapter 7.4.

Initialisation will be defined through the predicate `initialise`. This takes a string of words as input and a number to represent the position in the chart. Also included is a result variable similar to that used in section 12.3 in order eventually to record the final vertex in the chart. The boundary clause of the definition is:

```
initialise(Ver, Ver, []).
```

In other words, it succeeds if all the words have been scanned, where the first occurrence of `Ver` is the final vertex. It is this value which is passed to the second argument, the result variable. The recursive part of the definition appears somewhat more complicated.

```
initialise(Ver1, Vern, [Word|RestWords]) :-
    Ver2 is Ver1 + 1,
    foreach(word(Word, Cat),
        add_edge(Ver1, Ver2, Cat, [], [])),
    initialise(Ver2, Vern, RestWords).
```

The first word of the string is taken and, for each of its entries in the lexicon, an (inactive) edge is added to the chart before proceed-ing with the remainder of the string. The first clause of the tail of the definition increments the current vertex, `Ver1`, of the chart by 1 to give `Ver2`. This is achieved using two built-in predicates + – the built-in predicate for arithmetic addition – and `is` – the built-in predicate for the evaluation of arithmetic expressions. `foreach(X, Y)` is defined so as to find each possible means of satisfying `X` (through forced backtracking) and, for each case, car-rying out goal `Y`. The predicate is defined as follows.

```
foreach(X, Y) :-
    X,
    do(Y),
    fail.
foreach(X, Y) :-
    true.
do(X) :-
    X, !
```

Accordingly, the second clause of the tail of `initialise` finds each lexical entry for the particular word, `Word`, and adds an inactive edge to the chart – the fifth argument being the empty list. Because the edge names a lexical category the fourth argument list is also empty.

The definition of `add_edge` fulfils a number of functions. First, the chart must be checked to ensure that the edge to be added does not already exist; if so, nothing further needs to be done.

```
add_edge(Ver1, Ver2, Cat, Found, ToFind) :-
    edge(Ver1, Ver2, Cat, Found, ToFind), !.
```

If the edge does not exist, it needs adding to the chart. Here there are two cases depending on whether the edge to be added is either active or inactive. With respect to inactive edges, the edge – which will have the general form `edge(Ver1, Ver2, Cat, Found, [])` – is first asserted and then for each rule which contains `Cat` as its left-corner, an empty active edge from `Ver1` cycling back to `Ver1` is added to the chart. In addition, for each active edge which (starting at some vertex `Ver0`) ends at `Ver1` and is expecting a `Cat` next, a new edge must be added which spans vertices `Ver0` and `Ver2` with the dot moved one category to the right. This is achieved in our notation by moving the head category from the 'to find' list onto the front of the 'found' list – this is why the categories appear in reverse order in the found list. This latter part of the definition is the fundamental rule.

```
add_edge(Ver1, Ver2, Cat, Found, []) :-
    asserta(edge(Ver1, Ver2, Cat, Found, [])),
    foreach((Cat1 ==> [Cat|Cats]),
            add_edge(Ver1, Ver1, Cat1, [],
            [Cat|Cats])),
    foreach(edge(Ver0, Ver1, Cat1, Found1,
    [Cat|RestCats]),
            add_edge(Ver0, Ver2, Cat1, [Cat|
            Found1], RestCats)).
```

If the edge to be added between vertices `Ver0` and `Ver1` is active, it is first asserted and then any inactive edges starting at `Ver1` which can be combined with the new active edge via the fundamental rule are added.

```
add_edge(Ver0, Ver1, Cat, Found, [Cat1|RestCats]):-
    asserta(edge(Ver0, Ver1, Cat, Found,
    [Cat1|RestCats]),
    foreach(edge(Ver1, Ver2, Cat1, Found1, []),
            add_edge(Ver0, Ver2, Cat, [Cat1|
            Found] RestCats)).
```

The drive predicate for the program will take the form:

```
recognise(String) :-
    initialise(1, Vn, String),
    edge(1, Vn, s, Found, []),
    retractall(edge(_,_,_,_,_)).

recognise(String) :-
    retractall(edge(_,_,_,_,_)).
```

The first part of the definition sets the first vertex at 1 and, after initialisation and when no more rules may be invoked through their left-corners and all applications of the fundamental rule have been made, checks whether there is an inactive edge spanning the first and last vertices labelled s. The final goal removes all the edges asserted during the recognition process. The second rule is simply there to clean up any edges that may have been constructed during an unsuccessful parse. The complete listing for the program is given in section 12.8 as chart.pl.

It is a simple matter to change the recognition process above into a parser by including the structural information in the 'found' argument of edge. The necessary changes are given below.

```
initialise(Ver1, Vern, [Word|RestWords]) :-
    Ver2 is Ver1 + 1,
    foreach(word(Word, Cat),
        add_edge(Ver1, Ver2, Cat,[Word, Cat],
        [])),
    initialise(Ver2, Vern, RestWords).

add_edge(Ver1, Ver2, Cat, Found, []) :-
    asserta(edge(Ver1, Ver2, Cat, Found, [])),
    foreach((Cat1 ==> [Cat|Cats]),
        add_edge(Ver1, Ver1, Cat1, [Cat1],
        [Cat|Cats])),
    foreach(edge(Ver0, Ver1, Cat1, Found1,
    [Cat|Cats]),
        add_edge(Ver0, Ver2, Cat1, [Found|
        Found1], Cats)).

add_edge(Ver0, Ver1, Cat, Found1, [Cat1|Cats]):-
    asserta(edge(Ver0, Ver1, Cat, Found1,
    [Cat1|Cats])),
    foreach(edge(Ver1, Ver2, Cat1, Found, []),
        add_edge(Ver0, Ver2, ,Cat, [Found|
        Found], Cats)).
```

As data objects, charts are compatible with any combination of processing strategy; top-down/bottom-up, depth-first/breadth-first, left-to-right/right-to-left. The process just implemented has been bottom-up, employing as it does a left-corner strategy by keying rules via their left-corner but it is not especially difficult to produce a top-down chart parser using similar techniques. However, as a general approach to chart parsing the techniques implemented in this section are far from ideal. The major problem is the computational inefficiency of `asserta`. As noted in section 7.4, `asserta` is a rather slow operation. This is further compounded since all the asserted clauses have to be removed from the database – using `retractall` another slow predicate – before the next sentence can be recognised. In other words, the potential gains in speed which originally motivated the idea of chart parsing are lost in the particulars of the implementation. In addition, the approach suffers from a certain degree of inflexibility in defining alternative strategies. Certain gains in efficiency may be made by representing the chart as a list of edges which are then passed between the relevant predicates as arguments. Flexibility of control can be gained by placing new edges onto a list, usually called an **agenda**. Different strategies then arise depending on which item is chosen to be pursued next from the agenda.

12.7 Further Reading

King (1983) contains a number of useful tutorial introductions to various issues in syntactic processing as do a number of articles in the *Encyclopedia of Artificial Intelligence* (Shapiro, 1987). Winograd (1983) contains a great deal of detailed information on a variety of parsing techniques as does Allen (1995). Aho and Ullman (1972) and Grune and Jacobs (1990) provide technical presentations of much of this material. The relation between search strategies in general and parsing in particular is discussed in Thornton and du Boulay (1992). Pereira and Shieber (1987), Gazdar and Mellish (1989), Gal *et al.* (1991) and Covington (1994) also have a broad coverage on parsing techniques in relation to various Prolog implementations.

Problems with left-recursive rules for top-down parsers are discussed in Winograd (1983) and Gazdar and Mellish (1989). The particular reworking of the left-recursive rule for np is taken from Gazdar and Mellish (p. 158).

Pereira and Shieber (1987) and Covington (1994) have useful introductions to left-corner parsers. The compiled version of a left-corner parser is based on Matsumoto *et al.* (1983).

Deterministic parsing is discussed in Marcus (1980); see also Sampson (1983) and Thompson and Ritchie (1984) and Stabler

(1983). On oracles and shift-reduce parsing see Briscoe (1987). Technical accounts of this work can be found in Bornat (1979, chapter 18) and Chapman (1987).

Much psychological work on parsing stems from Kimball (1973) and Frazier and Fodor (1978). Introductions to this work can be found in Garnham (1985) and Garman (1990) as well as Moyne (1985), Smith (1991) and Allen (1995); see also Pulman (1987). Discussion of parsing prefences in relation to shift-reduce parsing can be found in Allen (1995) based on work by Shieber (1983) and Pereira (1985).

The implementation of the chart parser in section 12.6 is based on Gazdar and Mellish (1989, chapter 6) which not only contains a lucid introduction to chart parsing but also includes sections on more sophisticated programming techniques; see also Ross (1989). Other tutorial introductions can be found in Winograd (1983), Varile (1983), Thompson and Ritchie (1984) and Allen (1995).

12.8 Program Listings

(1) shift.pl

```
/* **********************************************

NAME: shift.pl

********************************************** */

?- op(1200, xfx, ==>).
?- reconsult('lex.pl').

recognise(String) :-
        config([], String-[]).

config([s], []-[]).

config([Cat2, Cat1| Stack], String-String1) :-
        (Cat ==> [Cat1,Cat2]),
        config([Cat|Stack], String-String1).

config(Stack, [Word|String]-String1) :-
        word(Word, Cat),
        config([Cat|Stack], String-String1).

s ==> [np, vp].
np ==> [det, n].
vp ==> [v, np].

/* ********************************************** */
```

(2) **lc.pl**

```
/* ********************************************

NAME: lc.pl

******************************************** */

?- op(1200, xfx, ==>).
?- reconsult('lex.pl').

recognise(Cat, [Word|String1]-String) :-
          word(Word, Cat1),
          link(Cat1, Cat),
          left_corner(Cat1, Cat, String1-String).

left_corner(Cat, Cat, String-String).

left_corner(Cat1, Cat, String1-String) :-
          (Cat2 ==> [Cat1|Rest]),
          recognise_list(Rest, String1-String2),
          left_corner(Cat2, Cat, String2-String).

recognise_list([], String-String).

recognise_list([Cat|Rest], String1-String) :-
          recognise(Cat, String1-String2),
          recognise_list(Rest, String2-String).

s ==> [np, vp].
np ==> [det, n].
vp ==> [v, np].

link(np, s).
link(det, np).
link(det, s).
link(v, vp).
link(Cat, Cat).

/* ******************************************** */
```

(3) **bup.pl**

```
/* ********************************************

NAME: bup.pl

******************************************** */

?- reconsult('lex.pl').
```

```
recognise(Cat, [Word|String], String1) :-
                word(Word, Cat1),
                link(Cat1, Cat),
                left_corner(Cat1, Cat, String,
                String1).
left_corner(Cat, Cat, String, String).
left_corner(np, Cat, String, String2) :-
                recognise(vp,String, String1),
                left_corner(s, Cat, String1,
                String2).
left_corner(det, Cat, String, String2) :-
                recognise(n, String, String1),
                left_corner(np, Cat, String1,
                String2).
left_corner(v, Cat, String, String2) :-
                down(np, String, String1),
                left_corner(vp, Cat, String1,
                String2).
link(np, s).
link(det, np).
link(det, s).
link(v, vp).
link(Cat, Cat).

/* ***************************************** */
```

(4) shift_or.pl

```
/* *********************************************

NAME: shift_or.pl

********************************************* */
?- op(1200, xfx, ==>).
%Definition of the oracle
action(1, shift, det, 2).
action(2, shift, n, 3).
action(2, shift, adj, 4).
action(4, shift, n, 5).
action(6, shift, v, 7).
action(7, shift, det, 2).
action(3, reduce, np ==> [det, n]).
action(5, reduce, np ==> [det, adj, n]).
action(8, reduce, vp ==> [v, np]).
action(9, reduce, s ==> [np, vp]).
```

```
arc(1, np, 6).
arc(6, vp, 9).
arc(7, np, 8).
arc(1, s, 10).

final(10).

recognise([State|Stack], []-[]) :-
                 final(State).

recognise([State|Stack], [Word|String]-String1) :-
      action(State, shift, Cat, NewState),
      word(Word, Cat),
      recognise([NewState, State|Stack], String-
      String1).

recognise([State1,State|Stack], String-String1) :-
      action(State1, reduce, Cat ==> [Cat1]),
      arc(State, Cat, NewState),
      recognise([NewState, State|Stack], String-
      String1).

recognise([State1,State2,State|Stack], String-
String1) :-
      action(State1, reduce, Cat ==> [Cat1, Cat2]),
      arc(State, Cat, NewState),
      recognise([NewState, State|Stack], String-
      String1).

recognise([State1,State2,State3,State|Stack],String-
String1) :-
          action(State1, reduce, Cat ==> [Cat1,
          Cat2, Cat3]),
          arc(State, Cat, NewState),
          recognise([NewState,     State|Stack],
          String-String1).

/* ********************************************** */


(5) chart.pl

/* **********************************************
NAME: chart.pl

********************************************** */

?- op(1200, xfx, ==>).
?- reconsult('lex.pl').

recognise(String) :-
      initialise(1, Vn, String),
```

```
        edge(1, Vn, s, Found, []),
        ('A sentence has been recognised'), nl,
        retractall(edge(_,_,_,_,_)).
recognise(String) :-
        ('No sentence has been recognised'), nl,
        retractall(edge(_,_,_,_,_)).

initialise(Ver, Ver, []).

initialise(Ver1, Vern, [Word|RestWords]) :-
        Ver2 is Ver1 + 1,
        foreach(word(Word, Cat),
            add_edge(Ver1, Ver2, Cat, [], [])),
            initialise(Ver2, Vern, RestWords).

add_edge(Ver1, Ver2, Cat, Found, ToFind) :-
        edge(Ver1, Ver2, Cat, Found, ToFind), !.

add_edge(Ver1, Ver2, Cat, Found, []) :-
        asserta(edge(Ver1, Ver2, Cat, Found, [])),
        write(edge(Ver1, Ver2, Cat, Found, [])), nl,
        foreach((Cat1 ==> [Cat|Cats]),
            add_edge(Ver1, Ver1, Cat1, [], [Cat|
            Cats])),
        foreach(edge(Ver0, Ver1, Cat1, Found1, [Cat|
        RestCats]),
            add_edge(Ver0, Ver2, Cat1, [Cat|Found1],
            RestCats)).

add_edge(Ver0, Ver1, Cat, Found, [Cat1|RestCats]):-
        asserta(edge(Ver0, Ver1, Cat, Found, [Cat1|
        RestCats])),
        write(edge(Ver0, Ver1, Cat, Found, [Cat1|
        RestCats])), nl,
        foreach(edge(Ver1, Ver2, Cat1, Found1, []),
            add_edge(Ver0, Ver2, Cat, [Cat1|Found],
            RestCats)).

foreach(X, Y) :-
        X,
        do(Y),
        fail.
foreach(X, Y) :-
        true.
do(X) :-
        X, !.
s ==> [np, vp].
np ==> [det, n].
vp ==> [v, np].

/* ******************************************** */
```

Solutions to Exercises

The following appendix offers some solutions to the exercises found in the text. In a number of cases these answers can be no more than suggestions since there are a number of possible alternative solutions.

Chapter 3: Facts

Question 3.1

```
spoken_in(german, austria).
spoken_in(german, switzerland).
spoken_in(french, canada).
spoken_in(french, belgium).
spoken_in(french, switzerland).
spoken_in(spanish, spain).
spoken_in(spanish, canary_islands).
```

Note the use of the underscore in `canary_islands`.

Question 3.2

```
speaks(spooner_bess, english).
speaks(spooner_ben, english).
```

An alternative:

```
speaks(bess_spooner, english).
speaks(ben_spooner, english).
```

Question 3.3

Some examples:

```
word(every, quantifier).
word(gave, verb).
word(under, preposition).
```

```
word(can, noun).
word(can, auxiliary_verb).

word(old, adjective).
word(old, noun).
```

Question 3.4

Some possible ways of expressing the facts.

(1) `language_family(dravidian).`
(2) `language_family(tamil, dravidian).`
(3) `extinct(latin).`
(4) `pidgin(tok_pisin, papua_new_guinea).`
(5) `word(pordo, esperanto, door).`
(6) `word(tante, noun, sing, fem).`
(7) `write_system(kanji, japanese).`
(8) `spoken_in(chamorro, guam, 51000).`

Note that the integer does not include a comma since this would change the predicate from an arity of three to four.

(9) `speaks(mary, warlpiri).`
     `speaks(mary, samoan).`

Note that this needs two facts to express the one sentence.

(10) `plural(ox, oxen).` or
     `word(ox, oxen, noun)`

where the first and second arguments represent the singular and plural forms respectively of the noun.

Question 3.5

(1) Ill-formed because `indo european` contains a space – should be changed to `indo_european`.
(2) Ill-formed since the predicate name `Language` begins with an upper case letter.
(3) Ill-formed since it does not terminate with a full-stop.
(4) Although factually incorrect, a well-formed Prolog expression.
(5) Ill-formed since predicates must not start with an integer.
(6) Well-formed.

Question 3.6

```
daughter_of(anglo_frisian, west_germanic).
daughter_of(high_german, west_germanic).
```

```
daughter_of(low_german, west_germanic).
daughter_of(old_english, anglo_frisian).
daughter_of(old_frisian, anglo_frisian).
daughter_of(german, high_german).
daughter_of(dutch, low_german).
daughter_of(english, old_english).
daughter_of(frisian, old_frisian).
```

Question 3.7

(1) The program does not contain a predicate spokenin – notice that the underscore is missing – with which to match the goal.
(2) The order of arguments – peru, spanish – is reversed in the goal from that in which the information is represented in the facts – spanish, peru.
(3) There are no speaks facts in the program and, hence, nothing to match with.

Question 3.8

(1) yes; since the goal matches with a fact.
(2) no; notice the second argument is biro not piro.
(3) no; there is no fact spoken_in(german, germany) in the program under consideration.
(4) yes; although the first disjunct fails for the same reason as for (3), the second disjunct is satisfied by a match with a fact and, therefore, so is the whole disjunction.
(5) yes; each conjunct is satisfied.

Question 3.9

(1) Swahili = english

Swahili is an ill-chosen variable name; Language would be more appropriate.

(2) Country = peru
(3) English = english
     UK = uk

Again, the variable names are ill-chosen.

(4) _123 = english

Recall that variables may begin with an underscore.

(5) yes; recall that the anonymous variable, _, may be instantiated to different values within a (compound) goal.

Question 3.10

(1)   Same answer.
(2)   Same answer.
(3)   English = english
      UK = australia
      Matches with the first fact.
(4)   Same answer.
(5)   Same answer.

Question 3.11

Make the relationship an argument to a new predicate, say, relation:

```
relation(spoken_in, english, uk).
```

Question 3.13

Example fact:

```
translation(german, berg, mountain).
```

This assumes that the translation is always from some language into English.

Chapter 4: Rules and Complex Names

Question 4.1

```
language(Language) :-
            spokenin(Language, Country).
```

Question 4.2

```
bilingual(Person) :-
            speaks(Person, Language1),
            speaks(Person, Language2),
            not(Language1=Language2).
```

Question 4.3

```
extinct(Language) :-
            language(Language, _, 0).
living(Language) :-
            not(extinct(Language)).
```

Question 4.4

(i) ```
     mother_of(Node1, Node2) :-
                    immediately_dominates(Node1,
                    Node2).
     ```

(ii) ```
     daughter_of(Node1, Node2) :-
                    immediately_dominates(Node2,
                    Node1).
     ```

(iii) ```
      sister_of(Node1, Node2) :-
                    mother_of(Node3, Node1),
                    mother_of(Node3, Node2),
                    not(Node1=Node2).
      ```
or
```
     sister_of(Node1, Node2) :-
                    daughter_of(Node1, Node3),
                    daughter_of(Node2, Node3),
                    not(Node1=Node2).
```

(iv) ```
     root(Node) :-
                not(immediately_dominates(Node1,
                Node)).
     ```

(v) ```
     leaf(Node) :-
                not(immediately_dominates(Node,
                Node1)).
     ```

## Question 4.5

```
subject(np) :-
     immediately_dominates(s, np).
object(np) :-
     immediately_dominates(vp, np).
```

Note that this definition will not work with the definitions in question 4.4 since the NPs are referred to by the constants np1 and np2. Neither matches with np.

Question 4.6

For discussion see chapter 5.2.3

Question 4.7

Note the amount of backtracking required before an answer is found.

Question 4.8

```
speaks(spooner(bess), english).
speaks(spooner(ben), english).
```
```

Question 4.9

Example entry:

```
word(chat, noun(masculine, singular)).
```

Question 4.10

Example entry:

```
word(cyning,  noun(gen(masc),  num(pl),  case
(nom))).
```

Question 4.11

```
immediately_dominates(s, np(1)).
immediately_dominates(vp, np(2)).

subject(np(X)) :-
      immediately_dominates(s, np(X)).

object(np(X)) :-
      immediately_dominates(vp, np(X)).
```

Question 4.12

Use Prolog to check your answers by typing the questions in at the Prolog prompt with the file `example.pl` loaded.

Question 14.12

```
tree(s(np(joe),  vp(v(climbed),  np(det(the),
n(mountain)))))).
```

Chapter 5: Lists and Recursive Rules

Question 5.1

```
spoken_in(english, [uk,usa,australia]).
```

Question 5.2

```
spoken_in(latin, []).

extinct(Language) :-
      spoken_in(Language, []).
```

Question 5.3

```
[[t,h,e], [c,l,i,m,b,e,r], [c,u,t], [t,h,e],
[r,o,p,e]]
```

Be careful that the first *t* is not in upper case since this would then be a variable.

Question 5.4

```
rule(s, [np,vp]).
rule(np, [det,n]).
rule(np, [det,n,pp]).
rule(vp, [v,np]).
rule(pp, [p,np]).
```

Question 5.5

Use Prolog to check your answers by simply typing in the questions at the Prolog prompt. No program need be loaded.

Question 5.6

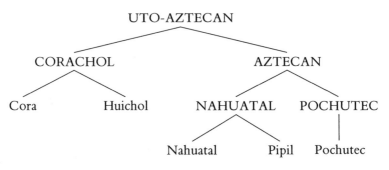

Question 5.7

```
language(Language) :-
     spoken_in(LangList, _),
     member(Language, LangList).
```

Question 5.8

```
belongs(Element, [Element|_]).

belongs(Element, [Head|Tail]):-
   belongs(Element, Head).

belongs(Element, [_|Tail]) :-
   belongs(Element, Tail).
```

The case where the head of the list is a list which is checked for Element.

Question 5.9

Prolog first reply states that spanish could be the head of some list (with the tail unspecified but represented by the variable _23). The second possibility is with spanish as the second element of a list with some head (represented by the variable _22) and with some tail (represented by the variable _27).

Question 5.10

```
subset([], List).

subset([Item|Tail], List) :-
          member(Item, List),
          subset(Tail, List).
```

Question 5.11

```
reply(Input, Output) :-
          member(Word, Input).
          keyword(Word, Output),
```

Some examples of keywords and possible responses.

```
keyword(hello, [hello,how,are,you,?]).
keyword(not, [are,you,sure,about,that,?]).
```

The following rule covers those cases where the sentence does not contain a keyword; the result is non-committal response. This rule must come after the previous one so that only applies after no keywords have been found.

```
reply(Input, Output) :-
          any_response(Output).

any_response([oh, really, ?]).
```

Question 5.12

```
tree(s, tree(np, tree(det,[],[]), tree(n, [],[])),
     tree(vp, tree(v, [], [!),
     tree(np,    tree(det,[],[]), tree(n, [],
     [])))))
```

Question 5.13

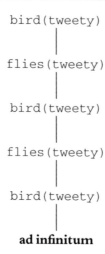

ad infinitum

Question 5.14

```
prefix(Prefix, List) :-
        concat(Prefix, Suffix, List).
suffix(Suffix, List) :-
        concat(Prefix, Suffix, List).
```

Recursive versions:

```
prefix([], List).
prefix([Head|Tail], [Head|Tail1]) :-
    prefix(Tail, Tail1).
suffix(List, List).
suffix(List, [Head|Tail]) :-
    suffix(List, Tail).
```

Question 5.15

```
member(Element, List) :-
        concat(List1, [Element|Tail], List).
```

Question 5.16

```
concat(List1, List2, List3, List4) :-
        concat(List1, List2, List5),
        concat(List5, List3, List4).
```

Question 5.17

```
plural(Singular, Plural) :-
          irregular(Singular, Plural).

plural(Singular, Plural) :-
          noun(Singular, 1),
          concat(Singular, [s], Plural).

plural(Singular, Plural) :-
          noun(Singular, 2),
          concat(Singular, [e,s], Plural).

plural(Singular, Plural) :-
          noun(Singular, 3),
          delete_last(Singular, Singular1),
          concat(Singular1, [i,e,s], Plural).

plural(Singular, Plural) :-
          noun(Singular, 4),
          delete_last(Singular, Singular1),
          concat(Singular1, [v,e,s], Plural).

delete_last([X], []).
delete_last([Head|Tail], [Head|Tail1]) :-
          delete_last(Tail, Tail1).

noun([t,r,e,e], 1).
noun([g,a,s], 2).
noun([s,p,y], 3).
noun([w,o,l,f], 4).

irregular([f,o,o,t], [f,e,e,t]).
irregular([o,x], [o,x,e,n]).
```

Question 5.18

```
(a) last(Item, [Item]).

    last(X, [_|Tail]) :-
            last(Item, Tail).

(b) delete(Item, [], []).

    delete(Item, [Item|Tail], Tail).

    delete(Item, [Head|Tail], [Head|Tail1]) :-
            delete(Item, Tail, Tail1).

(c) delete_all(Item, [], []).

    delete_all(Item, [Item|Tail], Tail1) :-
          delete_all(Item, Tail, Tail1).
```

```
        delete_all(Item, [Head|Tail], [Head|Tail1]) :-
              delete(Item, Tail, Tail1).
```

(d) ```
     replace_all(I, I1, [], []).

     replace_all(I, I1, [I|Tail], [I1|Tail1]) :-
               replace_all(I, I1, Tail, Tail1).

     replace_all(I, I1, [Head|Tail], [Head|Tail1]):-
               replace_all(I, I1, Tail, Tail1).
     ```

(e)  ```
     consec(X, Y, [X,Y|_]).

     consec(X, Y, [_|Tail]) :-
               consec(X, Y, Tail).
     ```

(f) ```
     reverse([], []).

     reverse([Head|Tail], List) :-
               reverse(Tail, List1),
               concat(List1, [Head], List).
     ```

(g)  ```
     palindrome(List) :-
               reverse(List1, List2),
               List = List2.
     ```

(h) ```
     same([],[]).

     same([Head|Tail], List) :-
           member(Head, List),
           delete(Head, List, List1),
           same(Tail, List1).
     ```

## Question 5.19

```
translate([],[]).

translate([Num|Tail], [Word|Tail1) :-
          num(Num, Word),
          translate(Tail, Tail1).

num(1, one).
num(2, two).
```

Question 5.20

```
member_tree(Node, tree(Node, Left, Right)).

member_tree(Node, tree(Node1, Left, Right)) :-
          member_tree(Node, Right).

member_tree(Node, tree(Node1, Left, Right)) :-
          member_tree(Node, Left).
```
```

Chapter 7: Built-in Predicates

Question 7.1

```
go :-
    nl,
    write('Which country are you interested
    in?'),
    nl,
    read(Country), nl,
    spoken_in(Language, Country),
    write(Language), tab(1), write('is spoken
    in'),
    tab(1),
    write(Country), nl.
```

Question 7.2

```
translate(List) :-
    translate(List, TransList),
    display(TransList), nl.

display([]).
display([Item|Tail]) :-
    write(Item), tab(1),
    display(Tail).
```

translate defined as for question 5.19.

Question 7.3

By using the predicate ascci as defined below, Prolog will reply
with the relevant ASCCI code for whichever character you type in
at the |: prompt.

```
ascci :-
    get0(C), nl,
    write(C), nl.
```

Example of interaction:

```
?- go.
|: a
97
yes
```

Question 7.4

See discussion in section 7.6

Question 7.5

```
op(300, xfy, &).
```

Note that the operator is right-associative

```
member(Element, Element & Tail).
member(Element, Head & Tail) :-
      member(Element, Tail).

concat(end, List, List).
concat(Head & Tail, List, Head & List1) :-
      concat(Tail, List, List1).
```

Chapter 8:   Finite State Grammars and Sentence Recognition

Question 8.1

(a)   Yes
(b)   Yes
(c)   Yes
(d)   Yes – although actually ungrammatical. Note that there is no restriction on which verbs may occur in any particular sentence frame. Solution: introduce subcategorisation information into frames and lexical entries: e.g.

      Vi – *vanished*   (i.e intransitive verb)
      Vt – *saw*   (i.e. transitive verb)
      Det N Vi
      Det N Vt Det N

(e)   Yes
(f)   No – no frame *Det N Conj Det N V*
(g)   No – no frame *Pro V Det N Prep Det N*
(h)   Yes – although ungrammatical; no distinction drawn between different subcategories of noun.
(i)   Yes – note that grammatical even if semantically odd.
(j)   Yes – although ungrammatical: no distinction between different case forms of pronouns.

Question 8.2

Examples of lexical facts:

```
word(joshua, n).
word(toward, prep).
```

Examples of sentence frames:

```
frame([n, v, pro]).
frame([pro, v, det, n, conj, det, n]).
```

Question 8.3

Simply add two lexical entries for *old*. No other changes need to be made to program.

```
word(old, adj).
word(old, n).
```

Question 8.4

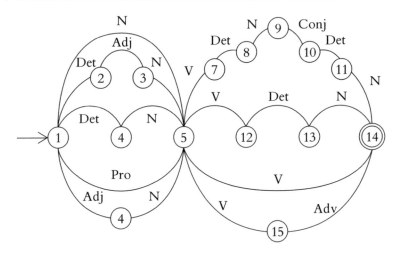

Question 8.5

Det N Vi
PN Vi
Det N Vt PN
PN Vt PN
Det N Vt Det N
PN Vt Det N
Det N Vt Det Adj N
PN Vt Det Adj N

Question 8.6

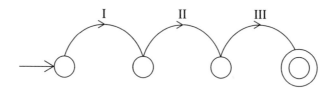

Question 8.7

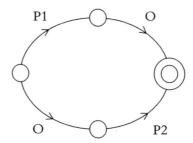

where P1 = {*all, no, more, other*}, P2 = *off* and O = the rest of the lexical items.

Question 8.8

```
initial(1).
final(7).

arc(1, det, 2).
arc(1, pn, 3).
arc(2, n, 3).
arc(3, vi, 7). etc.
```

Question 8.9

No: the names are only a means of distinguishing between different nodes. The numerical ordering usually used is simply a question of convenience.

Question 8.10

Compare the number of sentence frame facts that need stating with the number of arc facts for particular grammars.

Question 8.11

```
config([], 4).
```

Question 8.12

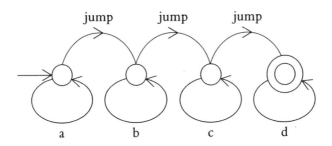

Question 8.13

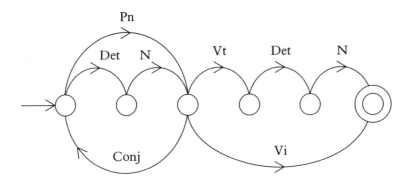

Question 8.14

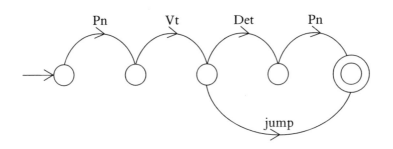

Question 8.15

Sentence frames represented with predicate cat taking a lexical category as argument and, if relevant, a star.

```
frame([cat(det), cat(adj, *), cat(n), cat(v)]).
```

String S recognised as a sentence if it can be matched to a sentence frame.

```
sentence(S) :-
     frame(SF),
     match(S, SF).
```

Matching is recursive, pairing off each word with a category from the sentence frame list.

```
match([], []).
match([Word|RestWords], [cat(Cat)|RestCats]) :-
                word(Word, Cat),
                match(RestWords, RestCats).
```

If the category of the word is starred then move on to the next word but stay in the same place in the sentence frame list in case another word of this category comes next.

```
match([Word|RestWords],[cat(Cat,*)|RestCats]):-
          word(Word, Cat),
          match(RestWords, [cat(Cat, *)|
          RestCats]).
```

If the head of the sentence frame list is a starred category and the next word is not of that category, then stay in the same place in the string list but move on a category.

```
match(Words, [cat(Cat, *)|RestCats]) :-
          match(Words, RestCats).
```

Question 8.16

```
sentence([Word|String]) :-
     recognise([Word|String], 1, Word).
```

recognise includes a third argument which is a record of the last word recognised. First part of the definition as normal.

```
recognise([], State, Word) :-
     final(State).
recognise([Word|String], State, Word1) :-
     word(Word, Cat),
     arc(State, Cat, State1),
     recognise(String, State1, Word).
```

This clause is added when the process breaks down. Then next arc is found and a report of a potential continuation is printed to screen.

```
recognise(String, State, Word) :-
    arc(State, Cat, State1),
    write('a '), write(Cat), write(' should
    follow: '),
    write(Word).
```

Chapter 9: Recursive Transition Networks

Question 9.1

As long as some limit is placed on n – say, no bigger than 5 – it is possible to write an FSTN for this language; it will look something like a ladder as the following shows.

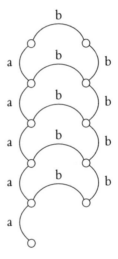

However, if n may be any number, then it is not possible to express as a FSTN since the corresponding diagram would need to have an infinite number of 'rungs' which, clearly, is not possible.

Question 9.2

PP

Question 9.3

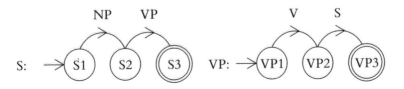

Question 9.4

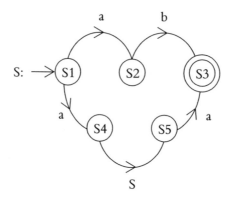

Question 9.7

```
config(s:3, [], []).

config(Network:State, String, Stack) :-
      arc(Network, State, Network1, State1),
      config(Network1:1, String, [Network:
      State1|Stack]).
```

The 'pop' rule could be partially evaluated in our example to:

```
config(Network:3,  String,  [Network1:State1|
Stack]) :-
      config(Network1:State, String, Stack).
```

because 3 is the final state of each network. However, in general this will not be the case and then partial evaluation will not be possible.

Question 9.8

```
config(Network:State, String, Stack) :-
      arc(Network, State, jump, State1),
      config(Network:State1, String, Stack).
```

Question 9.9

See discussion immediately following in section 9.5.

Question 9.10

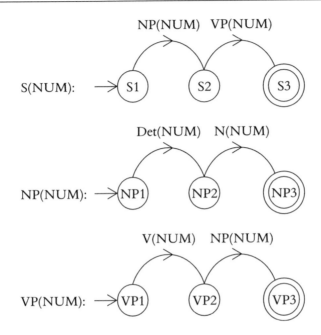

S(NUM): → S1 —NP(NUM)→ S2 —VP(NUM)→ S3

NP(NUM): → NP1 —Det(NUM)→ NP2 —N(NUM)→ NP3

VP(NUM): → VP1 —V(NUM)→ VP2 —NP(NUM)→ VP3

Chapter 10: Phrase Structure Grammars

Question 10.1

```
rule(s, [np, vp]).
rule(np, [det, n]).
rule(np, [det, n, pp]).
rule(det, [poss_np]).
rule(vp, [v, np]).
rule(pp, [p, np]).
```

The recognition procedure will not pick out either of the rules
rule(np, [det, n, pp]) or rule(det, [poss_np]) because the
call to rule in the definition of config requires that the list which
forms the second argument consist of two elements. The next
question addresses this problem.

Question 10.2

```
config([Cat|RestCats], String) :-
    rule(Cat, [Cat1]),
    config([Cat1|RestCats], String).
```

```
config([Cat|RestCats], String) :-
     rule(Cat, [Cat1, Cat2, Cat3]),
     config([Cat1, Cat2, Cat3|RestCats],
     String).
```

The general rule picks up a rule with a right-hand side category list
Cats and concatenates this list to the front of RestCats:

```
config([Cat|RestCats], String) :-
     rule(Cat, Cats),
     concat(Cats, RestCats, Cats1),
     config(Cats1, String).
```

Question 10.3

```
s(X) :-                          np(X) :-
    concat(Y, Z, X),                 concat(Y, Z, X),
    np(Y),          ,                det(Y)
    vp(Z).                           n(Z).

vp(X) :-                         pp(X) :-
    concat(Y, Z, X),                 concat(Y, Z, X),
    v(Y),                            p(Y),
    np(Z).                           np(Z).

det(X) :-
    poss_np(X).

np(X) :-
    concat(Y, Z, X),     concat is used twice to split
    concat(V, W, Y),     list into three sublists V, W
    det(V),              and Z
    n(W),
    pp(Z).
```

Question 10.4

It does not change the declarative meaning but it does change the
procedural meaning from a left-to-right to a right-to-left strategy.

Question 10.5

```
(1)   [the rain]
(2)   [the]
(3)   [walks]
(4)   [walks, slowly]
(5)   []
(6)   [simon, cut, the, rope]
(7)   []
```

Question 10.6

```
concat_dl(A-B, B-C, C-D, A-D).
```

Question 10.7

```
s(A-C) :-                np(A-C) :-
      np(A-B),                 det(A-B),
      vp(B-C).                 n(B-C).

vp(A-C) :-               pp(A-C) :-
      v(A-B),                  p(A-B),
      np(B-C).                 np(B-C).

det(A-B) :-
      poss_np(A-B).

np(A-D) :-
      det(A-B),
      n(B-C),
      pp(C-D).
```

Question 10.8

```
np(A, C) :-              vp(A, D) :-
      det(A, B),               v(A, B),
      n(B, C).                 np(B, C),
                               pp(C, D).

n([mountain|A], A).

rel_clause([that|A], B) :-
      vp(A, B).
```

Chapter 11: Definite Clause Grammars

The following solutions are not intended to be optimal in that no attempt is made to integrate all the various constructions into one consistent set of rules. Each is simply a potential solution to the individual question.

Question 11.1

```
s(L1, L3) :-
      np(Num, L1, L2),
      vp(Num, L2, L3).
```

```
np(Num, L1, L3) :-
      def(Num, L1, L2),
      n(Num, L2, L3).
v(plur, [likes|Rest], Rest).
```

Question 11.2

Because the variable Num appears as argument to each predicate, the rule incorrectly requires that the object NP agree with the verb with respect to number. The argument to np should be changed to something such as Num1.

Question 11.3

The determiner *the* is neutral with respect to number – it can either be singular (*the man*) or plural (*the men*). The anonymous variable is used since it can stand for either value.

Question 11.4

Standard rule for s but introducing person-argument Person to np and vp.

```
s --> np(Person, Number), vp(Person, Number).
```

Standard rules for np and vp but including Person argument which is passed to pronoun and v.

```
np(Person, Number) --> pronoun(Person, Number).
vp(Person, Number) --> v(Person, Number), adj.
```

Lexical entries for the various pronouns including person and number arguments.

```
pronoun(1, sing) --> [i].
pronoun(1, plur) --> [we].        Note anonymous vari-
pronoun(2, _) --> [you].          able since same form
pronoun(3, sing) --> [he].        for singular and plural.
pronoun(3, plur) --> [they].
```

Lexical entries for copular *be* including person and number arguments.

```
v(1, sing) --> [am].
v(_, plur) --> [are].             Note anonymous variable since
v(2, sing) --> [are].             plural form same for each person.
v(3, sing) --> [is].
```

Example of lexical entry for an adjective (no agreement features included).

```
adj --> [happy].
```

Question 11.5

The np-rules: each lexical category – det, adj and n – includes a gender argument Gen. Note that the adjectives also include a sub-categorisation argument – either 1 or 2 – to distinguish between those that appear before the noun – value 1 – and those that follow the noun – value 2.

```
np --> det(Gen), adj(1, Gen), n(Gen).
np --> det(Gen), n(Gen), adj(2, Gen).
```

The lexical entries for determiners including the gender argument: either masc or fem.

```
det(masc) --> [le].   det(fem) --> [la].
det(masc) --> [un].   det(fem) --> [une].
```

Lexical entries for adjectives including subcategorisation argument – 1 or 2 – and gender argument.

```
adj(1, masc) --> [beau]. adj(1, fem) --> [belle].
adj(2, masc) --> [gris]. adj(2, fem) --> [grise].
```

Lexical entries for nouns including gender argument.

```
n(masc) --> [timbre].  n(fem) --> [porte].
```

Question 11.6

Standard s-rule with agreement features.

```
s --> np(Agr), vp(Agr).
```

Rule introducing predicate np. Note that its agreement value Agr is the same as that for the verb (and, hence, the vp as a whole).

```
vp(Agr) --> v(pred, Agr), pred_np(Agr).
```

Somewhat simplistic rules defining a predicate nominal.

```
pred_np(sing) --> [a], n(sing).
pred_np(plur) --> n(plur).
```

Exemplar rules introducing copular *be.*

```
v(pred, sing) --> [is].
v(pred, plur) --> [are].
```

Question 11.7

s-rule which fixes subject np has having the case value nom.

```
s --> np(nom), vp.
```

vp-rule which fixes the object np as having the value acc.

```
vp --> v, np(acc).
```

np-rule which ensures the case value of the np is passed to the pronoun.

```
np(Case) --> pronoun(Case).
```

Exemplar lexical entries for the pronouns including case argument.

```
pronoun(nom) --> [i].   pronoun(acc) --> [me].
pronoun(nom) --> [he].  pronoun(acc) -->[him].
```

Question 11.8

```
s --> np(Agr), vp(Agr).
np(Agr) --> det(Agr), n(Agr).
vp(Agr) --> v(intrans, Agr).
vp(Agr) --> v(trans, Agr), np(Agr1).

det(sing) --> [every].
n(plur) --> [singers].
v(intrans, sing) --> [smiles].
v(trans, plur) --> [play].
```

Question 11.9

Some examplar vp-rules.

```
vp --> v(1).
vp --> v(2), np.
vp --> v(3), np, pp.
vp --> v(4), pp(from).
vp --> v(5), pred_np.
```

See question 11.10 for more details on this.

Some examplar lexical entries for verbs.

```
v(1) --> [ate].
v(2) --> [ate].
v(3) --> [put].
v(4) --> [detract].
v(5) --> [became].
```

Question 11.10

Rule for vp introducing np and pp complements. The pp includes
a preposition argument Prep which will be used to ensure pp is of
the correct form as determined by the particular dative verb chosen.

```
vp --> v(dative, Prep), np, pp(Prep).
```

Rule for pp which passes the Prep argument to the p.

```
pp(Prep) --> p(Prep), np.
```

Lexical rules for dative verbs. Entry includes subcategorisation argument and a preposition argument which is used to ensure pp of the
correct form – i.e. one headed by *to* or *for*.

```
v(dative, to) --> [gave].
v(dative, for) --> [caught].
```

Lexical entries for prepositions. A preposition with a to argument
is realised as *to*; similarly for for.

```
p(to) --> [to].
p(for) --> [for].
```

Question 11.11

vp-rule which states that consists of v followed by some comps as
determined by the particular verb chosen (represented by the argument Comps).

```
vp --> v(Comps), comps(Comps).
```

The recursive definition of comps. Boundary condition first: if no
-complements in the complement list then no need to find anything.

```
comps([]) --> [].
```

Recursive part of definition. If complement list is not empty, first find head complement and then proceed to find whatever remains in the complement list.

```
comps([Comps|RestComps]) --> comp(Comps),
comps(RestComps).
```

To find a complement np simply find an np. Similary for pp.

```
comps(np) --> np.
comps(pp) --> pp.
```

Question 11.12

s-rule. Subject np has a subject selection restrictions argument SubSR which is the same as that on the vp.

```
s --> np(SubSR), vp(SubSR).
```

The subject selectional restrictions SubSR on the vp are determined by the particular verb heading the vp and which are part of the verb's lexical entry. The lexical entry will also include selectional restrictions (ObjSR) for any object np that is subcategorised for and these restrictions will be passed to the object np.

```
vp(SubSR) --> v(intrans, SubSR).
vp(SubSR) --> v(trans, SubSR, ObjSR), np(ObjSR).
```

The subject selectional restrictions SubSR may be determined by an adjective if the vp is headed by copular *be*.

```
vp(SubSR) --> v(cop), adj(SubSR).
```

Rule for np which associates selectional restrictions with head noun.

```
np(SR) --> det, n(SR).
```

Exemplar lexical entries for verbs including subcategorisation and selectional restriction arguments. If intransitive then only subject selectional restrictions.

```
v(intrans, human) --> [prayed].
```

If transitive, then subject and object selectional restrictions. Anonymous variable used if no restrictions imposed on a particular position.

```
v(trans, _, animate) --> [frightened].
v(trans, animate, _) --> [admired].
v(trans, human, human) --> [married].
```

Lexical entries for adjectives including selectional restrictions imposed on subject np.

```
adj(female) --> [pregnant].
adj(animate) --> [dead].
```

Lexical entries for nouns with their semantic classification.

```
n(female) --> [woman].
n(human) --> [woman]
n(animate) --> [woman]
```

Question 11.13

Some examples.

```
v(fin(pres), sing) --> [takes].
v(fin(pres), plur) --> [take].
v(fin(past), _) --> [took].

v(fin(pres), _) --> [can].
v(fin(past), _) --> [could].
v(fin(pres), sing) --> [is].
v(fin(pres), plur) --> [are].
v(fin(past), sing) --> [was].
v(fin(past), plur) --> [were].
```

Question 11.14

Some examples.

```
aux(fin(pres)-base) --> [will].
aux(fin(past)-base) --> [would].

aux(fin(pres)-past_part) --> [has].
aux(fin(past)-past_part) --> [had].
aux(base-past_part) --> [have].

aux(fin(pres)-pres_part) --> [is].
aux(fin(past)-pres_part) --> [was].
aux(base-pres_part) --> [be].
aux(past_part-pres_part) --> [been].
```

```
v(fin(pres)) --> [bakes].
v(fin(pres)) --> [bake].
v(fin(past)) --> [baked].
v(base) --> [bake].
v(pres_part) --> [baking].
v(past_part) --> [baked].
```

Question 11.15

Standard s-rule.

```
s --> np, vp(fin(V)).
```

s-rule which passes a subcategorisation tense value Value (to be introduced as part of the subcategorisation requirements of verbs marked as 2 below) to the vp.

```
s(Value) --> np, vp(Value).
```

Standard vp-rule with auxiliaries.

```
vp(Value) --> aux(Value-Require), vp(Require).
```

vp-rules imposing various restrictions on the complements of certain verbs distinguished by a subcategorisation argument represented by a numeral.

```
vp(Value) --> v(Value, 1), np.
vp(Value) --> v(Value, 2), s(fin(Value1)).
vp(Value) --> v(Value, 3), that_c(base).
vp(Value) --> v(Value, 4), for_c.
vp(Value) --> v(Value, 4), vp(inf).
vp(Value) --> v(Value, 5), adjp.
```

Rule defining clauses headed by that.

```
that_c(Value) --> [that], s(Value).
```

Rule defining clauses headed by *for*; note that the following s is infinitival.

```
for_c --> [for], s(inf).
```

Rules introducing adjectival phrases with range of complements.

```
adjp --> adj(1), s(fin(Val)).
adjp --> adj(2), that_c(base).
```

```
adjp --> adj(3), for_c.
adjp --> adj(3), vp(inf).
```

Exemplar lexical entries for verbs.

```
v(fin(past), 1) --> [saw].
v(base, 1) --> [see].
v(fin(pres), 2) --> [believe].
v(fin(pres), 3) --> [require].
v(fin(pres), 4) --> [prefers].
v(fin(pres), 5) --> [is].
```

Exemplar lexical entries for adjectives.

```
adj(1) --> [confident].
adj(2) --> [insistent].
adj(3) --> [eager].
```

Question 11.16

Standard rules for s and vp.

```
s --> np, vp(fin(V)).
vp(Form) --> aux(Form-Require), vp(Require).
```

Next rules introduce passive vps which are always headed by past participle verb; first rule is with transitive verb (but note is missing following np usually required of transitive verbs)

```
vp(passive) --> v(past_part, trans).
```

Next two rules added to show dative verb.

```
vp(passive) --> v(past_part, dative), np.
vp(passive) --> v(past_part, dative), pp(to).
```

These two rules are for non-passive vps fulfilling standard sub-categorisation requirements.

```
vp(Form) --> v(Form, trans), np.
vp(Form) --> v(Form, dative), np, pp(to).
```

Examples of standard lexical rules for auxiliaries.

```
aux(fin(pres)-base) --> [can].
aux(fin(pres)-past_part) --> [has].
aux(fin(pres)-pres_part) --> [is].
```

Lexical rules introducing passive participle of *be* requiring a following passive vp.

```
aux(fin(pres)-passive) --> [is].
aux(fin(past)-passive) --> [was].
aux(past_part-passive) --> [been].
aux(base-passive) --> [be].
aux(pres_part-passive) --> [being].
```

Examples of standard lexical rules for main verbs.

```
v(past_part, trans) --> [hit].
v(fin(past), trans) --> [hit].
v(past_part, dative) --> [given].
v(pres_part, dative) --> [giving].
```

Question 11.17

Some examples:

```
np(np(PN)) --> pn(PN).
np(np(Det, Adj, N)) --> det(Det), adj(Adj), n(N).
vp(vp(V, S)) --> v(V), s(S).

pn(pn(john)) --> [john].
adj(adj(small)) --> [small].
```

Question 11.18

```
s(s(NP, VP)) --> np(NP), vp(VP, fin(Val)).

np(np(Pro)) --> pronoun(Pro).
np(np(N)) --> mass_n(N).
vp(vp(Aux, VP), Form) --> aux(Aux, Form-Require),
                          vp(VP, Require).
vp(vp(V), Form) --> v(V, Form).
vp(vp(V, NP), Form) --> v(V, Form), np(NP).

mass_n(n(fish)) --> [fish].
pronoun(pro(they)) --> [they].

v(v(can), fin(pres)) --> [can].
v(v(fish), base) --> [fish].
aux(aux(can), fin(pres)-base) --> [can].
```

Question 11.19

For the first two examples, recall that a PP may attach either as part of an NP or a VP. [See section 2.2 for some discussion and phrase structure trees.] For the third example, note that the two relevant analyses are [*her*] [*wet dog biscuits*] and [*her wet dog*] [*biscuits*].

Question 11.20

The gap information has to be included on the vp clause so as to match up with the definition of vp.

```
ind_ques --> wh_pro, vp(GapInfo).
```

Question 11.21

Examples:

```
ind_ques --> wh_p, vp(GapInfo).
ind_ques --> wh_p, s(gap(np)).

wh_p --> wh_pro(who)                    rc stands for rel-
wh_p --> wh_pro(which), n.              ative clause – see
wh_p --> wh_pro(which), n, rc.          question 11.25

wh_pro(who) --> [who].
wh_pro(which) --> [which].
```

Question 11.22

```
vp(GapInfo) --> v, np(GapInfo), pp(nogap).
vp(GapInfo) --> v, np(nogap), pp(GapInfo).

pp(GapInfo) --> p, np(GapInfo).
```

Question 11.23

```
vp(GapInfo) --> v, s(GapInfo).
```

Question 11.24

```
ind_ques --> wh_pro, s(gap(np)).

s(GapInfo) --> np(GapInfo), vp(nogap).
s(GapInfo) --> np(nogap), vp(GapInfo).
```

Question 11.25

```
np --> det, n, rc.
rc --> wh_pro, vp(nogap).
rc --> wh_pro, s(gap(np)).
```

Question 11.26

```
s --> neg_adv, aux(fin(Value)-Required), np,
vp(Required).

neg_adv --> [rarely].
```

Question 11.27

```
pronoun(i, me, my).
pronoun(you, you, your).
pronoun(he, him, his).

pronoun(nom) --> [Word], {pronoun(Word, _, _)}.
pronoun(acc) --> [Word], {pronoun(_, Word, _)}.
pronoun(gen) --> [Word], {pronoun(_, _, Word)}.
```

Question 11.28

```
v(pres_sing) --> [Word], {v(Word, _, _, _, _)}.
v(pres_plur) --> [Word], {v(_, Word, _, _, _)}.
v(past) --> [Word], {v(_, _, Word, _, _, _)}.
v(past_part) --> [Word], {v(_, _, _, Word, _, _)}
v(pres_part) --> [Word], {v(_, _, _, _, Word, _)}.
v(base) --> [Word], {v(_, _, _, _, _, Word)}.

v(takes, take, took, taken, taking, take).
v(tries, try, tried, tried, trying, try).
```

Question 11.29

All functors must start with a lower case letter; starting with a numeral is not possible.

Question 11.30

np-rule with agreement. Note that the agreement value of np, Num, is the intersection of the values for the det and n.

```
np(Num) --> det(Num1), n(Num2),
               {intersect(Num1, Num2, Num),
                   not(Num = [])}.
```

Exemplar lexical entries for determiners and nouns.

```
det([sing]) --> [every].
n([sing]) --> [climber].
```

Note that a determiner such as *the* will be associated with both singular and plural; similarly with a noun such as *sheep*.

```
det([sing, plur]) --> [the].
n([sing, plur]) --> [sheep].
```

Question 11.31

Part of (a simplistic) answer:

```
s --> np(Num), vp(Num),
          {write('Well done'), nl}.

s --> np(Num), vp(Num1),
          {write('You have the wrong agreement
          between
          subject and verb'), nl}.
```

Chapter 12: Alternative Parsing Strategies

Question 12.1

Assuming that the rules are expressed in the form:

```
s ==> [np(Num), vp(Num)]
word(men, n(plur)).
```

no change is necessary to the recognition procedure.

Question 12.2

Simply add parse arguments to the grammar rules and lexical facts:

```
s(s(NP, VP)) ==> [np(NP), vp(VP)].
word(men, n(n(men))).
```

As with 12.1, no further changes need to be made. Questions to the program take the form:

```
recognise(s(Parse), [every,child,booed,the,
villain]-[]).
```

Question 12.3

Reverse the order in which the categories on the right-hand side of the rule are searched for:

```
recognise(Cat, String-String1) :-
     (Cat ==> CatList),
     reverse(CatList, CatList1),
     recognise_list(CatList1, String-String1).
```

In order for this to work, the original string of words also needs reversing which can be done through a drive predicate.

```
recognise(String) :-
          reverse(String, String1),
          recognise(s, String1-[]).
```

Question 12.4

```
recognise([Cat1|Stack], String-String1) :-
          (Cat ==> [Cat1]),
          recognise([Cat|Stack], String-
          String1).

recognise([Cat3, Cat2, Cat1|Stack], String-
String1) :-
          (Cat ==> [Cat3, Cat2, Cat1]),
          recognise([Cat|Stack], String-
          String1).
```

Question 12.5

```
recognise(Stack, [Word|String]-String1) :-
          word(Word, Cat),
          concat(Stack, [Cat], Stack1),
          recognise(Stack1, String-String1).
```

Question 12.6

```
link(np, s).
link(det, np)
link(pn, np).
link(det, s).
link(pn, s).
link(v, vp).
link(advp, vp).
link(adv, advp).
link(intensifier, advp).
link(adv, vp).
link(intensifier, vp).
link(p, pp).
link(Cat, Cat).
```

Question 12.7

```
left_corner(pn, Cat, String1-String) :-
    left_corner(np, Cat, String1-String).

left_corner(det, Cat, String1-String) :-
    recognise(n, String1-String2),
    recognise(pp, String2-String3),
    left_corner(np, Cat, String3-String).
```

Question 12.9

As usual, add parse arguments to each grammar rule and lexical statement:

```
s(s(NP,VP)) ==> [np(NP), vp(VP)].
word(the, det(det(the))).
```

The only additional change (except for changing the predicate recognise to parse) is with the link facts which must also take this extra argument into account; for example:

```
link(np(_), s(_)).
```

Questions to the program take the form:

```
?-  parse(s(Parse),    [the,children,booed,the
villain]-[]).
```

Question 12.10

Include a parse argument in the definitions of left_corner as exemplified by:

```
left_corner(np(NP), Cat, String1-String):-
    recognise(vp(VP), String1-String2),
    left_corner(s(s(NP,VP)), Cat, String2-
    String).
```

link facts also need changing as for Question 12.9.

Question 12.12

Place the shift definition before that for reduction in the program.

Glossary of Terms

The following glossary covers various technical terms used in the text. Those entries marked with an asterisk refer to their specialised Prolog meaning.

Adjective: a class of words typically referring to properties or states which modify nouns or as the complement of the copular form of *be*. Examples: *The **small** man, Mary is **happy***.

Adverb: a class of words typically referring to the manner or time of an action which modify verbs. Examples: *Mary will be happy **soon**, The man walked **loudly** into the room*.

Agreement: a relationship between two items where one item requires the other to be in a particular form. Example: number agreement *The man* (singular) *smiles* (singular), *The men* (plural) *walk* (plural).

Ambiguous: an expression with more than one meaning.

Anonymous variable*: a special variable, represented by the underscore _, which counts as a 'don't care' variable. No value is output to screen once the variable has become instantiated to a value. Each use of the anonymous variable, even within the same clause, represents a new use and so need not be assigned the same value.

Assembler language: a low-level programming language which uses mnemonics instead of instructions expressed in the binary code of machine language.

Argument*: the names of the objects to which a predicate or function applies. The arguments appear between round brackets following the functor. For example, queen(england) and english are the arguments of the predicate speaks and england the argument of the function queen in the clause speaks(queen(england), english).

Arity*: the number of arguments taken by a predicate. For example, a binary predicate requires two arguments and a ternary predicate three. Unary predicates (one argument) are sometimes referred to as **properties**.

Artificial Intelligence: a term used to describe computer programs designed to perform tasks usually associated with human intelligence. Included in this is the ability to be able to understand natural language.

ASCII (pronounced 'askey'): short for American Standard Code for Information Interchange, ASCII is a numeric code for the various characters (letters, numerals and some special symbols) used to facilitate the transfer of information between different machines and programs.

Atom★: a string of letters, numerals and the underscore starting with a lower-case letter, or a string of special characters such as `-->` or any string of characters enclosed in single quotes. Examples: `john`, `spoken_in`, `013`, `'jiff strutt'`.

Automaton: an abstract computing device.

Auxiliary verb: verb accompanying a main verb used to express such distinctions as mood, aspect, and voice. Examples; *do, shall, may, can, will, have, be.*

Backtrack★: the process by which the Prolog interpreter retraces its steps to try alternative unconsidered possibilities whilst trying to satisfy a goal.

Base condition★: see *Recursive.*

Binary code: a coding system in which data is encoded as a series of 0s and 1s.

Body★: a term used to refer to the literals appearing to the right of : - in a rule. The body represents the **conditions** that must be satisfied for the head of the rule to be satisfied.

Bottom-up strategy: see *Search strategy.*

Bound★: see *Instantiate.*

Breadth-first strategy: see *Search strategy.*

Bridging assumptions: assumptions constructed from general knowledge used to establish the interpretation of referential expressions within a text. For example, because computers have keyboards we interpret *the keyboard* as the keyboard of the computer mentioned in the first sentence in *Ned likes this computer. However, the keyboard is not well-built.*

Built-in predicate★: a predicate pre-defined as part of the particular Prolog system being used. Often such predicates permit Prolog to behave in ways which would not be possible using 'pure' Prolog.

Call★: in attempting to satisfy a goal, the Prolog interpreter is said to call (or **invoke**) the relevant procedure.

Case: classification of different forms of noun depending on whether they are functioning as, say, the subject or object of a clause. In English the main contrast is between pronouns. *He* (nominative) *likes her* (accusative) vs. *She* (nominative) *likes him* (accusative).

Chart: a record of any words or phrases already located during the recognition or parsing process.

Clause★: a joint term used to refer to facts or rules.

Closed world assumption★: Prolog draws its inferences on the basis that the current program represents the only relevant source of information. Consequently, anything not recorded in the program is assumed not to be true.

Code: refers both to the act of writing a computer program in some programming language (in the sense of encode) and the resulting program.

Competence: a term used to refer to a speaker's (unconscious) knowledge of his or her language.

Compiler: a computer program which translates program statements from one form to another. For example, a compiler may convert instructions written in assembler language into machine code.

Compositionality: the idea that the meaning of a complex expression is a function of the meaning of its individual parts and the way they are syntactically combined.

Compound names★: complex terms consisting of a function symbol and some number of arguments.

Compound query★: a Prolog query consisting of more than one goal (each separated from the others by a comma, ,) each of which must be satisfied if the whole is to be satisfied.

Computer-aided instruction: the use of computers to facilitate the acquisition of knowledge in various domains.

Computational linguistics: see *Natural language processing*.

Condition★: see *Body*.

Conjunction: small class of words used to connect constructions. Examples: *and, or, but*.

Constant★: the name of a specific object or predicate. May be either an atom or numeral. Examples: speaks, john, 431.

Content scanning: a program designed to automatically analyse texts for their content.

Context (of utterance): those aspects of the situation of utterance which help determine its meaning. Context covers numerous factors such as the participants involved in the interchange, the temporal and spatial situation of the utterance, the immediately preceding utterances in the conversation, encyclopaedic knowledge, as well as the beliefs and intentions of the participants.

Cut★: a special symbol, ! , which prevents further backtracking from the cut.

Database: a store of information. In a computer database, the data is organised so that a program called a **database management system** can access and manipulate this information. The language in which the commands of the database management system are expressed is known as a **database query language**.

Debugging: the process of detecting, diagnosing and then correcting errors (known as **bugs**) in a computer program.

Declarative knowledge: typically described as knowledge *that* something is the case.

Declarative programming language: a programming language in which the programmer declares certain facts and rules about a domain from which the interpreter attempts to draw relevant conclusions.

Depth-first strategy: see *Search strategy*.

Determiner: class of words occurring with nouns often expressing notions of number or quantity. Examples: *a, the, this, some, many, every, two*.

Deterministic: a procedure in which there are no choices about how to continue at any point during the process.

Difference List★: a means of encoding a list in terms of two lists.

Disjunctive query★: a Prolog query consisting of more than one goal (each separated from the others by a semi-colon, ;), one of which must be satisfied for the whole to be satisfied.

Dotted rule: a phrase structure rule augmented with a dot on the right-hand side of the arrow. For example: $NP \rightarrow Det \bullet N$ represents the case where, in seeking an NP, a determiner has already been identified but the noun still remains to be found.

Drive predicate★: a predicate which controls a whole program by calling the main goals.

Element: see *List*.

Ellipsis: the omission of expressions from a sentence which can be recovered from the linguistic context.

Empty category: a syntactic category which has syntactic effects although with no lexical content. Sometimes also referred to as a **gap**.

Encyclopaedic knowledge: term used to refer to general knowledge about any and everything.

Expert system: a computer program which is able to solve problems in domains usually associated with (human) experts such as the diagnosis of medical complaints or the analysis of weather systems.

Extra-logical predicate★: a predicate which cannot be defined in 'pure' Prolog. In all cases they have a side-effect during the course of being satisfied. Some extra-logical predicates are concerned with input and output to the screen whilst others allow the program to be accessed and manipulated. Such predicates are supplied as built-in predicates.

Fact★: a statement that certain objects stand in a particular relationship.

Fail★: if a goal is not satisfied, it is said to fail.

Failure-driven loop★: a means of forcing backtracking so that all solutions to a particular goal will be found.

File type (or **file extension**): a code attached to a filename in order to identify the format of the file. It is separated from the filename by a full stop. In the text, the assumption is that Prolog files are identified with the file type .pl as in `myfile .pl`. Different implementations of Prolog may require different file types such as .prm or .pro.

Frame: a description of a stereotyped situation. For example, the frame associated with a lecture will include information about the participants typically involved in a lecture, the sort of place where a lecture will be delivered, how a lecture is usually conducted, and so on.

Function★: the atom which appears to the left of brackets of a structure in an argument position. For example, `queen` is a function in `speaks(queen(england), english)`.

Functor★: term referring either to a predicate or a function.

Gap: see *Empty category*.

Garden path sentence: sentences which tend to fool the (human) processor into making the wrong initial interpretation as in *The horse raced past the barn fell.*

Goal★: a Prolog clause interpreted as a question to be solved or as a 'goal to be satisfied'. In `?- speaks(john, english).` the goal is `speaks(john, english)`.

Grammar: the systematic description of a language. Will include statements about the phonology, morphology, syntax and semantics of the language.

Grammar Development System: a computer program designed to aid the writing and testing of grammars for various languages.

Head★: a term referring either to the literal on the left-hand side of `:-` in a rule or to the left-most element of a list.

High-level programming language: a programming language which allows the expression of instructions which reflect more the problem being solved rather than the exact details of how a particular computer is to solve the problem. Each statement in a high-level language corresponds to a number of machine language instructions. Examples of high level languages are Cobol, Basic, C, and Prolog.

Indexical: expressions which refer directly to the characteristics of the situation of utterance; e.g. *I* (current speaker), *here* (place of utterance), *now* (time of utterance), etc.

Indirect question: a question mentioned as part of indirect (reported) speech: *John wondered <u>who Bill saw</u>.*

Inference: a conclusion drawn from a set of assumptions.

Inference engine★: that part of the Prolog system which (automatically) attempts to satisfy goals by drawing conclusions from the current program.

Instance★: an instance of a clause is that clause with all of its variables replaced by some term.

Instantiate★: the assigning of a value to a variable. Alternatively, we can say the variable is **bound** to the value. A variable which has not been assigned a value is **uninstantiated**.

Intelligent tutoring system: computer-aided instruction where the system can determine and respond to the individual needs of the user.

Interface: the point of transfer of information between different components of a computer or information system. The **human-machine interface** is the means by which the computer communicates information to the user and the user issues commands and other information to the machine.

Interpreter★: see *Inference engine*.

Invoke★: see *Call*.

Iteration: the repeated occurrence of a particular type of item.

Kleene star: a means of expressing the possible iteration of categories. So, $X^★$ is taken to mean 'a sequence of zero or more instances of X'.

Labelled bracketing: a means of representing the syntactic structure of an expression using brackets to group the words into their various phrases. Example: $[_S [_{NP} John] [_{VP} [_V saw], [_{NP} Mary]]]$. See also *Phrase structure tree*.

Language generation: the production of linguistic utterances.

Lexicon: that component of the grammar which records information (phonological, syntactic, semantic, etc.) about the various words of the language.

List★: an ordered sequence of terms – referred to as **elements** – written between square brackets. The **empty list** contains no elements and is written [ ]. Non-empty lists consist of a head and tail.

Literal★: an individual predicate-argument structure.

Logic: the science of the formal principles of reasoning.

Logic grammar: the use of logic to encode a grammar.

Loop: a repeated instruction. During the execution of a program to be 'in a loop' refers to some process which is repeated without ever being completed.

Machine language: the basic language of a computer expressed in binary code.

Machine translation: the use of computers to translate from one (natural) language to another.

Match★: two terms match if either they are identical or the variables in both terms can be instantiated in such a way that substituting the variables with these values would result in them becoming identical.

Module: a self-contained element of something.

Morpheme: the smallest functioning unit of a word. For example, *developmental* is composed of three morphemes: *develop+ment+al*.

Morphology: that part of the grammar which describes the structure of words.

Natural Language: a human language such as English, Swahili or Piro. Contrasted with 'non-natural' languages such as computer languages, traffic signals, communication systems of animals, etc.

Natural Language Processing (NLP): the computational processing of (textual) natural language input. Sometimes also referred to as **Computational linguistics**. Here a distinction is drawn between the two terms. 'Natural language processing' is used to refer to actual computer systems designed to process natural language whilst 'Computational linguistics' is used to refer to the theoretical underpinnings of the enterprise.

Non-deterministic: a procedure where, at some point during the process, a choice has to be made from a number of possible alternative moves.

Noun: class of words typically referring to things or persons. Examples: *computer, baby, mountain, happiness.*

Number: grammatical distinction between singular and plural.

Operating system: a program which controls the whole operation of the computer. Includes functions ranging from controlling input and output to and from the keyboard, screen and disk to the formatting of disks and the creation and editing of text files.

Operator★: a functor which can appear between two arguments. For example, the predicate speaks is an operator in the clause queen(england)speaks english. Operators have to be defined by the programmer using the built-in predicate op.

OR-node★: a point within a search tree representing a disjunction of goals, one of which must be satisfied in order for the main goal to be satisfied.

Parse: both the process of assigning a syntactic description to a sentence and the resulting description. A program that performs this task is called a **parser**.

Parsing preference: the tendency of the human parser to prefer certain types of syntactic analysis over others.

Parsing strategy: see *Search strategy.*

Partial evaluation: replacement of calls to certain predicates with the relevant value if this is known.

Performance: language in use.

Person: grammatical distinction used to indicate the number and nature of participants in a situation.

Phonology: the study of the sound system of a language and of languages in general.

Phrase structure: description of the syntactic categories of words within larger expressions and how they are grouped together.

Phrase structure tree: a means of representing the phrase structure of an expression with the aid of a 'tree' diagram. The tree consists of a series of points or nodes labelled with the names of syntactic categories connected by lines or branches. Example:

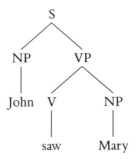

see also *Labelled bracketing*.

Phrase structure rules: statements about the possible structure of phrasal categories. For example, the rule *NP → Det N* is read as 'A noun phrase may consist of a determiner followed by a noun'.

Pragmatics: the study of the interpretation of utterances in context.

Predicate*: the name of a relationship or attribute. Prolog predicates always start with a lower case letter. Example: speaks is the predicate in speaks(john, english).

Preposition: a class of words typically used to refer to spatial, directional or temporal relationships. Examples: *under, on, near, towards, before, after, for.*

Procedure*: a set of clauses defining a particular predicate.

Procedural knowledge: knowledge about *how* to do something.

Procedural programming language: a programming language in which the programmer expresses instructions for various operations that the computer is to perform in order to solve a particular problem.

Program: a sequence of instructions or statements which can be used by a computer to perform a particular task. In Prolog a program consists of a set of procedures defining the relevant predicates for solving a particular problem.

Programming language: the language in which a programmer writes a program.

Programming code: the representation of data in a particular programming language.

Prolog: a high-level computer programming language based on the use of logic to represent problems and logical inference to solve these problems.

Pronoun: class of words which can be used to substitute for noun phrases. Examples: *I, my, she, they, who, whom, whose.*

Proof tree*: a graphical representation of the satisfaction of the various subgoals and their dependencies involved in the satisfaction of a main goal.

Proper noun (or **name**): a noun typically used to name an individual person or place. Examples: *John, English, France.*

Property*: see *Arity.*

Pull-down menu: a graphical menu of choices which appears when called up by the user.

Recognise: the process of determining whether a particular string of words is a sentence of the language or not. A program that performs this task is called a **recogniser**.

Recursive*: a definition of a predicate where part of the definition refers to the same predicate. In order for the definition to succeed there must be a non-recursive part of the definition, referred to as the **base** or **terminating condition**, which defines when the recursion stops.

Result variable*: a variable which is used to record a particular value at the end of a computation.

Reversible predicate*: the property of being able to compute any of the predicate's arguments from any of the others. For example, the definition of concat(L1, L2, L3) allows L3 to be computed given values for L1 and L2, or L1 and L2 to be calculated given L3.

Robust: a program is robust if it is able to respond in an appropriate manner to almost any possible input.

Rule*: a rule is a conditional statement of a form which might be expressed in English as 'Condition C1 holds if conditions C2 and C3 hold'. This is expressed in Prolog by the clause C1 :- C2, C3.

Satisfy*: a goal is satisfied if it can be shown to follow from the program. A goal will follow from the program if it matches either a fact or the head of a rule and each of the conditions constituting the body of the rule can also be satisfied.

Scheme: see *Frame.*

Search strategy: a means of attempting to find a solution to a problem which involves a number of possible alternative choices. Search strategies are classified along a number of dimensions in relation to a search tree. Assuming the search tree:

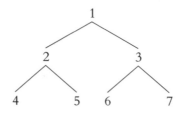

A **top-down** strategy starts at the top of the tree and works downwards. Exactly, which order the nodes will be visited depends on the choices along the other dimensions. One possibility is the order 1, 2, 4, 5, 3, 6, 7. A **bottom-up** strategy starts from the bottom of the tree and works upwards. One possibility is that the nodes would be visited in the order 4, 5, 2, 6, 7, 3, 1. A **depth-first** strategy works pursues each branch to its full depth as in the order 1, 2, 4, 5, 3, 6, 7 whilst a **breadth-first** strategy visits each node at the same level before moving deeper into the tree, as in the order 1, 2, 3, 4, 5, 6, 7. In addition, the nodes may either be visited in a **left-to-right** order (e.g. 1, 2, 3, 4, 5, 6, 7) or **right-to-left** (e.g. 1, 3, 2, 7, 6, 5, 4). Since parsing can be seen as a special type of search problem, parsing strategies can also be classified along the same dimensions.

Search tree: a graphical representation of the total computational space from which the interpreter attempts to find a solution to a specific goal given a particular program.

Semantics: the study of the meaning of linguistic expressions.

Simple object*: a term used to refer either to constants or variables.

Speech Recognition: the process of understanding spoken (rather than textual) input.

Speech Synthesis: the production of spoken (rather than textual) output.

Stack: a means of storing data in such a way that the last item stored is the first to be accessed.

Structure*: a complex expression consisting of a functor and some number of arguments where the arguments may themselves also be structures. For example, in speaks(queen (england), english) the whole expression is a structure consisting of the functor speaks and two arguments queen (england) and english. The first argument is also a structure consisting of the functor queen and argument england.

Subgoal*: a goal which has to be satisfied in order for another goal to be satisfied.

Syntax: the study of the way words may combine together in a language and in languages in general.

Tail*: the remainder of a list once its head has been removed. The tail is a list itself.

Term*: a term is either a constant, a variable or a structure.

Terminating condition*: see *Recursive*.

Text critiquing: programs designed to offer information on various properties of a text. They might include reporting spelling or grammatical errors as well as analyses of certain stylistic features.

Top-down strategy: see *Search strategy*.

Trace★: a means of following the course of a particular computation.

User-friendly: a computer application is user-friendly if it is easy to use and understand by an untrained user.

Variable★: a name standing for some object that cannot be named. They start either with an upper case letter or the underscore. Examples: `Language`, `Speakers_of`, `_language`, `_46`.

Verb: a class of words traditionally referred to a 'action' or 'doing' words although may name relationships and properties. Examples: *speak, climb, write, smile, give.*

Wh-question: a question asking for the identity of some item. Usually start with a word beginning "wh": *Who is that?*, *When will Jiff arrive?*

Writer's assistant: a program designed to help writers in the production of complex texts by providing various support tools.

Yes-no question: a question typically requiring a 'yes' or 'no' as answer: *Did Batkin hit the target?*

&-node★: a point within either a proof or search tree representing a conjunction of goals, all of which must be satisfied in order for the main goal to be satisfied.

Bibliography

Abramson, H. (1984) 'Definite clause translation grammars'. In *1984 International Symposium on Logic Programming*, Atlantic City, pp. 233–40.

Abramson, H. and V. Dahl (1989) *Logic Grammars*. Springer-Verlag; Berlin.

Aho, A. and J. Ullman (1972) *The Theory of Parsing, Translation and Compiling, Vol. I: Parsing*. Prentice-Hall; Englewood Cliffs, New Jersey.

Akmajian, A., R. Demers, A. Farmer and R. Harnish (1990) *Linguistics: An Introduction to Language and Communication*. 3rd edition. MIT Press: Cambridge, Mass.

Allen, J. (1995) *Natural Language Understanding*. 2nd edition. Benjamin-Cummings: Menlo Park, Cal.

Alty, J. and M. Coombs (1984) *Expert Systems: Concepts and Examples*. NCC: Manchester.

Antworth, E. (1990) *PC-KIMMO: A Two-level Processor for Morphological Analysis*. Summer Institute of Linguistics; Dallas, Texas.

Baecker, R. and W. Buxton (1987) (eds) *Readings in Human-Computer Interaction: A Multidisciplinary Approach*. Morgan Kaufmann: Palo Alto, Cal.

Baker, C. (1978) *Introduction to Generative-Transformational Syntax*. Prentice-Hall: Englewood Cliffs, New Jersey.

Baker, C. (1995) *English Syntax*. 2nd edition. MIT Press; Cambridge, Mass.

Ballard, B. and M. Jones (1987) 'Computational linguistics'. In Shapiro, pp. 133–51.

Barr, A. and E. Feigenbaum (eds) (1981) *The Handbook of Artificial Intelligence, 1*. William Kaufmann: Palo Alto, Cal.

Bates, M. (1978) 'The theory and practice of ATN grammars'. In L. Bolc (ed.) *Natural Language Communication with Computers*, Springer Verlag: Berlin, pp. 191–259.

Bates, M. (1987) 'Natural language interfaces'. In Shapiro, pp. 655–60.

Beardon, C., D. Lumsden and G. Holmes (1991) *Natural Language and Computational Linguistics: An Introduction*. Ellis Horwood: London.

Bennett, P., R. Johnson, J. McNaught, J. Pugh, J. Sager and H. Somers (1986) *Multilingual Aspects of Information Technology*. Gower: Aldershot.

Blakemore, D. (1992) *Understanding Utterances: An Introduction to Pragmatics*. Blackwell: Oxford.

Bornat, R. (1979) *Understanding and Writing Compilers*. Macmillan: Basingstoke.

Bratko, I. (1990) *Prolog Programming for Artificial Intelligence*. 2nd edition. Addison Wesley; Reading, Mass.

Briscoe, E. (1987) *Modelling Human Speech Comprehension: A Computational Approach*. Ellis Horwood: Chichester.

Brown, C. and G. Koch (1991) *Natural Language Understanding and Logic Programming, III*. North-Holland: Amsterdam.

Brown, G. and G. Yule (1983) *Discourse Analysis*. Cambridge University Press: Cambridge.

Burton-Roberts, N. (1986) *Analysing Sentences: An Introduction to English Syntax*. Longman: London.

Carbonell, J. and P. Hayes (1987) 'Natural language understanding'. In Shapiro, pp. 660–77.

Carlson, L. and K. Linden (1987) 'Unification as a grammatical tool'. *Nordic Journal of Linguistics*, 10, pp. 111–36.

Chapman, N. (1987) *LR Parsing: Theory and Practice*. Cambridge University Press: Cambridge.

Charniak, E. and D. McDermott (1985) *Introduction to Artificial Intelligence*. Addison-Wesley: Reading, Mass.

Clocksin, W. and C. Mellish (1987) *Programming in Prolog*. 3rd edition. Springer-Verlag: Berlin.

Coelho, H. (1987) 'Definite-clause grammar'. In S. Shapiro (ed.), pp. 339–42.

Coelho, H. and J. Cotta (1988) *Prolog by Example: How to Learn, Teach and Use It*. Springer-Verlag; Berlin.

Colmerauer, A. (1978) 'Metamorphosis grammars'. In L. Bolc (ed.) *Natural Language Communication with Computers*, pp. 133–89, Springer-Verlag; Berlin.

Corballis, M. (1991) *The Lopsided Ape: Evolution of the Generative Mind*. Oxford University Press: Oxford.

Copestake, A. and K. Sparck Jones (1990) 'Natural language interfaces to databases'. *Knowledge Engineering Review*, 5, pp. 225–49.

Covington, M. (1994) *Natural Language Processing for Prolog Programmers*. Prentice-Hall: Englewood Cliffs, New Jersey.

Covington, M., D. Nute and A. Vellino (1988) *Prolog Programming in Depth*. Scott, Foresman and Company: Glenview, Illinois.

Crystal, D. (1997) *The Cambridge Encyclopaedia of Language*. 2nd edition. Cambridge University Press: Cambridge.

Dahl, V. and H. Abramson (1984) 'On gapping grammars'. In *Proceedings of the Second International Conference on Logic Programming*, Uppsala, pp. 77–88.

Dahl, V. and M. McCord (1983) 'Treating coordination in logic grammars'. *American Journal of Computational Linguistics*, 9, pp. 69–91.

Dahl, V. and P. Saint-Dizier (eds) (1985) *Natural Language Understanding and Logic Programming, I*. North-Holland: Amsterdam.

Dahl, V. and P. Saint-Dizier (eds) (1988) *Natural Language Understanding and Logic Programming, II*. North-Holland: Amsterdam.

Dale, R. (1989) 'Computer-based editorial aids'. In J. Peckham (ed.) *Recent Developments and Applications of Natural Language Processing*, Kogan Page: London, pp. 8–22.

Dalrymple, M., R. Kaplan, L. Kartutunen, K. Koskenniemi, S. Shaio and M. Wescoat (1987) *Tools for Morphological Analysis*. CSLI Report 87–108. Center For the Study of Language and Information; Stanford, Cal.

Dowty, D., L. Karttunen and A. Zwicky (eds) (1985) *Natural Language Parsing: Psychological, Computational and Theoretical Perspectives*. Cambridge University Press: Cambridge.

Erbach, G. (1992) 'Tools for grammar engineering'. In *Third Conference on Applied Natural Language Processing*. Association for Computational Linguistics, pp. 243–44.

Evans, R. (1985) 'Program – a development tool for GPSG grammars', *Linguistics*, 23, pp. 213–43.

Franklin, J., L. Davis, R. Shumaker and P. Morawski (1987) 'Military applications'. In S. Shapiro (ed.), pp. 604–14.

Frazier, L. and J.D. Fodor (1978) 'The sausage machine: A new two stage parsing model', *Cognition*, 6, pp. 291–325.

Fromkin, V. and R. Rodman (1988) *An Introduction to Language*. 4th edition. Holt, Rinehart and Winston: New York.

Gal, A., G. Lapalme, P. Saint-Dizier and H. Somers (1991) *Prolog for Natural Language Processing*. John Wiley; Chichester.

Garman, M. (1990) *Psycholinguistics*. Cambridge University Press; Cambridge.

Garnham, A. (1985) *Psycholinguistics: Central Topics*. Methuen; London.

Gazdar, G. (1985) 'Review article: Finite state morphology'. *Linguistics*, 23, pp. 597–607.

Gazdar, G. (1993) 'The handling of natural language'. In D. Broadbent (ed.) *The Simulation of Human Intelligence*, Blackwell; Oxford, pp. 151–77.

Gazdar, G. and C. Mellish (1987) 'Computational linguistics'. In Lyons *et al.*, pp. 225–48.

Gazdar, G. and C. Mellish (1989) *Natural Language Processing in Prolog: An Introduction to Computational Linguistics*. Addison Wesley: Reading, Massachusetts.

Gazdar, G. and G. Pullum (1985) 'Computationally relevant properties of natural languages and their grammars'. *New Generation Computing*, 3, pp. 273–306.

Grune, D. and C. Jacobs (1990) *Parsing Techniques: A Practical Guide.* Ellis Horwood; Chichester.

Grosz, B., K. Sparck Jones and B. Webber (eds) (1986) *Readings in Natural Language Processing.* Morgan Kaufman: Los Altos, Cal.

Halvorsen, P.-K. (1988) 'Computer applications of linguistic theory'. In Newmeyer (Vol. II), pp. 198–219.

Hayes-Roth, F. (1987) 'Expert systems'. In S. Shapiro (ed.), pp. 287–98.

Hayes-Roth, F., D. Waterman and D. Lenat (1983) (eds) *Building Expert Systems.* Addison Wesley; Reading, Mass.

Heidorn, G., K. Jensen, L. Miller, R. Byrd and M. Chodorow (1982) 'The EPISTLE text-critiquing system'. *IBM Systems Journal*, 21, pp. 305–26.

Hirschman, L. and K. Puder (1988) 'Restriction grammar: A Prolog implementation'. In M. van Canegham and D. Warren (eds) *Logic Programming and its Applications Vol. II.* Ablex: Norwood, NJ, pp. 244–61.

Hogger, C. (1984) *Introduction to Logic Programming.* Academic Press; London.

Hogger, C. (1990) *Essentials of Logic Programming.* Clarendon Press; Oxford.

Hopcroft, J. and J. Ullman (1979) *Introduction to Automata Theory, Languages and Computation.* Addison Wesley; Reading, Massachusetts.

Hutchins, W. (1986) *Machine Translation: Past, Present, Future.* Ellis Horwood: Chichester.

Hutchins, W. and H. Somers (1992) *An Introduction to Machine Translation.* Academic Press: London.

Jackson, P. (1986) *Introduction to Expert Systems.* Addison Wesley: Wokingham.

Johnson, R. (1983) 'Parsing with transition networks'. In M. King (ed.), pp. 59–72.

Johnson, T. (1985) *Natural Language Computing: The Commercial Applications.* Ovum: London.

Johnson, T. and C. Guilfoyle (1989) 'Commercial markets for NLP products. In J. Peckham (ed.) *Recent Developments and Applications of Natural Language Processing.* Kogan Page: London, pp. 1–7.

Joshi, A. (1987) 'Phrase structure grammar'. In Shapiro (ed.), pp. 344–51.

Joshi, A. (1991) 'Natural language processing'. *Science*, 252, pp. 1242–49.

Kaplan, R. (1972) 'Augmented transition networks as psychological models of sentence comprehension'. *Artificial Intelligence*, 3, pp. 73–100.

Kearsley, G. (1987) 'Computer-aided instruction, intelligent'. In S. Shapiro (ed.), pp. 154–9.

Kimball, J. (1973) 'Seven principles of surface structure parsing in natural language', *Cognition*, 2, pp. 15–47.

King, M. (ed.) (1983) *Parsing Natural Language*. Academic Press: London.

King, M. (ed.) (1987) *Machine Translation Today: The State of the Art*. Edinburgh University Press: Edinburgh.

Koskenniemi, K. (1983) *Two-Level Morphology: A General Computational Model for Word-Form Recognition and Production*. University of Helsinki, Dept. of General Linguistics; Helsinki.

Kowalski, R. (1979) *Logic for Problem Solving*. North-Holland; New York.

Kowalski, R. and C. Hogger (1987) 'Logic programming'. In Shapiro (ed.), pp. 544–58.

Lesgold, A. (1987) 'Educational applications'. In Shapiro (ed.), pp. 267–72.

Lyons, J., R. Coates, M. Deuchar and G. Gazdar (eds) (1987) *New Horizons in Linguistics 2*. Penguin: Harmondsworth.

Marcus, M. (1980) *A Theory of Syntactic Recognition for Natural Language*. MIT Press: Cambridge, Mass.

Matsumoto, Y., H. Tanaka, H. Hirakawa, H. Miyoshi and H. Yasukawa (1983) 'BUP: A bottom-up parser embedded in PROLOG'. *New Generation Computing*, 1, pp. 145–58.

Matthei, E. and T. Roeper (1983) *Understanding and Producing Speech*. Fontana; London.

McCord, M. (1980) 'Slot grammars'. *American Journal of Computational Linguistics*, 6, pp. 31–43.

McTear, M. (1987) *The Articulate Computer*. Basil Blackwell: Oxford.

Minsky, M. (1972) *Computation: Finite and Infinite Machines*. Prentice-Hall; Englewood Cliffs, New Jersey.

Moyne, J. (1985) *Understanding Language: Man or Machine*. Plenum: New York.

Newmeyer, F. (ed.) (1988) *Linguistics: The Cambridge Survey, Vols I to IV*. Cambridge University Press: Cambridge.

Nirenburg, S. (1987) (ed.) *Machine Translation: Theoretical and Methodological Issues*. Cambridge University Press: Cambridge.

Obermeier, K. (1989) *Natural Language Processing Technologies in Artificial Intelligence: The Science and Industry Perspectives*. Ellis Horwood: Chichester.

O'Grady, W., M. Dobrovolsky and M. Aronoff (1992) *Contemporary Linguistics: An Introduction*. 2nd edition. St Martin's Press: New York.

O'Grady, W., M. Dobrovolsky and F. Katamba (1997) *Contemporary Linguistics: An Introduction*. Longman: London.

Oshern, D. and H. Lasnik (eds) (1990) *Language: An Invitation to Cognitive Science, Vol. 1*. Bradford Books, MIT Press: Cambridge, Mass.

Partee, B., A. ter Meulen and R. Wall (1990) *Mathematical Methods in Linguistics*. Kluwer Academic; Dordrecht.

Pereira, F. (1981) 'Extraposition grammars'. *American Journal of Computational Linguistics*, 9, pp. 243–55.

Pereira, F. (1985) 'A new characterization of attachment preferences'. In Dowty *et al.* (eds) pp. 307–19.

Pereira, F. and S. Shieber (1987) *Prolog and Natural-Language Analysis*. CSLI Lecture Notes, Chicago University Press; Stanford.

Pereira, F. and D. Warren (1980) 'Definite clause grammars for language analysis; A survey of the formalism and a comparison with augmented transition networks'. *Artificial Intelligence*, 13, pp. 231–78. Reprinted in B. Grosz *et al.* (1986), pp. 101–24.

Perrault, C. (1984) 'On the mathematical properties of linguistic theories'. *Computational Linguistics*, 10, pp. 165–76. Reprinted in Grosz *et al.* (eds) (1986), pp. 5–16.

Perrault, C. and B. Grosz (1986) 'Natural-language interfaces' in *Annual Review of Computer Science*, 1, pp. 47–82. Reprinted in Shrobe (ed.), pp. 133–72.

Pinker, S. (1994) *The Language Instinct: The New Science of Language and Mind*. Penguin: Harmondsworth.

Polson, M. and J. Richardson (1988) (eds) *Foundations of Intelligent Tutoring Systems*. Lawrence Erlbaum: Hillsdale, NJ.

Pulman, S. (1987) 'Computational models of parsing'. In A. Ellis (ed.) *Progress in the Psychology of Language*, Vol. 3, Lawrence Erlbaum: Hillsdale, NJ, pp. 159–231.

Ramsay, A. (1986) 'Computer processing of natural language'. In M. Yazdani (ed.) *Artificial Intelligence: Principles and Applications*, Chapman and Hall: London, pp. 69–110.

Reitman, W. (ed.) (1984) *Artificial Intelligence Applications for Business*. Ablex: Norwood, NJ.

Rennels, G. and E. Shortcliffe (1987) 'Medical advice systems'. In S. Shapiro (ed.), pp. 584–91.

Rich, E. and K. Knight (1991) *Artificial Intelligence*. 2nd edition. McGraw-Hill: New York.

Ritchie, G. and H. Thompson (1984) 'Natural language processing'. In T. O'Shea and M. Eisenstadt (eds) *Artificial Intelligence: Tools, Techniques, and Applications*, Harper and Row: New York, pp. 358–88.

Ross, P. (1989) *Advanced Prolog*. Addison Wesley; Reading, Massachusetts.

Sag, I. (1991) 'Linguistic theory and natural language processing'. In E. Klein and F. Veltman (eds) *Natural Language and Speech*, Springer-Verlag: Berlin, pp. 69–83.

Saint-Dizier, P. and S. Szpakowicz (eds) (1990) *Logic and Logic Grammars for Logic Programming*. Ellis Horwood: Chichester.

Saint-Dizier, P. and S. Szpakowicz (1990a) 'Logic programming, logic grammars, language processing'. In P. Saint-Dizier and S. Szpakowicz (eds) (1990), pp. 9–27.

Sampson, G. (1983) 'Deterministic parsing'. In King (ed.), pp. 91–116.

Schank, R. (1984) *The Cognitive Computer: On Language, Learning, and Artificial Intelligence*. Addison Wesley: Reading, Mass.

Shapiro, S. (1987) *Encyclopedia of Artificial Intelligence*. John Wiley; New York.

Sharples, M. and C. O'Malley (1988) 'A framework for the design of a writer's assistant' in J. Self (ed.) *Artificial Intelligence and Human Learning: Intelligent Computer-Aided Instruction*, Chapman and Hall; London, pp. 276–90.

Shieber, S. (1983) 'Sentence disambiguation by a shift-reduce parsing technique'. *Proceedings of 21st Annual Meeting of ACL*, Cambridge, Mass, pp. 113–18.

Shieber, S. (1984) 'Criteria for designing computer facilities for linguistic analysis'. *Linguistics*, 23, pp. 189–211.

Shieber, S. (1986) *An Introduction to Unification-based Approaches to Grammar*. CSLI: Stanford, Cal.

Shieber, S. (1988) 'Separating linguistic analyses from linguistic theories'. In U. Reyle and C. Rohrer (eds) *Natural Language Parsing and Linguistic Theories*, D. Reidel: Dordrecht, pp. 33–68.

Shrobe, H. (1988) (ed.) *Exploring Artificial Intelligence: Survey Talks from the National Conferences on Artificial Intelligence*. Morgan Kaufmann: San Mateo, Cal.

Shwartz, S. (1984) 'Natural language processing in the commercial world'. In W. Reitman (ed.).

Shwartz, S. (1987) *Applied Natural Language Processing*. Petrocelli: Princeton, NJ.

Slocum, J. (ed.) (1988) *Machine Translation Systems*. Cambridge University Press: Cambridge.

Smith, G. (1991) *Computers and Human Language*. Oxford University Press: Oxford.

Stabler, E. (1983) 'Deterministic and bottom-up parsing in PROLOG'. *AAAI-83*, pp. 383–86.

Sterling, L. and E. Shapiro (1986) *The Art of Prolog: Advanced Programming Techniques*. MIT Press; Cambridge, Massachusetts.

Swartz, M., and M. Yazdani (1992) (eds) *Intelligent Tutoring Systems for Foreign Language Learning: The Bridge to International Communication.* Springer-Verlag: Berlin.

Tennant, H. (1981) *Natural Language Processing: An Introduction to an Emerging Technology*. Petrocelli: New York.

Tennant, H. (1987) 'Menu-based natural language' in S. Shapiro, pp. 594–7.

Thomas, L. (1993) *Beginning Syntax*. Blackwell: Oxford.

Thompson, H. and G. Ritchie (1984) 'Implementing natural language parsers'. In T. O'Shea and M. Eisenstadt (eds) *Artificial Intelligence: Tools, Techniques, and Applications*, Harper and Row; New York, pp. 245–300.

Thornton, C. and B. du Boulay (1992) *Artificial Intelligence Through Search*. Intellect; Oxford.

Varile, G. (1983) 'Charts: A data structure for parsing'. In King (ed.), pp. 73–87.

Wall, R. (1972) *Introduction to Mathematical Linguistics*. Prentice-Hall; Englewood Cliffs, New Jersey.

Wanner, E. and M. Maratsos (1978) 'An ATN approach to comprehension'. In M. Halle, J. Bresnan and G. Miller (eds) *Linguistic Theory and Psychological Reality*, MIT Press: Cambridge, Mass, pp. 119–61.

Weizenbaum, J. (1976) *Computer Power and Human Reason: From Judgement to Calculation*. W.H. Freeman: San Francisco, Cal.

Wenger, E. (1987) *Artificial Intelligence and Tutoring Systems: Computational and Cognitive Approaches to the Communication of Knowledge*. Morgan Kaufmann: Los Altos, Cal.

Wilks, Y. (1987) 'Machine translation' in S. Shapiro, pp. 564–71.

Winograd, T. (1983) *Language as a Cognitive Process, Vol. I: Syntax*. Addison Wesley; Reading, Mass.

Winograd, T. (1984) 'Computer software for working with language'. *Scientific American*, 251, pp. 91–101.

Winston, P. (1984) *Artificial Intelligence*. 2nd edition. Addison Wesley: Reading, Mass.

Woods, W. (1987) 'Augmented transition network grammar'. In S. Shapiro (ed.), pp. 323–33.

Woolf, B. (1988) 'Intelligent tutoring systems: A survey' in H. Shrobe (ed.), pp. 1–43.

Index